26 OC

8

'BLITZED'

THE BATTLE OF FRANCE
MAY–JUNE 1940

'BLITZED'

THE BATTLE OF FRANCE
MAY–JUNE 1940

Victor F. Bingham
T.Eng(CEI), AMRAES, AFSLAET

Illustrations by
Lyndon Jones

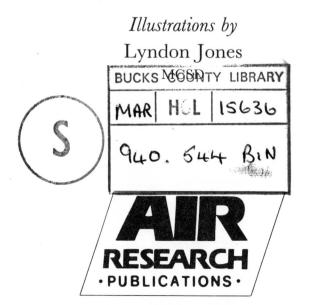

AIR
RESEARCH
· PUBLICATIONS ·

B03 273 194 7

First published 1990 by
Air Research Publications
34 Elm Road
New Malden
Surrey KT3 3HD
England

ISBN 1 871187 07 9

Typeset by Qualitext, Andover,
Hampshire SP10 5AP
Printed and bound in Great Britain
by LR Printing Services Ltd
Burgess Hill, West Sussex
RH15 9UA

Contents

Acknowledgements

The original unpublished manuscript of 'Blitzed' was written up in 1940–41 just as a record, a matter of interest. Then over the years it lay dormant gathering dust, to be awakened when two young Frenchmen contacted me in 1983 regarding the AASF. Through this research and the contact, a re-union took place in 1986 of about eighteen members of the AASF, who were brought together through the efforts of the two young Frenchmen, Gerard Faux and Denis Rigollet. The re-union took place in Vraux, where the villagers' hospitality was as outstanding as their welcome, as well as their interest in the Royal Air Force.

'Blitzed' was initially based on my diaries and notes, but further research and the help of friends and acquaintances has expanded and put more flesh on the bones of the original. So may I say a special thank you to the following, not in alphabetical order or preference:

To the villagers of Vraux, and in particular to Gerard Faux, Denis Rigollet and Bernard Pauzie for their help in France; Jacques De Vos for information and photographs in Belgium; Wing commander and Betty George of XV Squadron and the Blenheim Society; Squadron Leader Ken Campbell for his information and photographs on No. 73 Squadron; J. R. Heslop for the loan of his unpublished article on France 1940; Group Captain J. Wray for information on No. 53 Squadron, R. Pearce for information on No. 142 Squadron; E. Alwyn Benjamin for information on the 'Y' unit in France; J. Stevens ex-No. 218 Squadron for help from his AASF archives; R. Stride ex-No. 114 Squadron for help and contacts in the UK; Richard Searle of the RAE Farnborough library/archives; Staff of the Public Record Office, Kew; Staff of the RAF Museum Photographic Department; Flight Lieutenant G. Potter, H. Brown, R. Cooper, T. H. Davies, A. Drew and P. Robinson-Judd of No. 114 Squadron; J. I. Parry, G. Sweetman, O. Baum and L. 'Doc' Walls of No. 139 Squadron; Wing Commander W. Blackadder, P. L. Parrott and D. Brown of 607 Squadron; Wing Commander D. Annand of No. 26 Squadron; J. Kayll of No. 615 Squadron; Squadron leader Davies of No. 88 Squadron; Squadron Leader G. R. Wheeldon of No. 12 Squadron; Flight Lieutenant H. Cooper; S. J. Cain; R. Carless; D. A. Radford; C. Trett; J. Marr; R. A. Stamp; J. Wey; A. H. Phipps, Wing Commander G. Jordan; F. Fenwick; L. Lineker.

Thanks also to my wife for help and tolerance over continuous talk and correspondence on aircraft and the AASF and the BAFF, also as an unpaid telephone operator. Brickbats or bouquets can only be laid at my door, and opinions expressed are my own, unless stated otherwise; but I hope that 'Blitzed' will give a better understanding of the Royal Air Force's task in France 1939–40.

Introduction

The Battle for France never appeared, or appears, to raise the interest of the general public that the Battle of Britain did, yet the two small British contingents of the British Air Forces in France were of a far inferior number, and fighting greater odds, than the fighter squadrons of the Battle of Britain. To the British public, what was happening 'over there', appeared of little importance . . . until Dunkirk. The Battle of France was to Europe what the Battle of Britain was to the people of the British Isles, and to Europe at the time, of far greater significance. Our contribution of ground forces, ten British Army divisions to the French ninety-four, was during the 'Phoney War' to cause dissatisfaction amongst our Allies who saw the British ally "safe across the water". In the air our contribution was hardly enough to frighten the enemy, yet heroic deeds were to be enacted out of all proportion to those numbers, and carried out against enormous odds.

If the Battle of Britain was the first reverse that the Luftwaffe encountered, then the Battle of France was the first battle, the first testing time, the Luftwaffe's first encounter with the Royal Air Force. The Battle of France was lost on the ground more than in the air, for the British and French Armies could not comprehend the Blitzkreig tactics, tactics that clearly showed the German Generals in the forefront of their profession, with their officers and men no less professional. Yet those very theories had originated in Great Britain in the 1920s with Liddell Hart and J. F. Fuller, whilst in France a Major Charles de Gaulle was, in 1935, advocating the independent armoured force. Unfortunately for Great Britain and France, in fact for Europe, the message had not got through. The message would have had very little effect in Great Britain even if it had got through, for with disarmament in 1930, the pacifist and socialist influence in the 1930s, there was little hope of finding sufficient finance to set up any effective armoured force in the years before 1939.

In 1940, and in the years since, members of the British Army have frequently acquainted the British public with their opinion that, "The RAF never gave them help in France" or, "They never saw the RAF at Dunkirk" etc. This was hardly surprising when one considers that the British Expeditionary Force was evicted from France at Dunkirk within three weeks of the commencement of the campaign. Surely more a rout than a retreat. And how often were RAF airfields left unguarded to the advancing German Army? In some cases complete squadrons were exterminated in a week, aircraft patched up for the next sortie, crews killed or injured while attacking the German spearheads. For them there could be no foxhole or surrender, they were asked to carry out, and did carry out, near suicidal missions.

With the failure of the French and British Army to defeat the German Army breakthrough in France in May 1940, the decision had to be made to sacrifice the light bombers of the AASF and 2 Group Bomber Command in an attempt to slow or halt the German advance. These aircraft were flown by the pre-war regular aircrew, the 'seed corn' of the RAF's future. That the attempt failed is now part of history.

The events in the Battle of France proved and disproved many theories. It proved that the British Army appeared to be unable to operate without air superiority. It proved that without air superiority the day bombers could not help the army operations. It proved that day bombers required fighter escorts and that some of the RAF fighter tactics were better suited to the Hendon Air Display than fighting. It also showed that if the RAF failed in any way, then it was in its lack of full mobility, the failure to provide sufficient transport to ensure that mobility, and the failure to give the technical ground staff sufficient training in small arms and airfield defence. The British Army was at that time neither capable of, nor sufficiently trained, for anti-aircraft defence. With the eviction of the British Army* at Dunkirk, a scapegoat for their inadequancy was needed, so jibes against the French Army and the RAF were inevitable. Yet the RAF casualty list gives the lie to the latter, and the following text will I trust explain the basic movement of the battle.

Based on their experiences in France the RAF later formed the RAF Regiment and the Servicing Commandos. The Regiment was to defend airfields from attack whilst the Servicing Commandos units provided forward ground services with men trained to be mobile and defend themselves. Never again during the 1939–45 war, was the RAF to be dependent on another force to defend its ground sites and airfields. As the war progressed the media often lauded the youth of the members who became aircrew, yet many members of the British Air Forces France were below the age of 20 years. Many air gunners, radio operators and junior groundstaff were teenagers, yet all were to show gallantry and dedication in the action and sacrifice that was the Battle of France. No medal was struck for action in the Battle of France, very little recognition was given, yet the fighting and sacrifices made during those fateful days from 10th May to 16th June 1940 were probably the most outstanding of World War Two.

---

*The British Army left behind in France 120,000 vehicles, 2,300 pieces of heavy artillery, 8,000 Bren guns, 90,000 rifles and 7,000 tons of ammunition.

Preface

"If you want peace, prepare for war"

ON 3rd September, 1939, with the commencement of World War II, a number of Royal Air Force squadrons were in France on operational standby. They were back again on the same French soil where their fathers had fought in 1914-18. Politicans in Great Britain were bumbling along with their policies of appeasement and non-intervention, with socialism feeding on pacifism and politicians of the right failing to be positive enough. The Royal Navy and British Army, with larger budgets than the RAF, were still engaged in ways to take-over the RAF; yet it would be the latter service alone which would take offensive action against the German heartland.

'Blitzed' is about the Royal Air Force in France during 1939-40, and though mainly concerned with the British Air Forces France also concerns 2 Group operations in aid of the Allied forces, as well as a number of Armée de l'Air operations. It's mainly about the Air Component and the Advanced Air Striking Force squadrons, and their fight against superior forces. The choice of the title 'Blitzed' is precisely about what we were when the Battle of France finally ceased on 18th June 1940; blitzed but not beaten, more surprised by the professionalism of the German forces than in our inability to stop them; but having been blitzed, more determined than ever to see Germany beaten. Many groundcrew, including myself, from the BAFF and 2 Group, having lost their aircrew knew that they must take up the gauntlet, and so volunteered for aircrew training. It was not us alone, for all over Occupied Europe, the Empire and Commonwealth came young men who believed in freedom, heading towards Great Britain to join our ranks.

The following text covers the events in the RAF prior to and during 1939-40, the operational scene, the mistakes and background. It indicates the British and French Armies's lack of intellectual and physical concept of modern war. While the British Army was expecting air support, they apparently failed to appreciate the necessity for defending airfield areas. In many cases the troops were demoralised by the air and ground tactics used against them; yet in 1944 and 1945, the German troops were to experience far worse effects from Allied air superiority . . . without giving ground easily. The scene that is covered is set in Europe, during the first year of World War Two, the characters are not fictional but flesh and blood, they climbed into their aircraft knowing that once airborne, they had little chance of returning alive. This was the Battle of France, the aggressor was once again Germany.

The final chapters cover the aircraft use operationally in the Battle of France and explain their specifications, design features and their employment. From this review it is hoped that the reader will be able to evaluate the facts and therefore form a fairer opinion of each aircraft. Many historians hold a jaundiced view, which has been exaggerated in many cases by the failure to relate the aircraft to the operational scene at the time. For instance, the Battle as an aircraft and in performance was no worse than the Ju87; the Blenheim no worse than the Dornier Do17 . . . what distinguished the four aircraft types was one solitary factor, the Ju87 and Do17 operated in an environment where the German Luftwaffe held air superiority. When the reader considers the aircraft operated by the Royal Air Force, their evaluation should be on the basis of the operational background and not judged in hindsight.

It will be understood that every combat or attack cannot be covered, such coverage being only possible in individual squadron histories, but in this text I am trying to cover a wide spectrum of the battle, with discomfort, chaos, death and heroism every day occurrences. Aircrew were often assigned tasks out of all proportion to their numbers, targets were ill-defined due to the speed of the German advance, communications in many cases had broken down and choas prevailed in the back areas as retreating troops and refugees blocked the roads. The task of writing about all details is far outside the scope of one book, this book is about the Royal Air Force in the Battle of France. It illustrates the impossible task the RAF was asked to perform, and shows that the British Army's complaint of lack of RAF support is not borne out by facts. Last of all it is a salute to the aircrew of 1939–40, who by their sacrifice made victory in 1945 possible . . . it was their first battle and Britain's first battle in World War II.

Victor F. Bingham

Chapter One
The Thin Light Blue Line

Air Peace to Air War.

The Royal Air Force was fortunate that in its formative years, from 1919 to 1929, to have as its Chief of Air Staff, Sir Hugh Trenchard. Lesser men have criticised his defence of the RAF and his policies, yet here was a great man of self confidence, sincere, and with the will to ensure the continuity of the RAF; unfortunately it would appear that he did not have the politician's 'gift of the gab', and so has been criticised for this. Nevertheless, contrary to the opinions expressed by his opponents, Trenchard was never to imply that air operations alone would win a war, but he did champion the cause of independent air operations and an independent air force. In the early years of the air force that Trenchard created, served many young officers who would in the years ahead achieve fame and status as the commanding officers of Groups and Commands; men like Basil Embry, Keith Park, R. Pierse, C. Portal, R. Peck and others.

The existence of an autonomous air force was anathema to many of the Army and Navy 'brass', and many grounds would be raised over the years for the axing of the Royal Air Force and the transfer of its assets to the Army and Navy. Most of the grounds for this argument did not bear examination in the events of the 1939–45 war. One only has to point to the Royal Navy's complete under-rating of the U-boat and aircraft menace in pre-war years, and its abysmal record against these two threats until 1942. Many politicians, as well as 'experts', spoke of parity when discussing aircraft strengths of the RAF and Luftwaffe, usually interpreting this as a question of numbers which is always a misleading yardstick of air power. Yet this fallacy of mere numbers would continue through the years of peace and into the war years, without any comparison of performance or modern design.

Meanwhile, the Air Staff in the interwar years maintained the policy that the counter-offensive was the main element in our defence, which did of course result in our fighter defence becoming totally inadequate. This trend was not reversed until 1937, when 'Scheme K' was introduced, which called for an increase in fighter strength and the cutting down of first line bomber squadrons and reserves. By that date it was realised that there was no possibility of the RAF achieving numerical parity with the German Luftwaffe, so resources were then allocated to build RAF Fighter Command to a position that would make it capable of an adequate defence ... but only just. From 1937 to 1939 the Air Staff had demanded from the Government of Great Britain what they considered was practical in resources, whilst at the same time warning the Government of the perils if not provided. By September 1938 it was becoming more and more obvious that the 20 year peace was running to its close. Many politicians in Parliament and a considerable number of the British public, were not prepared to face the facts, preferring instead to put faith in a "piece of paper" brought back from Munich. It was not that they were not patriotic, rather that they were apathetic and pacifist, and so the peace ran to its close on 3rd September 1939.

To the eternal credit of Tranchard, his policies, and those of the Air Staffs that followed they had created a professional air force of dedicated servicemen. The RAF was not run on the jingoistic lines of the German Luftwaffe, but was formed of free serving enthusiasts, men who knew that the war was imminent and that they would be the spearhead upon whom the Hun hordes would fall. Not only were these the spearhead, they would form the nucleus of a force that would be the hammer that would smash Germany. The RAF of that period could consider itself most fortunate to have as head of its civil administration a man who devoted himself singlemindedly to the RAF and its affairs, that man was Arthur Street (later Sir Arthur Street), who was Under Secretary of State for Air. Another personality, far better known than Sir Arthur Street, was Air Marshal Sir W. Freeman, who was at that time the Air Member for Development and Production. He was responsibile for the pre-war planning of the organisation that would allow an increase in production when required, and whose 'Big bomber' policy the Air Staff were to adopt after Munich. This pre-war planning was able to make possible an increase in aircraft production of 100% during the first year of the war. Freeman's production organisation was the basis that Beaverbrook exploited upon being appointed by Sir Winston Churchill as the 'War Lord' of aircraft production, but what was finally achieved was the churning out of aircraft (the numbers game again) irrespective of their operational efficiency. Aircraft were being produced that were obsolescent, or leaving the factories with equipment no longer required and minus equipment that was operationally necessary. Many aircraft had to be modified at the squadrons by RAF personnel already overloaded with operational work.

Our French Allies were not so fortunate with their Armee de l'Air, for the years preceding 1939 found that Service operating obsolete bomber and fighter aircraft, and it was not until it was too late to rectify this situation that any effort was made. By August 1939 the fighter arm of the Armee de l'Air was only just beginning to

16

No. 73 Squadron Gladiators lined up at RAF Debden in 1938. (S/Ldr C. Campbell DFC)

modernise. Although one hundred and twenty of the Bloch 151/152 type had been received these were not completely equipped and it would be 1940 before any unit was operational upon them. The best and most modern of French fighters was the Dewoitine D520. Large orders for the aircraft were placed, but it was not until January 1940 that the first of the type was at an air force establishment for testing. To cover this transition period the French Government placed large orders with the USA for Curtiss Hawk 75 'Mohawks', but although this aircraft was manoeuvrable, it lacked the all-round performance of the Bf109. With regard to bombers, the Armee de l'Air units were operating, and would continue to operate into 1940, obsolete and obsolescent aircraft such as the Amiot 143 (maximum speed of 183 mph); Bloch 131 (maximum speed of 218 mph) and the Farman 221/222 (maximum speed of 210 mph). French aeronautical engineers and designers were neither short of ideas nor designs, but French politics nationalised aircraft factories and the lack of a sense of urgency meant failure to equip with modern aircraft. When the storm broke in 1940, the Armee de l'Air, in spite of its obsolescent equipment, took up the challenge alongside the RAF, whose Battle light bombers without fighter escort were just as vulnerable. Together the two Services fought against impossible odds.

17

Blenheim Mk Is of No. 139 Squadron lined-up for inspection at Wyton pre-1939. (Owen Baum)

The British Air Staff's decisions in 1936, their war plans and their re-equipment programmes would determine the RAF's wartime operations as from 1939. Unfortunately, the RAF was to enter World War II before the planned re-equipment could be completed. This, and the failure in France of the Allied Armies, ensured that the units allocated to the British Air Forces in France (BAFF) would be decimated. Even after the commencement of war, it was still planned to withdraw the Battle squadrons of the AASF to the UK for re-equipment with Blenheims, but only two Battle squadrons had been replaced before the onset of the German attack. By 1939, the short range light/medium bombers (Battle and Blenheim) that were destined under the war plans to go to France with the British Expeditionary Force, were based in the Oxfordshire/Berkshire area; whilst the long range striking force of Bomber Command were situated at bases nearest Germany, in the counties of East Anglia, Lincolnshire and Yorkshire. Bomber Command's strength at this date was 55 squadrons, but by the end of September 1939 this was reduced to 33 squadrons, the remaining squadrons being held in reserve to cover initial losses. These 33 squadrons included the ten Battle squadrons sent to France with the AASF. During this same period of time, Fighter Command of the RAF was approaching fighting trim and finally being equipped with Hurricanes and Spitfires. With a total strength of 35 squadrons Fighter Command was eleven squadrons under the strength considered sufficient to defend the UK. Of these 35 squadrons, six had been placed on a mobile basis, and of these six, four had been dispatched to France with the Air Component of the BEF. By May, 1940, the strength of Fighter Command had risen from 35 squadrons to 47, but of these only 38 squadrons were equipped with Hurricanes and Spitfires.

The Allied plans

The plan of the Western Allies as regards to the movement and employment of the RAF squadrons in the AASF (Advanced Air Striking Force) and the ACFF (Air Component of Field Forces) was in three phases. Phase I would take place from three days after mobilisation orders, and the 1st Echelon of the AASF (consisting of five Wings totalling ten squadrons) would fly over to France to bases in the Reims area. This would be followed by Phase II (ten to eighteen days after mobilisation), the first flight of the 2nd Echelon (Blenheims) of the AASF would fly over to prepared bases and satellites (the 2nd Echelon was ten bomber squadrons). During this same period the Air Component forces (two squadrons of reconnaissance aircraft) would move out to their bases. This would be followed by Phase III, which would take place nineteen to twenty-six days after mobilisation, when the second flight of the 2nd Echelon would move across the Channel. The whole plan envisaged the transfer to France within twenty-six days of mobilisation of twenty bomber squadrons (Bomber Command) of the AASF, two reconnaissance-bomber squadrons, six army-co-operation squadrons and four fighter squadrons of the Air Component.

On 4th April, 1939, a meeting took place between the Secretary of State for Air (Sir Kingsley Wood) and the French Air Minister (M.Guy le Chamber) to discuss amongst other things, French aircraft production. During the meeting the French 'Plan 5' was considered. This had visualised a production of 1,800 aircraft in the period between April 1938 and March 1939, but concern was felt as only 716 aircraft had actually been produced. The same plan also envisaged the production of 3,000 aircraft in the following year, but the rate of production at the time of the meeting was only 100 per month, rising to 150 aircraft per month in the Summer of 1939 and 200 per month in the Autumn. M.Guy le Chambre explained that their figure in the plan of 1,800 aircraft was only a goal to be reached under optimum conditions! He further explained that the French Air Force at that date consisted of 1,200 aircraft, which were out-of-date, with a further 5,000 aircraft obsolete but which could be used for other military purposes! Their fighters were only capable of about 240 mph and the bombers were too slow to be used except at night or with cloud cover. It was agreed that the United Kingdom should consider the possible supply to France of Merlin X engines with propellers, whilst the two Air Staffs would examine the possible standardisation in specifications for their air forces.

The next step was the setting up of advance airfields in the Reims area, and in May 1939 a stock of British bombs and pyrotechnics was

No. 105 Squadron Battles pre-war, flying line abreast. Note the lack of squadron code letters.

laid down in those airfields allocated to the AASF, with the transaction being disguised as a sale to the French.

A further meeting was then held on 25th July, when the following arrangements were made, two hundred and sixteen Merlin III engines were to be supplied by February 1940 and one hundred and seventy-five Merlin Xs by June 1940 . . . the latter to be delivered as parts so as to allow the French technicians to gain experience on their assembly. Further to this, three hundred and three DH Hamilton propellers would be delivered at the rate of thirty per month. During the month of August a number of RAF bomber squadrons were allowed to overfly France for experience; then on 24th August secret mobilisation of the AASF and Air Component was ordered, leave was cancelled, kit packed and equipment made ready for transfer. This was followed on 1st September by the opening of the AASF HQ in Reims, as it was now accepted that the AASF would proceed to their airfields in France whether war was declared or not.

The strengths of the competing powers now appeared like this:

	Germany	France	Gt Britain
Aircraft Production	8,295	3,163	7.940
First Line Strength	3,609	1,792	1,911
Reserves	900	1,600	2,200

Advanced Air Striking Force Movement

On 2nd September, 1939, ten Battle Squadrons (160 aircraft) were flown to France. These were Nos. 12, 15, 40, 88, 103, 105, 142, 150, 218 and 226; provision having already been made for the transfer of the servicing flights and essential personnel to be dispatched by air, so as to receive the Battles on their respective airfields in France, where stocks of fuel, oil, bombs and ammunition had already been laid down. The remaining personnel and stores left by sea on the same date. The transfers were:

Unit		Based at	Transferred to
HQ AASF		Abingdon	Chateau Polignac Reims
71 Wing	⎰ 15 Squadron	Abingdon	Betheniville
	⎱ 40 Squadron	Abingdon	Betheniville
72 Wing	⎰ 105 Squadron	Harwell	Reims-Champagne
	⎱ 226 Squadron	Harwell	Reims Champagne
74 Wing	⎰ 103 Squadron	Benson	Challerange
	⎱ 150 Squadron	Benson	Challerange
75 Wing	⎰ 88 Squadron	Boscombe Down	Auberive
	⎱ 218 Squadron	Boscombe Down	Auberive
76 Wing	⎰ 12 Squadron	Bicester	Berry-au-Bac
	⎱ 142 Squadron	Bicester	Berry-au-Bac

The first difficulties encountered, with one or two exceptions, was that there were no permanent buildings on the airfields, and the airfields were remote for the most part from all but small villages and the billeting arrangements presented problems. From examination of the facts it would appear that a lot depended on the degree of efficiency of the local French Air Company (who were charged with all arrangements on each airfield) in preparing the way. No. 71 Wing appears by the records to have been the most unfortunate, for the French Air Company there were expecting only five Officers and thirty other ranks, no arrangements having been made for accommodating or feeding the remainder of the two squadrons.

John Marr of No. 40 Squadron remembers the day of arrival:

"The first night was spent in the Betheniville Village hall on straw-filled palliasses, which still had all the harvest bugs in them! This made everyone scratch a lot and from then on decide the concrete floor was the lesser of two evils. Washing was done in the stream which flowed through the village and I remember the local ladies soon organised a laundry system for us as it took a long time for the workshops to organise a bathhouse for us. Feeding was chaotic because the French Army were supposed to organise it. When the RAF kitchens and supplies arrived, it seemed to consist of nothing else but pilchards. I have never eaten a pilchard since those days!"

At the airfield itself, things were even worse, two tents had been provided, but one was used by the French guard! Three petrol filling points were available but the bomb dump was only partly constructed, while no trenches had been dug. Officers were quickly billeted on local families, but the other ranks slept on the floor of the local cinema . . . unfortunately this already held many residents of the biting kind, so there was more scratching than sleeping! The feeding of the men was carried out by the French Army, with their style of rations . . . a little different to RAF fare!

The Anglo-French plan was to have one squadron on each airfield, but at this point the satellite landing grounds for the 2nd Echelon were not ready . . . to be fair, the French had not guaranteed that they would be . . . so the plan to move the 2nd Echelon in was abandoned. This move was finally cancelled on 21st September, when at a conference at General Gamelin's HQ, the French Air Force Commander in Chief (General Vuillemin) suggested that these Blenheim Squadrons might be better left in England for use against a possible German attack through Belgium. The Air Staff were in agreement with this suggestion, especially as they felt that the move (going by past experience) usually resulted in lowered operational efficiency for about eighteen days. With the satellite landing grounds not ready, this meant that the five main airfields reserved for the 2nd Echelon would have to be taken up, if the distribution of one squadron per airfield was to be achieved, so on or about 12th September the following moves took place:

No. 15 Squadron moved from Betheniville to Conde-Vraux,
No. 105 Squadron moved from Reims-Champagne to Villeneuve-Vertus,
No. 150 Squadron moved from Challerange to Ecury,
No. 88 Squadron moved from Aubervie to Mourmelon-le-Grand,
No. 142 Squadron moved from Berry-au-Bac to Plivot.

Plivot was destined to be the base for strategic reconnaissance, so within a few days of No. 142 Squadron's move, they were moved back to Berry-au-Bac, and on 8/9th December, No. 12 Squadron moved from Berry-au-Bac to Amifontaine.

In general the movement of the motor transport was in array; there were delays in unloading, no arrangement for feeding personnel and no guidance provided for vehicles to proceed to their destinations or for the en-route refuelling of the vehicles. For instance, No. 15 Squadron's Motor Transport (MT) convoy eventually arrived at Conde-Vraux on the evening of 19th September. The safe arrival of the motor transport at their various destinations was officially considered to be entirely due to the resourcefulness of their personnel, and the extreme helpfulness of the French civil and military authorities on the way.

Blenheim Mk IV N6231 at Wyton, August, 1939. (Owen Baum)

Air Component Movement

Transfer of the aircraft took place over a number of days, the first priority being the four squadrons of Hurricanes Nos. 1, 73, 85 and 87 which arrived in France on 8/9th September, 1939.

	Unit	Based at	Transferred to
60 Wing {	1 Squadron	Tangmere	Le Havre-Octeville
	73 Squadron	Digby	Le Havre-Octeville
	85 Squadron	Debden	Rouen-Boos
	87 Squadron	Debden	Rouen-Boos

By 17th September most of the ground parties had arrived, though once again the road convoys suffered delays. The first reconnaissance squadron to arrive was No. 53 Squadron with twelve Blenheims, these being initially based at Plivot, but on 11th October the squadron was moved to Poix. On 2nd October Nos. 4 and 13 Squadrons arrived with their Lysanders for tactical reconnaissance, and the eventual allocation of squadrons to airfields was thus:

	Unit	Based at	Transferred to
50 Wing	HQ	Odiham	Athies
50 Wing {	4 Squadron	Odiham	Mons-en-Chaussee
	13 Squadron	Odiham	Mons-en-Chaussee
	53 Squadron	Odiham	Plivot (then to Poix)
70 Wing	HQ	Upper Heyford	Roye-Amy
70 Wing {	18 Squadron	Upper Heyford	Roye-Amy
	57 Squadron	Upper Heyford	Roye-Amy
51 Wing	HQ	Andover	Abbeville
51 Wing {	2 Squadron	Hawkinge	Abbeville
	26 Squadron	Catterick	Abbeville
	59 Squadron	Andover	Poix

23

Operational control

The control of the AASF was vested in AVMP. Playfair, while that of the Air Component was AVM C. Blount. Besides these two components two further air missions were scheduled to go to France, the No. 1 Air Mission was led by Air Marshal A. S. Barratt, who was to represent the British Chief of Air Staff at the HQ of General Vuillemin (Commander in Chief of the French Air Force); the No. 2 Air Mission being led by Air Commodore F. P. Don, who was to represent the Commander in Chief RAF Bomber Command at the HQ of General Mouchard (Commander of the 1st French Air Army. In a report within the Royal Air Force regarding the AASF Battles' employment, it was acknowledged that the aircraft's relatively short range and light defensive armament made it unsuitable for deep penetration raids; whilst the use of the aircraft for the purpose of dropping leaflets at night was objected to by Bomber Command, as their night flying training had been restricted to night take-offs and landings. On 3rd September, 1939, Air Vice Marshal Slessor wrote to Bottomley in regard to the report, with a view to considering how to use the AASF Battles, and also stressed the limitation of their equipment . . . yet little appears to have been considered to providing these aircraft with fighter escorts during bombing operations. In early December the AASF Command began the first rotation of squadrons for re-equipment, Nos. 15 and 40 Squadrons being routed home for re-equipment with Blenheims, and their place was taken by Nos. 114 and 139 Squadrons with their Blenheims.

With the arrival of No. 114 Squadron at Vraux, the villagers were again to have an RAF squadron billeted on them. Airmen were once again to be allocated to lofts and barns. T. H. Davies records the following:

"Our little bunch were allocated a billet in a farm at the extreme end of Vraux. A vertical ladder ascended to the top of the hayloft; underneath was a galaxy of mooing cows which were fortunately quiet in the nocturnal hours. The farmyard was a huge rectangle, the old farmer and his wife lived our end – on the base but next to the cowshed. The farmer quickly appraised the position upstairs and secured some sacks of animal feed which served as excellent bedding – taking into account the circumstance.

The environment to me was totally strange, and out of my experience. It was enough to climb up and down those stairs with kit for those number of months. And more laughable, the latrine situated the other side of the stables – just far enough to reach in an emergency but suicide at night. I assume the latrines were typical war pattern but consisted of a deeply dug type of slit trench with a large tree trunk slung across. One said one's

No. 73 Squadron Hurricanes 'showing the flag' over France, September 1939. Only one aircraft is carrying squadron code letters. (S/Ldr C. Campbell, DFC)

prayers before entering on the natural function!''

The first weakness to manifest itself in the communications structure and command linkage, was the weakness in instituting instructions for bombing or reconnaissance sorties. Information would first of all come from French reconnaissance to AASF HQ, then the request for a sortie would be passed to Bomber Command HQ for approval. This approval would then pass to AASF HQ, thence to Wing HQ, and thence to the Squadrons! This was rectified in January 1940, when the title of British Air Forces France was given to an overall structure commanded by Air Marshal A.S. Barratt; this absorbed the AASF and Air Component, as well as the No. 1 and 2 Air Missions, also divorced the AASF from the operational control of Bomber Command. The Air Component was also renamed as RAF Component British Expeditionary Force (or RAFCBEF for short!). This new command structure partly came about because of a review of the original structure by Air Officer Commanding in Chief Bomber Command, who stated that the requirements needed ''buttoning up'', and was certainly influenced by the War Office demanding control over a number of their own aircraft ... when the Blitz hit them the

Army staff were not even capable of controlling their own troops' movements.

Prior to this, on 21st September, 1939, at his Headquarters General Gamelin had suggested to Air Chief Marshal Sir C. Newall (Chief of Air Staff) that two further fighter squadrons should be dispatched to the defence of the BEF area, leaving the four existing squadrons at Rouen and Le Havre. This suggestion was politely rejected, partly because this was not part of the original agreement and partly because the numbers of of fighter squadrons left in the UK for Home Defence was below the requisite number. However, it was agreed that two further fighter squadrons would be positioned, so as to be immediately ready for operations, should such an emergency arise in France. Nos. 1 and 73 Squadrons were moved on 8/9th October from the BEF area to a position in advance of the AASF airfields. Then, on 15th November, on warnings being given by intelligence sources of an imminent German attack, Nos. 607 and 615 Squadrons with their Gladiators were flown across to Merville, which had been vacated by Nos. 85 and 87 Squadrons due to the airfields's surface being in a muddy and unusable condition; these two squadrons being moved to Lille-Seclin. From Merville Nos. 607 and 615 Squadrons moved to Vitry-en-Artois, the fighter position now being:

> Two Hurricane fighter squadrons (85 and 87) were in the BEF area at Lille-Seclin.
> Two Gladiator fighter squadrons (607 and 615) were in the BEF area at Vitry-en-Artois.
> Two Hurricane fighter squadrons (1 and 73) were in the AASF area Verdun-Metz at Vassincourt and Etain-Rouvres.

No. 607 Squadron landed at Merville to find continuous torrential rain and the subsequent mud. The squadron then moved on to Vitry-en-Artois and again barns and haylofts were the billets for the airmen. Sergeant D. Brown, who was with the squadron, remembers the place under snow:

> "We were billeted in a farmhouse in the main street. The name of our host was Maurice Villeman, and four of us shared his front room which had a tiled floor, but a nice fireplace. Our beds consisted of two low trestles with three tapered boards, a straw palliasse and four blankets. Washing facilities were primitive but adequate. Later on some of our officers lent us their proper camp-beds, which they did not need as they were living in the one and only hotel. Gradually the snow eased and a partial thaw set in. Flying then became possible. The airfield became soggy and rutted, but every night it froze and we became expert at replacing broken tailwheel struts. We later found that this was the coldest winter for 100 years!"

26

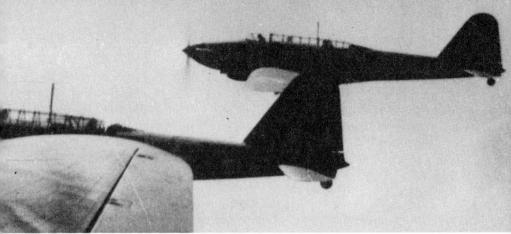

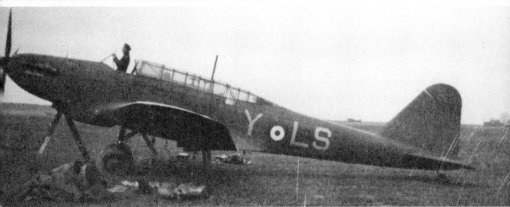

Snaps from the front. Top: No 15 Sqn.
Battles over France – Aug. 39. Above:·
P2177 of No 15 Sqn at Vraux, Oct. 39.
Right: Curly Baldwin and Mick Mitchell
of No 15 Sqn at their billet, Farm Guiset,
Vraux, holding young Bernard Guiset.
Bottom right: the scene at Vitry with No
607 Sqn Gladiators and French guard.
Below: Airmen Freeman, Mills and Davies
of No 114 Sqn in 'scruff order'.

The German Enemy

In 1935 with the disclosure that Germany now possessed its own Air Force, it appeared to knowledgeable politicians and airmen that a war between Germany and Great Britain was patently obvious. This would become even more obvious as Germany's re-armament programme was speeded up even more, and the Luftwaffe under Hermann Göring began to reach parity in numbers with the RAF . . . eventually to substantially exceed it. To the onlooker this contest in numbers appeared as if the two air forces were sparring prior to a fight, a deathwish to engage in mortal combat. Yet, while the RAF was expanding in an effort to defend the UK, the German Luftwaffe was being prepared as a weapon of aggression; long range artillery to strike ahead of the German Army, an Army which at the behest of its leader was to conquer and humiliate Austria and Czechoslovakia; then to attempt the conquest of the the the remainder of Europe. The Luftwaffe was by 1939 basically a tactical air force, mainly subjugated under the blitzkrieg tactics to the German Army's determination of targets, attacking ahead of the army spearheads any supply dumps, airfields, and troop or armoured formations.

While a large amount of tactical and practical experience had been gained for the Luftwaffe by the "Kondor Legion" in Spain, some of the experience was to be wrongly analysed, as was to be proved in the Battle of Britain; but in the Battle of France the Luftwaffe's over-whelming air supremacy and tactics were to prove unbeatable. This, combined with a German Army led by Generals who were the best of their profession, proved the total decimation of the Allied forces. At the end of the Battle the Luftwaffe would have to lick its wounds inflicted by the RAF and Armée de l'Air, and a number of units had to return to Germany to re-equip and re-organise. The Luftwaffe command structure ran down from the Oberkommando der Luftwaffe (Air Force High Command) to the Air Fleet (Luftflotten), to the Fliegerkorp (Air Corp), then to the Geschwader (equivilent to an RAF Group). Each Geschwader had a number of Gruppes, each having approximately thirty aircraft. In each Gruppe were Staffeln with each Staffeln having nine to ten aircraft . . . though the strength of each Gruppe or Staffeln varied according to the date in the war and its duties. By May 1940 the Luftwaffe had a strike force of 1,444 bombers, which were in Air Fleets 2 and 4; with a fighter force of over 1,000 Bf109s; ready to strike in the West upon initiation of *Fall Gelb* (Plan Yellow). In the bomber force was KG1 with He111s; KG2, KG3, KG76, KG77 and KGr606 with Dornier Do17s; plus Gruppen re-equipping with Ju88s. During the winter of 1939–40 high level reconnaissance Do17s were often seen and a number were caught and destroyed by RAF Hurricanes. With the coming of 10th May, 1940, these reconnaissance tactics and low level flights were to reward the Germans tenfold.

For the attack in the West the Germans had 'Army Group B' in the north, and 'Army Group A' in the south, ready to punch through the Ardennes; and though the *Panzerwaffe* was well equipped to defend itself from the skies, having 2,600 of 88mm AA guns and 6,700 light AA guns, (postwar research has determined that it fought its early battles at a numerical disadvantage as regards tanks) and the Allied Armies in France were defeated by an enemy force having an inferior number of tanks, but with an organisational efficiency and effectiveness in handling their tanks and aircraft, beyond the conceptual strategy of the Allied Armies. For the offensive in May 1940, the German Army was to employ one hundred and thirty-six of its one hundred and fifty-seven divisions.

The original attack in the West was to operate under the plan codename *Fall Gelb*, which was a rehash of the First World War *Schlieffen Plan*. This was an attack through the Low Countries, which was objected to by Field Marshal Erich von Manstein . . . considered by many as Germany's military genius . . . who felt that the strike through the Low Countries was its weakness. Against this he drew up a plan, which was a variation of *Fall Gelb*, called *Sichelschnitt* (Scythe Stroke). In this plan, the northern 'Army Group B' would strike through the Low Countries as a decoy to draw the French and British Army into a trap. With the movement northwards of these armies to help the Belgians, then 'Army Group A' would strike through the Ardennes, scythe through France to the Somme, and thus cut off the Allied Armies trapped in the Low Countries. The Ardennes being considered by the French Command as impenetrable by armoured forces, the defences there were held by middle-aged French reservists, whilst the regular forces moved into Belgium. The *Sichelschnitt* plan was originally turned down by the German High Command, but eventually it was brought to the attention of Hitler, who had it adopted . . . still known as *Fall Gelb*.

The initiation of *Fall Gelb* almost commenced in November 1939, but bad weather conditions and a certain amount of resistance by the German High Command was against this; the resistance was not because of their consciences, but due to lack of final military preparations. Nevertheless, German preparations and reconnaissance continued, but the weather in the 1939–40 winter was extremely bad and eventually *Fall Gelb* and its operation drifted into 1940.

Chapter Two
The Battle of France Commences

Operations Commence

On 6th September, 1939, a telex was received at both the Air Ministry and Bomber Command from the AASF, which read, "AASF now ready to operate at full strength, though operations will be on a restricted basis on account of lack of full rearmament and refuelling facilities." So from this date photo-reconnaissance patrols over and along the enemy front line commenced. Many were carried out without interruption, except for flak. Yet what is surprising is that even at this date there was a disagreement about the use of the Battle squadrons. Bomber Command were against their use by night, whilst the Air Staff felt that they were not equipped for deep penetration raids, but could be used effectively against an invading army, no move being made to upgrade their armament.

From 15th September the Blenheims of the Air Component's Nos. 18 and 57 Squadrons were cleared to make photographic sorties. Aircraft taking off from a forward base at Metz and proceeding to carry out vertical air photography over the Ruhr. During the winter months a lot of this would be curtailed by the freezing of the camera equipment at altitude. Then on 11th October, No. 57 Squadron moved to Poix, a grass airfield near Amiens.

On 20th September three Battles of No. 88 Squadron, while on photo-reconnaissance, were bounced by a section of Bf109s. Two of the Battles were shot down, but K9243, flown by Flying Officer King, escaped and his air gunner, Sergeant F. Letchford, managed to shoot down one of the attackers.

Three Battles of No. 103 Squadron were, on 27th September, carrying out reconnaissance of the Franco-German frontier, when three French Curtiss 75s made an aggressive approach. So the Battles fired off recognition signals and descended to ground level. The French fighters then flew off, but almost immediately three Bf109s attacked. The first aircraft hit was K9271 flown by Flying Officer Vipan, with observer, Sergeant Vickers, who was severely injured in the attack. The Merlin engine was spluttering and Vickers was in pain, so the pilot force landed the aircraft near to Rohrbach, one undercarriage not coming down. A French soldier told him that the Battles had shot down an enemy fighter, pointing to a column of dense black smoke rising from a nearby wood. Sergeant John Vickers was taken to the hospital, and became the first British airman to be

A No. 142 Squadron Battle crossing the Laon-Reims road at Berry-au-Bac.

Sgt. Observer Vickers of No. 103 Squadron. (R. Carless)

awarded a French decoration, being awarded the Medaille Militaire before he died on 7th October.

Still no fighter escorts were being provided for the Battles, and on 30th November, No. 150 Squadron were to suffer as a consequence. Five of their aircraft were out on reconnaissance when they were attacked by fifteen Bf109s, the enemy attacking in groups. Within minutes four Battles and one Bf109 had been shot down and a further Bf109 gone down in spiral dive. The sole remaining Battle, K9283 flown by Squadron Leader MacDonald, had both its port and auxiliary fuel tanks holed, with the flaps and other equipment damaged. The landing at base was satisfactory until almost the end of the landing run, when the aircraft swung due to a burst tyre, the aircraft then burst into flames and was destroyed. From this recce' six crew members were killed or missing, the remainder injured or wounded, and K9283, K9284, K9387, N2028 and N2093 lost. Bob Pearce, who served on Battles of No. 142 Squadron with the AASF, carried out thirteen operational sorties in France and says of those times:

"On service with 142 Squadron, there was no feeling of being in the least bit intrepid. On the contrary, the aircraft was regarded not only with affection, but also with pride. We much preferred our Battles to the Blenheims which were at that time entering squadron service. Everyone knew that Blenheims were unable to maintain height on one engine. It didn't occur to us that the Battle had all the flying characteristics of a brick, should its solitary engine cease to function.

"When filling the ammunition pans, we tended to use plenty of tracer bullets, on the principle that the enemy would be deterred if he saw what was approaching him."

At this period of the war the air gunner, with his proudly worn 'winged bullet' insignia, was usually an armourer or wireless operator, and in the case of the Battle and Blenheim, the latter trade. The air gunner was regarded first as a 'tradesman' and only secondarily as aircrew; thus, when an operation was planned, only the pilot and observer attended the briefing. Then at the aircraft the air gunner joined the crew, when he would be provided with the 'colour of the day' cartridges.

No. 142 Squadron were at this time based at Berry-au-Bac, the aircraft being taxied across the main Reims-Laon road to dispersal points in the periphery of a wood. The young airmen found that living and working in a foreign country was quite a novelty, being billeted in a farm at Ville-au-Bois, where a very good relationship was soon established with the locals.

There were occasions that brightened up the tedium of routine work, such was the day when Flying Officer Trent of No. 15 Squadron decided to carry out practice dive bombing. It was the custom of the squadron either to practice dive bombing with 8½lb practice bombs on a target on the airfield, or to carry out dummy dive bombing attacks on the airfield's 'Red House'. Wing Commander George takes up the story:

> "An exercise of the latter variety threw the whole place into a state of alarm, when it was realised that the aircraft he was flying was in fact bombed up. Moreover, it was a nice day, and Len had not bothered to take his helmet, and therefore could not be contacted. I well remember doing the only thing possible, which was to leap into an aircraft and try to head him off. Fortunately he was taking his time about climbing and I managed to catch up with him and contrive to thwart him every time he showed signs of peeling off, which made him very cross until he evetually got the message and landed, and was persuaded to look in the bomb bay (four 250lb HE)."

This took place at Vraux, where No. 15 Squadron had moved, after being at Bethenivile with No. 40 Squadron. Both squadrons, along with other AASF squadrons were engaged on reconnaissance patrols of the frontier areas, mostly without interruption by the enemy. On one patrol a No. 15 Squadron pilot, Sergeant Pilot Day, was blinded by the sun as the squadron swung away from Hunland, and he carried on into enemy territory. Within a short space of time he found himself alone! He landed ten minutes after the squadron.

In the BEF area No. 87 Squadron was now based at Merville, although it did make temporary moves to other airfields during the winter of 1939–40. Merville as an airfield would become almost unusable during the winter months, but at this period the squadron was enjoying the late summer weather. One of the flight commanders was Flight Lieutenant Vose-Jeff, who was to shoot down the squadron's first enemy aircraft. Stan Cain was a member of the squadron and remembers Jeff as:

Pilot Officer L. Trent of No. 15 Squadron. (W/Cmd. H. George DFC)

The Maison Rouge HQ building at Vraux Airfield. (T. Davies)

"Outstanding amongst a bunch of outstanding people, he was a leader, and had the admiration and respect of the whole squadron."

He also remembers the flimsy four gallon petrol tins,

"Made of thin tin and packed two in a wooden crate. Owing to bad packaging and careless handling, they leaked about 30% of the fuel by the time we got them."

Other units as well as the squadrons were deployed to France and formed part of the BAFF; some were Air Stores Parks (which prepared replacement aircraft), mobile Direction Finding Units, 'Y' intercept unit, various HQ units as well as Communication Flights, the latter units flying Tiger Moths and Magisters. E. Alwyn Benjamin* was a member of the 'Y' intercept unit, which was responsible for intercepting and decoding Luftwaffe radio signals. The personnel were accommodated in small cottages at Fismes, not far from Reims.

"The wireless huts were on a steep hill with their aerial masts nearby – a perfect give-away to any German pilot or observer."

Some of the smaller units were fairly isolated away from the main RAF units, one of these was the mobile direction finding station of 75 Wing HQ based at St Hilaire. The DF station later moved to Mourmelon, where the nine airmen came under the charge of Corporal J. R. Heslop:

"We were all regular airmen, well known to each other, and we revelled in our comparative freedom to do as we pleased, while at the same time paying close attention to our work.

"Until the main party arrived we had been fed by the French Army. I still recall with horror the garlic flavoured haricot beans, the horsemeat stew, the execrable coffee. How different it was to the local cafes where traditional French cuisine was on offer. We drank with members of a "Char d'assaut" (tank unit) in the local cafe most evenings. We exchanged songs as the evening wore on, played French billiards and generally enjoyed the evening meal there too.

---

*Pre-war trained Post Office wireless operator. Commissioned in the Middle East in 1942.

"The children of the village had been pleased to see us. We were friendly and indulgent. They joined in the football and in the strange game of cricket. During the winter, snowball fights had been frequent. I gained the nickname of 'Monsieur Le coup de neige' after using the phrase to them in describing a direct hit with a snowball, my mangled French rendering it as 'un coup de neige'!''

AASF HQ had been established as from 2nd September at Chateau Polignac, and immediately the place was organised and communication and office routine established. Arthur Phipps was a member of the HQ team:

"When I first saw the Chateau Polignac in daylight, I realised that it must be the most prominent building on the outside of the town and, being at a main road junction opposite to the Pommery Parc, could not fail to be located by enemy aircraft."

He was also looking forward to French cooking,

"As this was my first time in France, I was looking forward to the delights of French cuisine. Our first (and for some of us, the only) meal at a cavalry barracks of stewed horse meat seemed revolting, but we were assured that the horse had only recently died!''

Flight Sergeant G. Jordan was attached to No. 1 Air Mission to France:

"On Monday, 4th September, we proceeded in convoy to St Jean-les-Deux Jumeaux on the Marne. The village had been completely evacuated, in order to accommodate the personnel of GQGA (Grand Quartier General Aerien) which was the HQ of the French Chief of Air Staff, General Vuillemin. The purpose of the Mission was liaison between GQGA and the British Air Ministry, an officer flew to London with dispatches once a week in a Dragon Rapide owned by Isle of Man Airways."

The BAFF/AASF Headquarters were in communication with the UK and Bomber Command through Typex sets, which were encoding/decoding cypher machines. The HQ complete with Typex were moved to Nancy, and with them moved H. Cooper, a Wireless and Electrical Mechanic, responsible for the servicing of the Typex sets. Two flats were taken over in Nancy for the Typex section, one for working and the other for accommodation. Mobile transmitting was also practised:

"We moved regularly to mobile sites with the mobile transmitter in a van, in case we were chased by the fellows from the nearby border beyond the Vorges mountains."

Quite a number of Magisters were used for communications in France, and eighteen were lost there during the campaign. Also used were Tiger Moths. G. Wheeldon* was a regular Sergeant Pilot attached to No. 50 Wing HQ at Athies with the aircraft parked at Mons-en-Chaussee. The Wing was commanded by Wing Commander F. M. F. West VC. MC. Wheeldon remembers:

> "He instructed me to fit a strap to the rudder pedal of the Tiger so that he could fly it with his good leg (West had lost a leg in the 1914–18 War), which he did on several occasions."

The official reason for the use of the Tiger Moth was to fetch and carry the camera packs to and from the Lysander and Blenheim squadrons, but on one flight:

> "... returning from Amiens to Mons-en-Chaussee, I found myself flying in supercooled rain and I watched the ice building up on the leading edges and interplane struts. Being a Tiger, it stayed up in the air and on arrival at Mons I broke a lump off one of the main struts and found the 'nose' was about 1 inch thick."

Sergeant Wheeldon was fortunate as an NCO pilot to be operating on detachment:

> "I had a very good time up to the Blitz. In the Tigers we were restricted to a maximum height of 1,000ft. and we never saw any enemy aircraft."

What may seem surprising now, is the fact that on a squadron at that time, NCO pilots were on a separate and lower plane to the officers, there being a distinct barrier; yet quite often on fighter squadrons, NCO pilots were flying as wingmen to Flight or Squadron Commanders ... having acquired more flying experience. When the Blitz commenced Wheeldon was posted to No. 98 Squadron for a refresher course on the Battle, then on to operations with No. 12 Squadron ... and survived.

The RAF fighter squadrons commenced their patrolling on 11th October, and on the 30th of the month opened their score with Pilot Officer Mould of No. 1 Squadron shooting down a Do17. This was followed by No. 87 Squadron shooting down an He111 on 2nd November. By this date Nos. 1 and 73 Squadrons had been transferred from the Air Component to the AASF, this took place on 8th October. They were numbered 67 Wing; No. 73 Squadron being commanded by a tough Irishman, Squadron Leader Knox, and No. 1 Squadron by Squadron Leader 'Bull' Halahan.

On 6th November, Pilot Officer Ayerst of No. 73 Squadron chased a single He111 about 40–45 miles into Germany, when he saw nine fighters coming up to his altitude of 14,000ft, and from his rear. Thinking they were Hurricanes he allowed them to reach his height

*Retired as Squadron Leader G. R. Wheeldon.

35

The He111 shot down by Flying Officer Vose-Jeff of No. 87 Squadron. 2 November, 1939. (S. J. Cain)

and about 300–400 yards on the starboard side, noticing them making a climbing turn he decided to join the formation and only then realised that they had black crosses on the wings ...Bf109s! Ayerst then spotted two more formations climbing fast, so decided to make a quick getaway as the odds were getting a little one-sided. Heading for French territory he had the enemy formation on his tail, so he stuffed the nose down to 2,000ft, but they followed him 4–5 miles inside French territory, where a formation of French Curtiss 75s and Morane 406s chanced on the scene and joined combat. By the time the fight had finished the French had claimed nine enemy aircraft but after debriefing this was reduced to three Bf109s – and Ayerst had five bullet holes in his aircraft.

On 8th November, Flying Officer 'Cobber' Kain, who was to become the first RAF ace of World War 2, opened up his own score, and that of No. 73 Squadron's, by climbing to 25,000 ft and shooting down a Do17 which crashed in the village of Lubbe. Fighter patrols were made by the Hurricanes at least three times a day and Flight Lieutenant R. Lee of No. 85 Squadron on 21st November shot down an He111 off Boulogne and so opened up his unit's score.

No. 67 Wing during 23rd November claimed the shooting down of four Do17s and three He111s during the day, with Kain shooting down a Do17 which force landed. Sergeant C. (Ken) Campbell* of No. 73 Squadron made an attack on a Do 17 formation:

---

*Retired as Squadron Leader C. N. Campbell DFC.

No. 73 Squadron 'B' Flight pilots on transport to dispersal. 'Ken' Campbell on right at back. (S/Ldr. C. Campbell DFC)

"I then saw eight aircraft approaching the airfield from Germany, flying at about 26,000ft. As they got nearer I recognised them as Dorniers, meanwhile, I had been climbing. The Dorniers were flying in loose formation and as I turned to follow them, still about 1,000ft below, they must have panicked as they suddenly split up and one came diving down some quarter mile in front of me.

"I immediately pushed my throttle on to full boost and dived after him. I gradually caught him up ... by that time I was 300 yards behind the Dornier, I saw tracer bullets flying over my left wing. I immediately put on some right rudder, causing my Hurricane to skid to the right and looking back saw another Dornier diving on my tail.

"Looking forward again I saw flashes from the rear gunner of the Dornier. I held my fire until he was in my sights at 200 yards, then pushed my firing button for a burst, then skidded to the right again ... We were by now diving almost vertically towards the ground and had lost the Dornier that had been on my tail. I centred my sights and gave another burst of fire at the Dornier and black smoke streamed from his port engine and the aircraft steepened its dive into the vertical. I followed it down and saw it crash beside a railway line and pinpointed it as being near the village of Sancy-le-Hant.''

After an attack on a British Hurricane formation by French fighters, it was decided to paint red-white-blue stripes on the tails, in the hope that our Allies would recognise which side the Hurricanes were on ... but before long there were red faces in an RAF Mess, when Hurricanes picked on a Potez 63 in mistake for a Bf110!

The guns on some of the Hurricane squadrons had by now been re-harmonised from their peacetime setting of 400 yards down to 250 yards, and during January 1940 rear armour was being fitted. This armour covered the area from the bottom of the spine to the top of the head; with this and the bullet proof windscreen, our fighter pilots were now in a better position to wage combat.

During the winter months, RAF Hurricanes and Armée de l'Air Curtiss 75s and Morane 406s carried out fighter affiliation exercises with the AASF Battles. These determined that although the Battles' 'jinking' in formation was effective to a point, if the fighters attacked in two groups, with one approaching from astern and the other from abeam and slightly below, there was no way of countering this. In spite of this the Battles were still poorly armed and unarmoured, still no self-sealing tanks and still no escorts for every patrol ... the only concession was the removal of the long-range fuel tank in the fuselage. To provide cover for the blindspot on the Battle a Vickers Gas Operated (VGO) machinegun on a hinged, pivoted mounting was now installed. Of dubious use, it was aimed to the rear by means of a mirror and sights.

No. 26 Squadron with their Lysanders arrived at Abbeville on 3rd October, to find that they had been beaten there by No. 2 (AC) Army Co-op. Squadron. The main party arrived by sea and train, only to find no motor transport available and the billets about 5 miles away at Plessiel, with the best billets already taken by No. 2 Squadron! So the NCOs and men complete with full kit and rifles marched there, singing. Both their presence and singing appeared to be appreciated by the French inhabitants. The billets for the men of the Air Component turned out to be, as with the AASF, mainly stables or lofts, whilst the Officers and some NCOs found accommodation in old houses and chateau. Life in general was a little spartan, and the early chores were the digging of dirt latrines, anti-aircraft pits and shelters.

The Lysanders' main task was to be tactical reconnaissance by eye and camera for the Army, so the first tasks were mosaics along territory adjacent to the Belgian frontier, short landing practice and reconnaissance exercises. The Lysanders were not the only ones exercising, for by 20th October solitary Ju88s were seen overflying Abbeville on reconnaissance. On the third day the Hurricanes bagged one but the following day the reconnaissance aircraft got away. When the Hurricanes bagged the one on the fifth day the reconnaissances ceased.

The Armée de l'Air fighter force had a good day on 6th November. After a force of Bf109s had shot down two French reconnaissance aircraft, nine Hawk 75s of GRN/22 pounced and despatched four Bf109s. Three of the enemy pilots escaped and became POWs, whilst the fourth died in his aircraft. Unfortunately, as regards reconnaissance, the Ardennes area was only weakly monitored, even though Intelligence had warned of German troop concentrations and a possible attack in November. As the area was considered by the French GHQ to be impassable for an armoured force, very little consideration was given to thoroughly reconnoitre the area by air and this persisted right until the Blitzkrieg commenced on 10th May.

Over the winter months German reconnaissance aircraft had continuously come in from the Luxembourg direction and in over Champagne, some being intercepted and shot down by Nos. 1 and 73 Squadrons' Hurricanes. In one case the crew baled out, less the pilot, who feigned death until his attacker (a No. 1 Squadron Hurricane) came alongside, when the 'dead' pilot then attempted to shoot his attacker down with a 'free' machinegun. The attempt was not completely successful and although the Hurricane was damaged the Dornier pilot baled out to captivity. He was later entertained at the No. 1 Squadron Mess before being despatched to a POW camp. Hurricanes and Bf109s did not meet in combat until 22nd December, when a three aircraft section of No. 73 Squadron was patrolling Metz-Longuyon from their airfield at Rouvres. The section was directed by RT towards an unidentified aircraft, then as the section was warned that the aircraft had turned behind them, five Bf109s swept in and behind . . . resulting in two Hurricanes being shot down before combat could be joined.

On 30th October, Blenheim L1246 of No. 57 Squadron, crewed by Sergeant Farmer, Sergeant Proctor and AC. Partlow, were on photographic-reconnaissance, but due to bad visibility it was not possible to take photographs, so the pilot descended to make a visual assessment. On climbing away the aircraft was attacked by two Bf109s. Upon landing at Orly one undercarriage collapsed with the port wing and tail unit being damaged. By the end of 1939 the two squadrons on strategic reconnaissance, Nos. 18 and 57, had lost twelve Blenheims, No. 18 Squadron losing four and No. 57 Squadron losing eight. Six were lost through enemy action, two crashed in England landing after a reconnaissance, one lost in flying accident, one landed in Belgium with frozen controls, and two crashed in France.

On 3rd January, 1940, two Blenheims of No. 18 Squadron took off to carry out a photographic reconnaissance over Germany. Although one landed safely in England with 90 photographs, the other Blenheim was shot down SSE of Aachen, inside Belgium, by three enemy fighters. With the re-organisation of the RAF units in France into the BAFF, the various Wings etc. were renumbered. These were as follows:

50 Army Co-op Wing
No. 4 Squadron
No. 13 Squadron
No. 53 Squadron

60 Wing HQ at Seclin
No. 85 Squadron at Seclin
No. 87 Squadron at Lille-Marq

63 Wing HQ at Merville
No. 3 Squadron at Merville
No. 79 Squadron at Merville

70 Bomber Wing
No. 18 Squadron
No. 57 Squadron

75 Wing HQ at St Helaire-Le Grand
No. 88 Squadron at Mourmelon
No. 103 Squadron at Betheniville
No. 218 Squadron at Auberive

51 Army Co-op Wing
No. 2 Squadron
No. 26 Squadron
No. 59 Squadron

61 Wing HQ at Vitry
No. 607 Squadron at Vitry
No. 615 Squadron at Abbeville

67 Wing HQ at Bussy-la-Cote
No. 1 Squadron at Vassencourt
No. 73 Squadron at Rouvres

71 Wing HQ at Chateau-Fagnieres
No. 105 Squadron at Villeneau
No. 114 Squadron at Vraux
No. 139 Squadron at Plivot
No. 150 Squadron at Ecury

76 Wing HQ at Neufchatel
No. 12 Squadron at Amifontaine
No. 142 Squadron at Berry-au-Bac
No. 226 Squadron at Reims-Champagne

Weather over the winter months was so severe that not only were the engines hard to start, but machine guns froze up and the intercom/radio sockets became damp and resulted in 'howling' and lack of communication. All this resulted in reduced flying activity, and in one case, the escape of an He111; this had been intercepted by three No. 73 Squadron Hurricanes over Etain, but with frozen guns and flat batteries there was not much anyone could do. Special engine tents were sent out to the Battle and Blenheim squadrons, which, in conjunction with paraffin heaters, eased the engine starting problems a little. Harry Brown of No. 114 Squadron remembers the winter as:

"Very, very bad, cold and plenty of snow, we had temperatures of 40° below, we could not get our aircraft airborne. We later had blow-up tents over the engines with flameless heaters in them."

No. 87 Squadron were at Merville for a period during the bad weather of the winter. Stan Cain remembers an incident that could have been tragic:

"During this period of bad weather and snow and ice, we had to run-up the engines to keep them warm as our starter acc's could not stand the pace. We had to resort to hand starting and all had to have a go at winding. I was assisting on one occasion when the engine misfired which resulted in me being thrown into the propeller; as she had only backfired I only got a swipe from the flat of the prop' and got off with some bruising. While I was in the sickbay our Warrant Officer Discip' came to see me. His words were, "Hello Cain, I hope you realise how lucky you are, if you

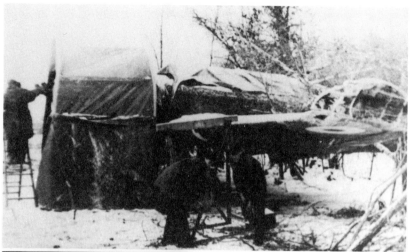

A No. 142 Squadron Battle being repaired after a low flying accident. Maintenance under such bad conditions was normal. (R. Pearce)

Armourers bombing up a Battle light bomber with 250 lb GP bombs.

had damaged that prop' you would have been paying for it for the rest of your service!'' I have yet to decide if he was joking or not.''

Bomber Command as well as the BAFF were by now far from convinced of the use of bomber aircraft against an advancing army. Their statement was:

"Bomber aircraft have proved extremely useful in *support of an advancing army*, but it is not clear that a bomber force used *against an advancing army*, well supported by all forms of anti-aircraft defence and a large force of fighter aircraft, will be economically effective.''

It was intended that the Battles would be loaded with four 250lb. bombs fused with an 11 second delay, and to make their attacks from around 50ft. The Blenheims were to have a mixed load of two 250lb. general purpose bombs fused with an 11 second delay, plus 20lb. or 40lb. bombs, and to make their attacks from heights up to 1,000ft. It was intended that the aircraft should make a low approach in formation, break formation at the last moment and to deliver individual attacks at about 30 second intervals, reforming after the attack.

41

During February and March 1940 the Battles of No. 142 Squadron went to Perpignan for night flying training, whilst on the fighter side it was business as usual. On 2nd March Flying Officer Kain and Sergeant D. Sewell of No. 73 Squadron sighted seven He111s that were being engaged by French ack-ack, the enemy aircraft clawing for height as they headed for Germany. As the two Hurricanes closed the gap, six Bf109s dived into the attack. Kain hit one and possibly damaged another. Sewell was put out of action as the Bf109s closed in and shot his radiator up. Kain's engine was struck by a cannon shell and set on fire. Both force landed in France and got back to base safely. Flying was more or less uneventful until 23rd March when, during the morning, several combats took place, with No. 73 Squadron claiming five enemy aircraft shot down and two damaged. In one incident seven Do17s escorted by three Bf110s were intercepted, followed by combats with formations of Bf109s. One Hurricane was lost during the day, which was Kain, who was leading a section of three to attack nine Bf109s. During the combat, Pilot Officer Perry shot a Bf109 off Kain's tail whilst Kain was shooting at another enemy aircraft,which left the scene trailing smoke. Two Bf109s then pounced on Kain's tail and hit his gravity tank, the aircraft was immediately engulfed in flames and Kain forced to bale out. In spite of his burns, Kain turned up at the squadron the same evening.

Previously the Bf109s had shown marked reluctance to cross the lines, but now large formations of them were sweeping across as far as Metz. These offensive tactics increased as April approached and Bf110s were more frequently seen. The Bf110s qualities were originally rated much higher than they turned out to be and the AOC had offered a dinner in Paris to the first pilot to bring down a Bf110 on the Western Front. This had been won in March, when three pilots of No. 1 Squadron, attacked a formation of nine BF110s north of Metz, setting one on fire which crashed on French soil. The AOC's personal Percival Q6 collected the three for dinner at Maxim's.

The combat took place on 29th March over Bouzonville. Closing quickly into the attack the Hurricane pilots soon found that they could easily out manoeuvre the Bf110 at the medium altitude and the rear gunners appeared to have great difficulty bringing their guns to bear on the attacking fighters during the manoeuvring. The result of the dogfight confirmed one Bf110 shot down and shots traded with the others but these hightailed it quickly for German airspace. It was also established that though the Bf110 was no dogfighter it certainly had a faster top speed than the Hurricane, even a Mk. 1 fitted with DH. or Rotol variable pitch propeller.

The Hurricanes had gone to war fitted with the Watts two-blade

Pamphlet dropped by the AASF Battles and Blenheims on early 'Nickel' raids. ('Doc' Walls)

Der Führer spricht!

„Gar uns ist dieser Bolschewismus aber eine Pest ...
Jede weitere deutsche vertragliche Verbindung mit dem
derzeitigen bolschewistischen Rußland würde für uns ganz
wertlos sein. Weder wäre es denkbar, daß national-
sozialistische deutsche Soldaten jemals zum Schutz des
Bolschewismus eine Hilfspflicht erfüllen, noch wollen wir
selbst von einem bolschewistischen Staat eine Hilfe entgegen-
nehmen." (Reichstagsrede vom 30. Jan. 1937.)

„Zu einem einzigen Staate haben wir kein Verhältnis
gesucht und wünschen auch zu ihm in kein engeres
Verhältnis zu treten: Sowjet Rußland."
(Reichstagsrede vom 20. Feb. 1938.)

„Die Regenten des heutigen Rußlands sind
blutbefleckte gemeine Verbrecher."
(Mein Kampf, Seite 750.)

Also sprach Adolf Hitler.

wooden propellers and no rear armour. The bomber squadrons at this stage would say, "What's rear armour?" but combat with the Bf109s had soon shown the lack of performance of the Hurricane during manoeuvring, especially going into the dive. A report at the time summarises it clearly:

"This engagement proves again that the Me109 dives faster than the Hurricane and demonstrates the necessity of having constant speed airscrews fitted to AASF Hurricanes at the earliest opportunity."

The First 'Nickel' (leaflet dropping operation) flown by the AASF Battles was carried out by a No. 88 Squadron aircraft, P2247, on 18th March. Other Battle Squadrons then commenced this type of operation. On 28th March, four No. 88 Squadron aircraft took off on a reconnaissance over Germany, but 10/10th cloud down to the safety height on return prevented P2247 from landing, the other three aircraft having landed. So after remaining in the air for five hours without any chance of weather improvement, the crew baled out. On 20th April, four No. 218 Squadron Battles took off on a 'Nickel' operation over Germany but only three aircraft returned as P2201 was shot down near Kreilsheim. On 4th April, 1940, Air Marshal Portal took command of Bomber Command, and a quick review of the situation caused him to correspond with the CAS. In this he expressed his doubts and fears regarding their use of the light bomber squadrons:

"I am convinced that the proposed employment of the units is fundamentally unsound, and if persisted in, it is likely to have disastrous consequences on the future of the war in air . . ."

43

Meanwhile, those light bomber squadrons and the other squadrons of the BAFF had suffered the rigours of the hard cold winter. The aircraft out in the open were hard to keep serviceable, even when large portable tents were issued to cover the engines. Personnel were in general billeted in small villages in lofts above farm animals or farm implements, shivering in their blankets at night having heaped gas capes and anything else they could on top. Washing and shaving was done from the farm pump. Officers were accommodated in slightly better conditions, as were some of the NCOs; but in general squadron personnel's inconvenience was on par with the Army's. The Crossley, Ford and Bedford motor transport was hard to start in the sub-zero conditions and the procedure first thing in the morning was the removal of plugs and placing them on a fire to warm up whilst a small fire was lit under the engine sump to warm the oil, the engines being hand started in those days. At the airfields most of the servicing personnel sections were housed in small tents, in which things like aircraft machine guns etc. were stripped and cleaned. Only at these sections was there any possibility of having a fire, so scavenging for firewood was a number one priority during the cold winter days. With the fire then a 'brew-up' of tea could be accomplished and only with the fire and tea could the coldness in the bones be diminished. Sometimes once a week, though mostly fortnightly, a 'liberty' lorry or coach would make a run to Reims or the nearest large town, so that personnel could have a hot bath and good meal, a taste of civilisation and the fleshpots!

The French villagers, after a short period of acclimatisation, welcomed the RAF personnel. T. H. Davies of No. 114 Squadron says of the time:

"The farmer and his family were 'salt of the earth' and very anti-Nazi. The elder had experience of the first war in the trenches. On returning from guard – cold and miserable – walking in the snow covered fields at night – still two on, four off – the old man would have us in and give us hot milk and lovely French panay. Another time I recollect sitting in the squarish kitchen, which served all purposes, appreciating the lovely heat. The farmer constantly offered the enclosed stove small twigs from a pile nearby, an endless task interrupted by a copious draught of wine."

Most aircraftsmen had been limited on departure from the UK to one uniform, a pair of boots and gumboots, and a change of under clothes. So it did not take many months wear before the trousers were stiff enough almost to stand up on their own! From P. Robinson-Judd, an armourer with No. 114 Squadron, came the following description of those times:

*Not in Russia, but a No.
607 Squadron Gladiator
running up at Vitry in
the 1939–40 winter.
(W/Cmd. Blackadder
DFC)*

"For me, the salient features of my stay in Vraux were the intense cold and attendant discomfort. The absence of any sort of billet heating or toilet facilities. The frozen cookhouse bread and the cans of margarine. The bleak airfield guard duties, wearing a woolly balaclava adorned with icicles and the appalling conditions of the 'back road' following the thaw – some beautiful mornings spent on the airfield in spring, and of course the final elimination of the squadron as a light bomber unit."

That elimination was still in the future and other actions and alterations were to take place before that date. In January 1940 the decision was made to withdraw Nos. 607 and 615 Squadrons to Rouen, so as to exchange their Gladiators for Hurricanes. Squadrons went on armament training to Perpignan and enemy invasion alerts were sounded.

For the French fighters the last day in March was disastrous, the Morane 406 proving an inferior weapon. Eleven of this type of aircraft of Groupe de Chasse III/7* were flying in staggered formation between 20,000 and 25,000ft on patrol in the Morhange area, when twenty Bf109s pounced out of the sun. Within five minutes two 406s were going down in flames, another one out of control and the remainder had been damaged beyond repair.

No. 607 Squadron commenced re-equipping with Hurricanes in mid-April, followed by No. 615 Squadron, whose second Flight did not proceed to Abbeville for this purpose until 9th May, 1940. Also in April another Lysander unit, No. 16 Squadron, was dispatched to France, making a total of five Lysander squadrons; Nos. 2, 4, and 13 attached to Corps, with Nos. 16 and 26 formed as a pool for GHQ to allocate as necessary. A Cierva Rota autogiro had also been flown by No. 26 Squadron earlier on, along with the Lysanders at Lille, but this crashed in early November, 1939.

---

*French fighter unit designations: 7th Escadril (Squadron) of the third group.

An RAF ground gunner in France with twin Lewis machine guns.

Flight Lieutenant D. Annand of No. 26 Squadron. (W/Cmd. D. Annand DFC)

One of No. 26 Squadron's pilots was Flying Officer D. Annand*, who, was a Flight Commander flying Lysanders:

"For security we flew with the two Brownings loaded, ringsight 'on', Lewis gun loaded and ready (sometimes a VGO). One never flew straight and level (photography being the exception), but weaved from side to side, looking over one's shoulder. The two coloured flares fired out of the Lysander roofing (changed every night at 0001 hours) were to identify yourself to British and French fighters, and 'friendly' ground troops if necessary. When the balloon went up we lost many Lysanders, as they were vulnerable."

The long-range photo-reconnaissance squadrons of the Air Component with their Blenheims, found the weather conditions during the winter months impossible, in general, for the photographing of the areas in Germany assigned to them. On top of this there was also the possibility of Allied fighters shooting them down whilst on photo-reconnaissance! This happened to Pilot Officer Hitch and crew of No. 59 Squadron on 18th March, 1940, when he was attacked by an RAF Hurricane. Although a landing was made at Poix, the aircraft was a write-off.

It was not only the fighters either. Flying Officer J. Wray** returning to No. 53 Squadron from a spell in hospital, was ferrying out a new Blenheim for No. 59 Squadron from Odiham to Glisy, when French ack-ack near Crecy-en-Ponthieu shot him down . . . and so back to hospital; fortunately he was able to return back to flying duties within the year.

The Air Component Lysanders, as well as the Blenheims of the BAFF, were having their share of ground problems, as many of the airfields and advanced landing fields were roughly flattened grass fields and, on soft ground, easily rutted. In the winter months these

---

*Retired as Wing Commander and went back to sea as a navigating officer.
**Retired as Group Captain DFC after 32 years service.

were often studded with molehills, which resulted in tailwheel assemblies and sternframes continually being damaged. One of the fitters who had to contend with this problem was 'Doc' Walls of No. 139 Squadron:

> "We had cracked sternframes on our Blenheims, and many hours I've struggled to align 'Shadow factory' spares with Filton airframes."

About the middle of February, 1940, the squadron moved from Betheniville to Plivot, some 10 Km east of Epernay. Of the airfield, 'Doc' Walls recalls:

> "The airfield was a vast improvement on Betheniville, being much flatter, and in an area of flat land stretching to the south, east and west; the northern side where the village stood, ran down towards the River Marne. The airfield had been provided with numerous dugouts, heavily sandbagged for aerodrome defence. Surprisingly, these were never manned and were not equipped with ack-ack or even machineguns."

Between the 6th and 16th March the squadron, like other squadrons, went on detachment to Perpignan for armament training. During this period they lost P4926, which crashed into the sea; the pilot and observer were killed, but the air gunner, LAC Brown, swam ashore. With the return of the squadron to Plivot, the next date of interest was on 11th April, when an alert was sounded and the squadron placed on two hours readiness and the *four* ground defence Lewis machineguns manned.

On 8th May the HQ ZOAN (French) warned the HQ (North) BAFF during the night to expect air attacks at dawn. Little notice was taken for it had been one of many.

A Battle of No. 142 Squadron with Fordson tractor and fuel bowser in the snow at Berry-au-Bac. (R. Pearce).

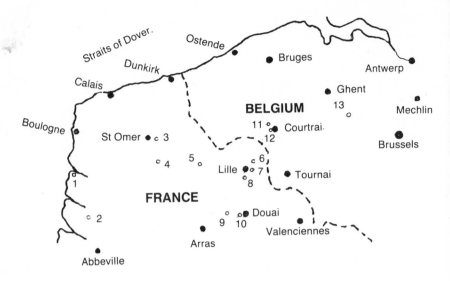

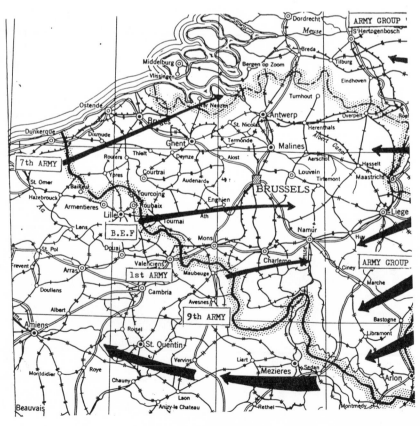

The battle begins

By midday on 9th May, 1940, the German High Command had issued orders for the attack in the west to commence the following morning. So as dawn broke on 10th May, ten DFS230 gliders landed at Fort Eban Emael (Belgium), and a further thirty gliders of the same type landed alongside the canal bridges near to Maastricht. Demolitions took place at most points along the Belgian border, and one of the Maas bridges was 'blown' by a Belgian Sergeant before it could be captured by the enemy airborne forces. The main German attack appeared to be in the direction of Maastricht, Tongres and Gembloux, but as alarmist reports of German Army movements had been received at French Army Headquarters in the early hours of the morning, very little attention was now paid to the fresh reports. At dawn also came the Luftwaffe attacks, with bomber strikes on at least seventy airfields in France, Belgium and Holland, as well as other targets. With this, No. 501 Squadron was flown over to Betheniville, No. 3 Squadron left Kenley and flew to Merville, while No. 79 Squadron flew to Mons-en-Chaussee.

The AASF Battle Squadrons were then placed on a '30 Minute readiness', with Barratt impatiently waiting on General Gamelin to give the orders to attack the German spearheads. Upon requesting permission to attack, Barratt was informed at 0800 hours by the French Army GHQ that operations were limited to fighter and reconnaissance only. The BEF and French Army moved across the frontier into Belgium to take up position along the Dyle, whilst middle-aged French reservists were left to hold the frontier facing the Ardennes. Meanwhile in the Ardennes, Panzer units of 'Army Group A' were moving forward under cover of darkness, with their aim to strike through to Sedan – *Sichelschnitt* was starting to unfold. At Maastricht and other breakthrough points 20mm and 37mm anti-aircraft weapons were quickly brought up and deployed, ready for retaliatory attacks by the Allied air forces.

At BAFF Headquarters, Barratt was making repeated requests, as was General d'Astier of the French Air Force, to be allowed to attack. Reconnaissance aircraft, *those that got back*, reported enemy armoured columns and troop formations stretching miles back into Germany, making the target of a lifetime. Gamelin refused to acquiesce to Barratt's requests, (maybe for fear of a bombing war, for which France was not prepared). At 12.00 hours, with his patience exhausted and still no permission given, Barratt authorised Playfair to send off his Battle squadrons. The enemy's direction of advance was now clear, for armoured columns covered by Bf109s and supported by Ju87 dive bombers, were thrusting towards Maastricht, with large numbers of flak guns being brought up to cover the Maastricht bridges at Vroenhoven and Veldwezelt.

The first attack was by thirty-two Battles of Nos. 12, 103, 105, 142, 150, 218 and 226 Squadrons, which took off to attack the enemy columns advancing through Luxembourg. Mobile flak guns and fighter defences took a heavy toll of the unescorted low-flying Battles, their unprotected fuel tanks flared as they were hit by flak or aircraft shells. Many burnt before they hit the ground, others were cannoned into oblivion and only nineteen aircraft returned to their bases near Reims. No. 142 Squadron had supplied eight Battles to take part in this operation, the aircraft taking off at 12.00 hours in two sections. K9367 was forced to return due to its undercarriage not retracting and of the other seven, three failed to return:

L5231	F/O. Roth,	Sgt. Algie,	AC. Morris,	failed to return
?	P/O. Laws,	Sgt. Miller,	AC. Langton,	failed to return
L5238	Sgt. Spear,	Sgt. Brooks,	LAC. Nugent,	failed to return
L5517	F/O. Martin,	Sgt. Trescothic,	Cpl. Todd.	
L5580	Sgt. Heslop,	Sgt. Hemmings,	LAC. Gillam.	
P2246	P/O. Corbett,	Sgt. Irvine,	LAC. Gaston.	
L5242	F/O. Gosman,	Sgt. Pollack,	LAC. Cave.	

On return a white Very light was shot up from P2246, to indicate dead or wounded on board. The Battle touched down but slewed off the runway as it slowed down. The pilot, Pilot Officer Corbett, was unconcious in the cockpit with two tracer bullets in his right ankle, the observer was dead and the gunner injured. From the other three crews, visibly shaken, came the story of their low level attack at 200ft. along a road in Luxembourg. The Germans had motorbike combinations, in the sidecars of which were mounted machineguns; these had dispersed to the side of the road and, combined with rifle fire from the troops, had shot down the three aircraft, as well as damaging the others.

At 15.30 hours a second attack of thirty-two AASF Battles took-off to strike again at the German 16th Army advancing through Luxembourg. Without fighter cover the Battles had little defence as the German fighters covering the columns swept down to attack. A further ten Battles failed to return.

Meanwhile, in Holland, reports were received that Waalhaven Airfield (Rotterdam) was in German hands after an attack by German paratroops assisted by Ju 52/3m transports. It was decided to put in an attack on this target, BAFF, at 12.05 hours, requested Bomber Command's help to carry out this operation. As it was considered that a bombing attack might cause unnecessary civilian casualties, it was decided to send in six Fighter Command Blenheim 1Fs of No. 600

Battle L5540 of No. 150 Squadron, shot down during an attack on a German column on the Luxembourg-Gevenmacher road. F/O Roberts, Sgt. Ward and AC1 Mayrick became POWs. 10 May 1940.

Battle L5231 of No. 142 Squadron shot down on 10 May during an attack on German troops in Luxembourg. F/O Roth, Sgt. Algie and AC Morriss became POWs.

Squadron 'B' Flight. The six Blenheims swept in low to attack the airfield and were 'bounced' from above by twelve Bf110s, resulting in the loss of five aircraft. The RAF had not relearnt about 'The Hun in the sun'. As a result of further requests, nine Blenheim IVs of No. 15 Squadron, No. 2 Group, took off at 14.00 hours to the same target. The attack was led by Squadron Leader Lawrence. Going into a shallow dive from 3,000 ft. the crews claimed the hangars hit, as well as the destruction of sixteen aircraft on the airfield and a number of unloaded flak guns.

All the aircraft returned safely, although Pilot Officer Trent, who was number three in the leader's section, took a seagull through the forward perspex, which covered his observer, Sergeant Prior, with gore. L8852, flown by Flying Officer Dawson-Jones, received a hit in his port mainplane that resulted in a square yard of damage. Several aircraft were damaged by flak but no personnel were injured.

No. 40 Squadron, as had No. 15 Squadron, sent off two Blenheims to reconnoitre the battle area but whereas No. 15 Squadron's aircraft had returned safely with a few flak holes, L8776, flown by Flying Officer Burns and crew, failed to return. The other aircraft, L8833, flown by Squadron Leader Paddon and crew, returned to base at Wyton but landed on fire.

The target for No. 40 Squadron was an attack on Ypenburg Airfield near the Hague. Twelve Blenheim IVs, led by Squadron Leader Gleed, took-off and carried out their attack, but lost L8828 and L8831. Next in were twelve Blenheim IVs of No. 110 Squadron, who had been detailed to attack Ju52/3m troop transports on the beaches north of the Hague. Six of the aircraft were detailed to carry out a low-level attack escorted by six Blenheim 1F fighters. This was carried out successfully by the bombers and all returned safely, but during the straffing of the beach one of the Blenheim 1F fighters was hit by return fire from the ground and forcelanded there. The crew escaped injury and managed to set fire to their aircraft.

In the morning of 10th May, the Hurricanes of No. 1 Squadron were ordered to carry out patrols. This was followed in the afternoon by more patrols, until when nearing Sedan they were told over the R/T. of an enemy formation. As the five Hurricanes neared their prey this turned out to be thirty Do17s with a fighter escort of fifteen Bf110s. The flight climbed to 7,000ft, then turned to port and dived into the rear of the formation. At the very last moment the Bf110s broke left and right in line astern. The end of the fight resulted in ten confirmed enemy aircraft shot down for the loss of one Hurricane, with the pilot safe; the tails being blasted clean off two of the Bf110s.

No. 87 Squadron had been dispatched to Senon when the German attack began, and engaged two or three attacks on the airfield by Do17s. It was then recalled to the BEF area where, at Lille-Seclin, it joined No. 85 Squadron in combatting a number of small air raids over Belgium, the fighting usually taking place at heights from 7,000 to 12,000ft.

The first notice that No. 85 Squadron had of the attack, was the sound of enemy aircraft engines overhead and the crack of ack-ack firing, but it was not long before a section of each flight was airborne. Within forty minutes they were back with ammunition exhausted, ready for refuelling and rearming, claiming the downing of three Hs126s and one He111. One Hurricane was damaged and its pilot injured. By the end of the day the squadron had increased its score to 17 enemy aircraft destroyed, but with two more Hurricanes unserviceable.

Another unit that was woken up to the war with a shock in the early hours was the HQ Typex Section, whose accommodation was on the high part of Nancy. The first that H. Cooper saw were He111s which passed close by at the end of their bombing run.

"Bear in mind that they were bombing Nancy without opposition from low level, and we were on a high part on the western side of the town; as a consequence when completing their bombing run they were extremely close to the top of the hill. I'm surprised they didn't see the masts shining, because they were stainless steel. Anyway, they were bombing Nancy not us, and one could see the buildings to the east of the town coming apart. They were maybe a dozen aircraft all running in from east to west, the only opposition was an ack-ack gun on a low trajectory from the road towards Toul.''

Heinkel 111 shot down on Toul Airfield on 10 May 1940. L to R: guard, Sgt. Gamblin, H. Cooper and F/Lt. Barrow. (H. K. Cooper)

A No. 501 Squadron Hurricane being refuelled and re-armed at Bethenville. One airman near the cockpit keeps watch while the pilot talks to a colleague.

During the day No. 501 Squadron had flown over from Tangmere to Bethenville and immediately opened up their score, with Flying Officer A. Pickup shooting down a Do17 fifteen miles north of Vouziers, after a burst of 140 rounds. The following day the squadron claimed the shooting down of two Do17s, two He111s and two Bf110s.

On 11th May, the Luftwaffe struck at French airfields as well as three AASF ones. The most effective attack was the strike at Vraux, which was a classic example of how to destroy an operational squadron on the ground. The Blenheims of No. 114 Squadron had been rearmed, refuelled, and prepared for an operation, when nine Dornier Do17Zs of 4/KG2 swept across the airfield at 06.30 hours. The nine Do17s had taken off from Aschaffenburg, and led by their Staffelkapitän, Oberleutnant Reimers, flew to the French border across Luxembourg at a height of just two to three metres, crossing the Maginot Line without incident. The attack on Vraux was made at approximately 50 metres (160ft.), dropping 50Kg bombs and machine gunning the Blenheims. The fuel dump was also hit. With the aircraft not fully dispersed and the airfield unprepared, No. 114 Squadron was eliminated as an operational unit within a few minutes. One of the Do17s, U5 + GM, was flown by Leutnant Bornschein, and from this aircraft Stabsfeldwebel Borner filmed the attack. The film was immediately developed on landing and rushed to General Loerzer, who expressed satisfaction and appreciation.

Top: No. 114 Squadron Blenheim N6232 damaged by bomb blast of a near miss during the attack by 4/KG2. (R. Stride). Above: Wrecked No. 114 Squadron Blenheim and fuel dump burning at Vraux after the attack on 11 May 1940. (M. Judkins). Below left: A Dornier 17Z of 4/KG2 used on the raid on Vraux at its base at Aschaffenburg. (B. Kruger). Below right: Berthold Kruger, lead observer of the 4/KG2 raid on Vraux. Photo taken in 1945. (B. Kruger)

None of the Dorniers were damaged by groundfire from the airfield, but on the return flight the lead aircraft, U5 + LM, flying low to avoid detection, clipped a tree and was badly damaged. Later on it was sprayed with groundfire which badly injured the pilot, so an emergency landing was made at Frankfurt-Rebstock by the observer. The disappearing enemy aircraft left behind eight Blenheims on fire, and the remainder damaged by blast and bomb splinters. Fortunately no RAF or French personnel were killed and only two had minor injuries. The RAF were having their first taste of Blitzkrieg. Two unfortunates were airmen sitting on the pole of a dirt latrine, being blown into the pit by the bomb blast! A number of unexploded bombs were found on the airfield by the armourers, and although suspected of being delay fused, were later found to be unarmed ... probably dropped from too low an altitude.

The next aircraft for the slaughter of that day were eight Battles of Nos. 88 and 218 Squadrons, being ordered off without a fighter escort to attack German troop concentraions near the Luxembourg border. Flying low they were decimated by flak before they reached the target area only one Battle, carrying an injured crew and riddled by flak, made it back. To follow this came Blenheim IVs of 2 Group, which included eleven aircraft of No. 110 Squadron, who took-off at 14.50 hours to attack troops and bridges around Maastricht (Albert Canal bridges).

Going in to the attack the squadron closed up its formation, but concentrated flak forced the formation to open up. Engines screaming at full boost, the attack was pressed home. Flak took its toll – tortured metal, flames and death as the aircraft wheeled across the sky. On return all but one of the aircraft were damaged, and two failed to return:

L9175 Flying Officer Gratton, Sergeant Paterson, LAC. Allom.
N6208 Sergeant Bennett, Sergeant Colling, AC. Hannah. The pilot and air gunner were injured in a French hospital and the observer dead.

Next in were twelve Leo 451 bombers of Groupe de Bomb I/12 and Groupe de Bomb II/12 escorted by eighteen Morane 406 fighters of Groupe de Chasse II/6. The target was again the Albert Canal bridges at Maastriccht. Again a flak screen met the attack and again the Bf109s were there to give battle, but this time there was an escort. Although all the bombers were damaged, only one crash landed. A similar attack in the afternoon by six Leo 451s of the same units got a different reception, the escort being totally overwhelmed by Bf109s and slaughter followed.

During the opening of the battle on 10th May, 67 Wing (now including No. 501 Squadron) had claimed forty bombers for the loss of ten Hurricanes. the Luftwaffe admitted the loss of 83 aircraft, not including the Ju52s on that first day of the Blitz. No. 607 Squadron at Vitry-en-Artois had for a few days been maintaining a section of three Hurricanes at 'readiness' half-an-hour before dawn each day. On 10th May the section comprised of W. F. Blackadder (Flight Commander), Peter Parrott and another pilot. They were at their Mess in the village as dawn was breaking, heard the sound of aero-engines overhead, then in rushed their transport driver to warn of enemy aircraft flying over (these were a force of He111s that had attacked Arras). Piling into the truck the driver took the pilots as fast as possible to the airfield, where the fitters had the Hurricanes ready. Pausing only to grab their helmets and 'chutes the pilots ran to their respective aircraft; Peter Parrott:

> "At this point I saw two Heinkel 111s at about 5,000ft. disappearing to the north-east, and I was cursing my luck at being too late. However, I started the engine of the Hurricane, then chocks away, and without waiting to warm-up the engine, opened the throttle wide and took-off straight from the parking spot, there being nil wind.
>
> "As I climbed away I saw two more He111s only a little way ahead of me, and took up the chase. While I was climbing the EA were pulling away from me, but as soon as I levelled off at the same height as them I started to overhaul them, although they were probably at least two miles ahead of me, and my overtaking speed was not all that great. I eventually started to come within range and then realized that I was approaching the Belgian frontier near Charleroi. As, for the previous four months, I had continually been warned that I must under no circumstances violate Belgian neutrality, I decided that I must open fire at long range. This I did and was rewarded with the sight of tracer being returned by the top gunner. Having exhausted my ammunition with no apparent effect on the enemy I broke off the attack and returned to Vitry, wondering if I would be reported by the Belgians for crossing the frontier. It was not until I had landed that I was told of the invasion of the Low Countries."

Air Commmodore Lord Runciman, previous CO, talks to pilots of No. 607 Squadron at their dispersal (D. R. Brown)

No. 607 Squadron was to engage in combat with many other bomber formations* during the day, and No. 3 Squadron fought at least three major combats, one with a force of 20–30 He111s escorted by fighters. The battles were waged throughout the day and across the whole front.

Squadron Leader Joe Kayll had been posted from No. 607 Squadron to take over No. 615 Squadron early in 1940, and was at Le Touquet re-equipping with Hurricanes. Without any warning on 10th May, Le Touquet was bombed and the squadron lost three Hurricanes on the ground, but ironically no Gladiators. The damaged Hurricanes were immediately replaced with new ones, and the half-trained squadron returned to Merville the following day, leaving their Gladiators behind. The first patrols were over the Louvain-Wavre Canal and Liege-Namur, having numerous combats as there were no shortage of targets. No. 53 Squadron was, on 11th May, trying to carry out photo-reconnaisance, but low cloud and the loss of one aircraft during the first four sorties resulted in a failure to achieve results. Further low-level reconnaissance sorties of the Albert Canal area were only partly successful and resulted in the loss of two more Blenheims that failed to return and two more damaged.

On the fighter front, No. 85 Squadron caught a group of enemy aircraft in the Tongres-Maastricht area, and in the following combat claimed eight enemy aircraft 'kills' for the loss of one Hurricane. The Luftwaffe was, however, operating in force, so no respite could be expected. Fighter Command appeared reluctant to release more squadrons to the French campaign although fighter squadrons were operating from southern England along the French coastal belt. In hindsight, this was perfectly understandable, as squadrons and aircraft would be disappearing into the melting pot in France quicker than they could be formed and trained.

No. 11 Group was, from 10th May, providing fighter cover on the left flank of the Allied Armies, and for the first two days encountered very little enemy opposition. At this period the group only had a maximum of sixteen fighter squadrons available and, although the Blenheim fighter squadrons were employed initially, these were withdrawn for night operations. Up to five Spitfire squadrons were employed during the latter part of the campaign, but were not allowed inland, the Hurricanes bearing the brunt of the fighting over land.

In the afternoon of 11th May, No. 1 Squadron Hurricanes attacked a formation of forty enemy bombers escorted by fifteen Bf110s, and in the melêe Flying Officer Richey was forced to bale out of his crashing

*The Commanding Officer of No. 607 Squadron, Squadron Leader L. E. Smith, who had just returned from leave, was shot down on his first patrol.

Hurricane. The Squadron Operational Record Book recorded, 'The first of many!' At the end of the fight, confirmation of the results was found in the wreckage of eight Me110s and one Hurricane in the locality.

Amongst many airfields and units under attack on the 11th was No. 150 Squadron at Ecury-sur-Coole, an attack on the airfield being delivered at 06.10 hours by between 18–24 enemy aircraft. It was estimated that about one hundred and fifty 50Kg bombs were dropped which set fire to part of the adjacent wood. The armoury tent, the pyrotechnic store and Battle P2334 were set on fire and destroyed. There were eighteen bomb craters on the airfield and five unexploded bombs on the edge of the airfield. In spite of this there were ten Battles serviceable for further operations.

'Panther' (codename for AASF HQ) instructed Nos. 105 and 150 Squadrons to be prepared to bomb with their bombs tail-fused for 11 second delay, and at 14.05 hours issued orders for the bombing. These operations started the following day, when three 'B' Flight aircraft took off at 14.45 hours to attack a mechanised column between Neufchateau and Bertrix.

Heavy flak was encountered from the crossroads before the target area and a direct hit was made on P2336, which was seen to explode with the wreckage crashing in flames. The remaining two Battles attacked the mechanised column from 100 feet with their eight 250 lb. GP. bombs, then made their way back to base.

No. 105 Squadron, like No. 150 Squadron, only had two aircraft return from the attack, whilst No. 226 Squadron were attacked on the ground. Enemy aircraft dropping between 12 and 16 HE bombs followed by a low-level machine gunning of the airfield and village.

The River Meuse, or River Maas as it is known in Belgium and Holland, has formed for France a natural barrier against the threat of invasion from the east. In Belgium it forms a wide slow-running water barrier, and the Belgians tried to keep it that way by restricting the number of bridges crossing it. In the Maastricht area, there were two road bridges crossing the river in the town, whilst outside the town, two roads led over bridges crossing the Albert Canal. The bridges in the town and at Kanne were successfully blown by the Belgians, but the bridges on the Maastricht-Vroenhoven and Maastricht-Veldwezelt roads were captured by the German 1st Paratroop Regiment, and now Reichenau's sixth Army was advancing over them. This was the target for the Allied air attacks.

Another bridge over the Albert Canal was at Briegden. This had not been attacked by German paratroops, but neither had it been blown. This was because the Pioneer troops detailed to the blowing-up of the

How the British Press pictured the invasions.

bridge, had been killed when bombs fell on their barrack blocks. General d'Astier was at this time forced to call on the RAF for support to attack the German spearheads, as the French bomber force units were either in the process of re-equipping with new aircraft, or in changing bases, and like the RAF, insufficiently mobile.

Although the XVI Panzer suffered some delay due to the bombing around Maastricht, the cost to the Allied air forces was high. The first two attacks on 12th May were by Nos. 103 and 139 Squadrons. Of the latter squadron, seven out of nine Blenheims were lost between

Tongres and Maastricht. The nine aircraft had taken off from Plivot to attack an enemy troop column, fighter cover having been promised over the target area. Enroute the Blenheims were attacked by about thirty Bf109s, which were sweeping the area. The 'A' Flight Commander, Squadron Leader Scott flying N6216, appeared to receive a direct hit on his bomb load. In the resulting explosion his wingmen also disappeared, one minus a wing cartwheeled to destruction. Fighters queued to get in shots at the formation, so the Blenheims broke, engines screaming, punctured fuel tanks leaking burning fuel and one by one crashed. 'B' Flight Commander, Squadron Leader Tideman (P4923), was seen to go down and another Blenheim dived away in flames. The Commanding Officer, Wing Commander Dickens, and his wingman, Flight Lieutenant Pepper (L9416), managed to fight through, with maximum boost pulled and flying right down on the 'deck'. Somewhere on the way back the wingman was to force land in Allied territory. Only one other aircraft made it to the target. Being late, the pilot had made a fast low approach and attack evading the defending fighters, then beat it back to Plivot. The Commanding Officer's aircraft was so badly damaged that it was written off, two crews made it back on foot, but an analysis of the raid once again proved how out of date the target information was. The squadron had run into flak well before the target, indicating a German advance that had been far more rapid than estimated.

The two AASF Blenheim squadrons were now more or less eliminated as an effective force, although an attempt would be made to raise an operational force by the posting of six No. 114 Squadron crews to fly No. 139 Squadron aircraft.

Meanwhile, a near suicidal attack was called for on the bridges over the Albert Canal near Maastricht. The unit selected was No. 12 Squadron, known in Service parlance as 'Shiny Twelve', 'Dirty Dozen' and other far ruder names. Six Battles were to be supplied with volunteer crews, to attack the Vroenhoven (Maastricht-Tongres road) bridge, and the Veldwezelt (Maastricht-Hasselt road) bridge. The Vroenhoven bridge being constructed of concrete and the Veldwezelt bridge of metal, both being approximately 350 feet long and 30 feet wide.

Although all the squadron's aircrew volunteered, in the end there were only five aircraft serviceable. The crews selected were:

P2204	F/O. Garland	Sgt. Gray	LAC. Reynolds	} Veldwezelt bridge.
L5439	P/O. McIntosh	Sgt. Harper	LAC. McNaughton	
L5527	Sgt. Marland	Sgt. Footner	LAC. Perrin	
P2322	F/O. N. Thomas	Sgt. Carey	Cpl. Campion	} Vroenhoven
L5241	P/O. T. Davey	Sgt. Mansell	LAC. Patterson	

61

The wireless operator/air-gunners on all the aircraft were basically groundcrew, and for their flying duties on operations were paid an *extra 1/6* per day (present day coinage approximately 7 ½ pence). Now, two days after the bridges had been captured by the enemy, these volunteers were being asked to attack the bridges, without fighter escort and in fact, with little hope of returning. No wonder the Germans were amazed at such madness.

Garland, at the briefing, opted to lead his section on a low-level attack, whilst Thomas and his wingman decided to dive bomb their target. Bf109s of JGr21 and JG27 had been assigned to guard the area of the bridges and a large number of flak-guns ringed the area. The effectiveness of the defence had already been proven, and this attack was going to be no different. AASF Hurricanes were sent to provide cover over the bridges, but were already outnumbered before the Battles went into the attack.

In the attack Garland was seen going in low, with pieces being shot off his aircraft by the intense light flak. Then, wreathed in flames, he dived into the western end of the bridge and exploded. McIntosh arrived at the target in flames, unloaded his bombs and crash landed, being pulled from the wreckage by his crew. Marland's aircraft was seen to stagger from the flak on fire, attempted to climb away, went into a stall and flicked over into the ground. At the other bridge both Thomas and Davey dived into the attack and almost blew themselves up with their bombs. Thomas, hit by the flak, managed to keep his badly shattered Battle flying, then the engine failed and he was forced to land, the crew being taken prisoner by a nearby German road convoy.

Davey's Battle was hit, but staggered away with its fuel tank on fire, so he ordered his crew to bale out. Coaxing the aircraft on he eventually crash landed near his base, the observer parachuted to safety and returned to the squadron, but the air-gunner was taken prisoner after injuring himself on landing.

The attempt on the bridges left a number of wrecked aircraft strewn around the canal and the countryside, both Allied and Luftwaffe. For the attack Garland and Gray were posthumously awarded the Victoria Cross. Their air-gunner, LAC. L. Reynolds, who shared their peril and death, received no award. For this he had been paid 1/6 a day, such was the princely reward for the 'part-time' aircrew's love of flying.

Still on 12th May, at 07.50 hours, twelve Blenheims of No. 15 Squadron took-off to attack the bridges in the Maastricht area. The two sections being led by Squadron Leader Glen (P6917) and Squadron Leader Lawrence (L9024). The plan of attack was to

F/O 'Red' Eames on a BSA and F/Lt. Lawrence of No. 15 Squadron. (W/Cmd. H. George DFC)

approach the area from the south at 5,000 feet and to attack individually in a shallow dive, releasing the bombs at the lowest possible altitude. Hurricanes had orbitted the target area ready for the attack, but as the Blenheims swept in the Bf109s dived on fighters and bombers alike. As the Blenheims swept lower the flak finished off what the Bf109s had missed, the flak hosing up with such intensity that it appeared that none could survive, metal tore off the wings and fuselage, aircraft in flames fell to earth.

Sergeant Hall and crew* in P6914 crashed on the canal bank at Gellik. Pilot Officer 'Red' Eames, pulling away at zero feet, lifted his aircraft over a row of poplars near Gellik to find facing him a flak battery. He engaged this with his forward gun before pulling away and joining up with Squadron Leader Lawrence. At 11.30 hours six damaged aircraft landed at Wyton; Pilot Officer Robinson (L8800) with smashed hydraulics, flaps and undercarriage, made a wheels-up landing; Pilot Officer Eames (L8850) was injured in the leg and wrist from a shell that exploded between the seat and rudder bar; Flying Officer Webster (L8851) received a bullet wound in his foot.

Apart from the six aircraft that failed to return, three others were damaged beyond unit repair. Not only were the aircrew shaken by their experience, but the groundcrews were bowled over by their loss of aircraft and crews. As with most squadrons of the period, the aircrew and groundcrew were mainly regular air force personnel. The Squadron was a close-knit community and a strong bond spanned everything, it was ''our aircraft'' and ''our aircrew'':

L8847 F/O. Basset	Sgt. Middlemass	LAC. Cavanagh	
L8849 F/O. Douglass	Sgt. Shorthand	LAC. Davies	} Failed
N6151 Sgt. Pepper	Sgt. Booth	LAC. Scott	to
P6911 F/O. Oakley	Sgt. Avent	LAC. Woods	return.
P6912 P/O. Frankish	Sgt. Roberts	LAC. Cooper	
P6914 Sgt. Hall	Sgt. Perrin	LAC. McDonnel	

*The villagers buried the crew in their churchyard; then in 1985 a memorial was raised and they were duly honoured by the villagers, relatives and surviving comrades.

At 08.10 hours, twelve Blenheims of No. 107 Squadron, led by Wing Commander Basil Embry, took off from Wattisham to attack the same area allotted to No. 15 Squadron. Even before the target area was reached intense flak was hosing up at the formation and the formation opened out to reduce the possibility of hits. Then, as the flak ceased, in came the Bf109s, Embry* called for the squadron to close up tight, having practiced this to allow the gunners to bring their weapons to bear. Even as they closed ranks they were hacked out of the sky, shattered remnants of the squadron attempting to fight their way out and claiming the downing of two enemy fighters in the process. Fortunately, Embry was still leading the squadron, a pilot and squadron leader who was prepared to investigate or try anything that would improve protection or efficiency, but four crews failed to return:

L8748 F/O. R. Rotherham	Sgt. R. Brown	LAC. E. Coote
P4914 P/O. O. Keedwell	Sgt. J. Merritt	AC2. L. Berridge
P4905 F/O. W. Edwards	Sgt. V. Luter	LAC. W. Palmer
L8733 P/O. S. Thornton	Sgt. L. Mellorship	AC2. J. Mayor

The defensive fire of the Blenheim was nearly nil. Originally the air gunner in his Bristol turret had one Vickers 0.303in. VGO. machine-gun and little armour. Initially the fuel tanks were unprotected, self-sealing tanks only being fitted during early 1940. The pilot had one Browning 0.303in. machinegun in the port wing for aggressive use. Neither the pilot nor the observer had much armour protection early on, apart from the bomb bay and bombs behind and below them. One pilot claimed he sat on his tin helmet when flying, as he knew which was the most important part to protect!

During the day the RAF flew 140 bomber sorties, from which 24 aircraft failed to return. During the afternoon of the 12th, further raids were flown; twice by No. 103 Squadron, and once each by Nos. 105, 150, 82 and 218 Squadrons. Some of the Battle squadrons carried only two crew as they were dive bombing with the pilot releasing the bombs. From these sorties Battles K5512, K9353, K9485, P2183, P2336 and P2693 failed to return.

As can be seen, with the failure of the armies to prevent the enemy striking through Maastricht, Tongres, Gembloux and the Ardennes, the decision by the Air Ministry to fling in the light/medium bombers of the AASF and 2 Group, meant the sacrifice of their crews. Even if not said in so many words, the sacrifices were made to prevent any further incursion and to save the Allied forces. Air Marshal Arthur Barratt knew it when he committed his BAFF forces, but he had little option. It has been said that it almost broke him.

Fighter aircraft of the RAF and Armee de l'Air were continually

---

*Retired from the RAF as Air Chief Marshal GCB, KBE, DSO, DFC, AFC.

flying sorties, either as escorts or on standing patrols, trying to break the established German pattern of Blitzkrieg. The RAF fighters were too few and the French fighters (excluding the Dewoitine 520) too inferior to have significant effect on the armada sent against the Allies. Combat reports indicated that in fighter *v.* fighter combat, the Bf109E could out dive the Hurricane by a quick flick into a dive. The Merlin on the Hurricane just spluttered in protest if asked to do the same.

'B' flight of No. 1 Squadron on the 12th tangled with a heavily escorted enemy bomber formation. The mood of the squadron was changing from a quiet acceptance of the war, to a more vicious and deadly aim, to wipe out all Germans, 'B' Flight's pilots were in just that mood. During the combat, one of the pilots, Flying Officer Leslie ('Leo') R. Clisby DFC RAAF, having shotdown a Bf110, proceeded to knock hell out of two He111s that got in his way. Whilst one turned away damaged the other went down to force land in a field. Spotting the enemy pilot getting out and running off, Clisby landed nearby, gave chase, and brought him down with a rugby tackle. His fellow pilots reckoned he only wanted to try out his revolver! The Flight's results were five enemy aircraft destroyed for the loss of one Hurricane, which force landed on fire, but the pilot was alright.

During the day, No. 85 Squadron claimed to have knocked down seven enemy aircraft for the loss of one Hurricane, the pilot of which baled out behind the German lines. However, he evaded capture and collected information on German forces in the area before he escaped to the Allied lines, where he was able to give this to the army. Air Component fighters during this 24 hours flew 110 sorties over the BEF area and claimed the downing of eighteen enemy aircraft for the loss of five Hurricanes. Some fighter squadrons lost count of the number of enemy aircraft shot down. C. H. Trett was not only a member of No. 1 Squadron, but a keen diarist of the squadron's activities:

> "During the next five weeks (from 1st April 1940) this figure was to leap to 124 confirmed, our own pilot losses being a remarkable 3. Aircraft were shot down on many occasions, but the pilots kept on returning after being missing for days . . . The pilots of course were outstanding and no praise could be high enough for their efforts."

At first light on 12th May, six Battles of No. 103 Squadron took-off to attack bridges in the Sedan sector, a hit being made on a bridge north of Villers. Although other bridges were attacked, no definite claim was made for their destruction. The French had provided a fighter escort and although there was light flak pumped up at them, all aircraft returned safely. One pilot was injured and force landed his aircraft near Challerange. Next in were four Battles of No. 150 Squadron, who had been detailed to attack pontoon bridges north of

Officer aircrew of No. 1(F) Squadron with their CO S/Ldr. 'Bull' Halahan, at Vassincourt. (S/Ldr. C. Campbell DFC)

Villers and northwest of Romilly-Allincourt. In spite of intense flak none of the aircraft were lost and the French fighter escort kept the enemy fighters away.

Wing Commander 'Bull' Halahan led No. 1 Squadron over Maastricht in an attempt to provide fighter cover for the British bombers. While shooting down a Bf109 and an Arado, he received a hit in the engine and was forced to land with wheels up. Flying Officer Lewis claimed a Bf109, but his aircraft was set on fire and he had to bale out. This he did successfully, but the locals put him in the 'cooler' because of doubts as to his identity.

With the advance of the British 2 Corps into Belgium on the 10th, the Air Component Lysanders had spearheaded their entry. No. 4 Squadron crossed the Belgian frontier at 09.15 hours and proceeded as far as Brussels, but it was not until the 13th that enemy troops were sighted. On this day one Lysander failed to return . . . a similar story would be repeated as each day went on.

Heavy losses and bad weather prevented any operations by 2 Group on 13th May, but this day was marked by the Luftwaffe concentrating its resources on the Sedan area, where no fewer than five Panzer Divisions were massed for the assault. The Luftwaffe were ordered to pin down the French defences while the ground forces established themselves across the Meuse. Ju87s of StG77 dive bombed the artillery positions, while waves of Do17s of KG2 plastered the rear areas. During these operations, another attack was taking place at Houx and Dinant, supported by Ju87s of StG1 and Dornier 17s of KG76 and KG77.

Luftwaffe activity on this day amounted to over 600 sorties, with the majority being flown by KG2, KG3, KG53, StG2 and StG77. A number of bombers fell victims to the French fighters and BAFF Hurricanes. Of the French fighters only the Dewoitine D520 could fight on fairly equal terms with the Bf109 and Bf110, provided that the combat took place at medium altitude.

'Sichelschnitt' sweeps forward

Even though Allied Command attention was concentrated on the German attack from the north into Belgium, the French aerial reconnaissance had detected the German attack through the Ardennes. Panzer Group Kleist of 'Army Group A' was moving forward with its armoured and supply columns stretching as far back as the Rhine, and considerable numbers of tanks and other vehicles were enroute to the Meuse around Dinant, Givet and Bouillon. Later on during the 13th, two more Panzer Divisions, the 3rd and 7th, had forced bridgeheads across the Meuse at Dinant, and the torrent of German forces breaking through the Ardennes was now becoming a flood.

During the day Curtiss hawk 75s of Groupe de Chasse I/15 caught twelve Ju87s returning from a bombing mission and in a short space of time shot down the lot without loss. Shortly afterwards they found a further group of Ju87s, and shot some more down before the Curtiss fighters ran out of ammunition. This was a rare occasion when there were no Luftwaffe fighters handy.

The number of bombers in the AASF had now dwindled from 135 serviceable on 10th May, to just 72. An order was issued that the AASF Blenheims were to be rested for twenty-four hours and the Battles only despatched on one operation. This operation was carried out by No. 226 Squadron, at the request of the French, to prevent a portion of their army being cut off. The attack was flown by two separate flights of Battles and the attack was carried out at low level. The one flight hit German troops and transport around Breda, while the other flight, led by Flight Lieutenant Crooks, went in to close the roads in Breda. Going in to the attack Crooks realised that there were civilians in the streets, so he flew down the main street first as a warning. He then returned and bombed the buildings at the cross roads; this brought down buildings and a factory across the roads.

In the air and leading the Panzer attacks were Loerzer's Fliegerkorp II and VIII, which comprised approximately 1500 aircraft, roughly equivalent to the combined British and French air forces in France. The attacks opened with the Do17s concentrating on targets behind the lines, with the tank operations covered by the Ju87s. A cover of Bf109s patrolled overhead or strafed retreating troops, some were not averse to shooting up refugees.

The squadrons of 2 Group had been stood down due to the previous day's losses and for the absorption and preparation of new aircraft and crews. On the BEF Front the Lysanders flew contact patrols over British troops, but were proving vulnerable to enemy aircraft attacks and some failed to return from sorties over the front line. No. 85 Squadron Hurricanes were engaged on a number of tasks, becoming heavily engaged in one combat near Lille with a superior force of enemy aircraft, the impression of the RAF pilots being that there were Hun aircraft everywhere. No. 3 Squadron, carrying out forward patrols near Wavre-Louvain, claimed four enemy bombers downed before lunch, but lost two Hurricanes in a mid-air collision later on in the day.

Just before midnight, twenty ground staff of No. 139 Squadron were transported to Belgium, where they were to set up a temporary landing strip to receive replacement Blenheims from Britain. The party travelled all night to their destination, which turned out to be a large farmhouse with four large flat fields. For three days they worked hard to level out the worst parts until it was usable . . . but no aircraft appeared. One of the party was Owen Baum, a wireless operator:

"During the night we had seen flashes and heard explosions to the north-east, and by the Sunday morning the explosions were getting louder. There was a lot of military traffic moving on the nearest road, and at midday we had a shock. A lone dispatch rider called at our field kitchen for food and told us that the Germans were only a mile or so away."

'Doc' Walls of No. 139 Squadron:

"That morning we were erecting a windsock on a makeshift pole when a Blenheim flew over. He then turned and circled at low level, finally landing. To our surprise he was from a home-based squadron out on recce' to establish the German advance positions. It was pure luck that he had spotted our windsock and then our vehicles.

"He advised us to drop everything and make for Cherbourg as quickly as we could, the German advanced columns were already well south of us. Our exodus was immediate, abandoning everything but rifles and small kit (destroying everything that was not removeable) we boarded our three-tonner and a low loader. Suffice to say, we were lucky, we did reach Cherbourg, and we were able to board one of the last ships to leave that port."

On 14th May, four Battles of No. 150 Squadron took-off at 15.24 hours and headed for Sedan to bomb the pontoon bridges over the river there. None of the aircraft returned and so nothing is known of the operation, although with the mass of Bf109s flying in the area it can only be assumed that there was one end. The aircraft and crews were:

L4946	F/O. Ing	Sgt. Turner	LAC. Nolan
K9483	P/O. Posselt	Sgt. Bowen	AC. Vano
P2182	P/O. Boon	Sgt. Fortune	AC. Martin
P5232	Sgt. Barker	Sgt. Williams	AC. Summerson

No. 12 Squadron were still short of aircraft and crews after the mauling on the 12th, but still put up five Battles and crews to attack

A No. 73 Squadron Hurricane being refuelled and rearmed at Rouvres. (S/Ldr. C. Campbell DFC).

troop and MT columns heading from Sedan to Givonne. Yet in spite of diving bombing the targets the flak and machinegun fire was intense and accurate and as they pulled away from the area in came the Bf109s. Only one Battle returned which was L5538 crewed by Pilot Officer J. McElligott, Sergeant B. Long and LAC. T. Burgess.

No. 1 Squadron were also to lose two experienced pilots on 14th May, when 'B' Flight attacked fifteen Bf110s. Flight Lieutenant Hanks got one, but in the fight received a cannon shell in the gravity tank which was not self-sealing. The aircraft caught fire, so he spun down and baled out. Lewis, Moulds and Boot each got a Bf110, but Clisby and Lorimer were shot down, Clisby diving into the ground after shooting down two aircraft. Clisby, his dark-blue RAAF uniform getting the worse for wear, had been dined the night before by Noel Monks of the Daily Mail. His remark about it was, "Brother, these old rags will see me through" . . . so passed an Australian, an ace with at least 14 confirmed kills, an airman the RAF and RAAF could be proud of.

The German advance in all directions continued, the 1st Panzer Division heading to Cherery. It was near there that the tanks of the French 4th and 7th caught them while they were refuelling, but quick action by the Panzer's anti-tank screen and lack of infantry support for the French tanks soon restored the situation in the Panzer's favour. In all this melée, lack of communication and identification resulted in Ju87s attacking Guderian's Panzer Corp.

Tail unit of Battle
P2332 of No. 12
Squadron that failed to
return 14 May 1940.
(J. De Vos)

Typical of all the retreat, muddle and confusion Owen Baum remembers:

"People on foot, on cycles, pushing handcarts, in cars and vans, jammed the road. Whole families with all their dearest possessions were hauled along on farm wagons by sweating horses. Months before, we had been greeted in France with smiles and handshakes. Now it was all abuse and jeers, or demands from stranded car owners for petrol.

"The next two days were the worst. German planes began to strafe the roads and the roadside fields. We saw many dead in the fields, young and old people; horses and their wagons in the deep ditches, and family possessions everywhere."

No. 615 Squadron were ordered to escort a Blenheim reconnaissance aircraft up the Louvain-Wavre Canal towards the German border to check how many bridges were still standing. Joe Kayll* remembers:

"The Blenheim flew under two bridges that remained with great skill, and returned to Merville with a wounded top gunner."

On 15th May No. 615 Squadron was ordered into Belgium to an airfield near Courtrai, just over the border from France. Their sister squadron, No. 607, were carrying out offensive patrols ahead of the British Army, but these were not always successful as the squadron was often heavily outnumbered and had to return to Vitry with no

---

*Commanding Officer of No. 615 Squadron.

ammunition left. The 'A' Flight Commander of No. 607 Squadron, W. F. Blackadder,* says of those times:

"As the Army advance became a withdrawal and the Army Co-operation squadrons were more and more depleted we seemed to be used in their place. The confusion was considerable as to the whereabouts of the German Panzers."

The 14th May was a portent of the future of the BAFF and 2 Group and mirrored what had already happened to the bomber squadrons of the AASF. Totally overwhelmed by flak defences and fighters, with the German advance threatening their airfields, the writing was already on the wall.

A number of Panzer Divisions were now across the Meuse in strength, advancing in a cut and thrust manner at a speed too fast for the Allied GHQ to comprehend. Although a counter attack by the French Army was made at Sedan, it petered out and failed. An attack was then called up against the pontoon bridges and was carried out by ten Battles of No. 103 Squadron. Although there was no fighter opposition the flak was sufficient to make the attack not a total success. The French then requested an attack on the enemy at Sedan. This was first carried out by the Armée de l'Air, with all available aircraft being thrown in, including night bombers like the Amiot 143 with a maximum speed of 183 mph. This attack was torn asunder by flak and fighters, the losses so heavy that no reserves were available for any more operations that day.

The second attack was put in by the Battles and Blenheims of the AASF, a total of 71 aircraft, in an attempt to allow the French 2nd Army to regroup and counter attack. It had been decided to transfer six No. 114 Squadron crews to fly the remaining No. 139 Squadron aircraft. These six were assigned to their aircraft, whilst two other crews of No. 114 Squadron were to fly replacement aircraft L9464 and L9466. The two No. 114 Squadron aircraft took off at 15.00 hours for Sedan, but short of the target the first aircraft was seen to strike the ground by the second aircraft's observer. This aircraft, flown by Sergeant G. Potter, was within minutes attacked by several Bf109s, who proceeded to tear chunks out of the Blenheim. The next action is briefly described by G. Potter:

"I jettisoned my 40 lb. bombs, as they were prone to explode when hit, and kept my two 250 HE's. I did not get a chance to use them as the 109s kept up attacks on me for a good ten minutes." ·

What was not said was that the aircraft was severely damaged.

In general the attacks went in between 15.00 and 16.00 hours, and

*Flight Lieutenant Flight Commander, demobbed as Wing Commander.

71

Potez 63-11 recce aircraft at Mourmelon-le-Grand Airfield in 1940. (Gerard Faux)

Bloch MB131 of 14 Groupe Aerienne Autonome at Mourmelon-le-Grand 1940 . . . not one of the best French aircraft. (Gerard Faux)

whilst six No. 82 Squadron aircraft of 2 Group bombed the road east of Breda more slaughter took place around Sedan. The attack cost the AASF forty aircraft, over 50% casualties; four from No. 12 Squadron, one from No. 88 Squadron, three from No. 103 Squadron, six from No. 105 Squadron, four from No. 139 Squadron, four from No. 142 Squadron, four from No. 150 Squadron, ten from No. 218 Squadron and three from No. 226 Squadron . . . plus the one from No. 114 Squadron already mentioned.

Bob Pearce of No. 142 Squadron said of the attacks:

> "Unfortunately when the time arrived to attack German troop columns the troops were not intimidated by either the noise of the diving aricraft or by the Browning gun mounted in the leading edge of the wing. Neither did they seek shelter from the rear-gunner's bullets as the plane climbed away. Instead, in an orderly manner, they left their vehicles, made their way into the adjacent verges and field, lay on their backs in serried ranks and, with their rifles held vertically, awaited the arrival of the attackers. Thus the final run was through a hail of bullets. It was no comfort to remember that the radiator, beneath the engine, would quickly lose its coolant if hit."

As dusk approached on 14th May a number of 2 Group Blenheim squadrons were called on again. Twenty-eight aircraft from Nos. 21, 107 and 110 Squadrons set off with a Hurricane escort, with Embry leading the last two squadrons. The bomb run commenced and again a barrage of fire darkened the sky as the flak batteries blasted the sky, and so the Blenheims ran in, but flak hit the bombers and clawed a number out of the sky and damaged five others. Whilst three of the Wattisham aircraft failed to return, one crew escaped. Although the attacks on the Sedan bridge head appeared to have caused some alarm to the local German Command, and in spite of the troops being fatigued, it was still sufficiently strong for the French counter attack to founder.

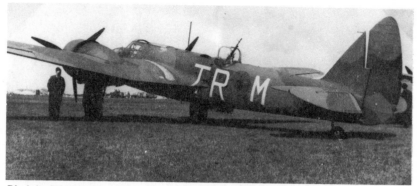

Blenheim IV 'Tac-R' of No. 59 Squadron with toned down roundels and no fin flash.

The Lysanders of the Air Component on this date were flying contact patrols and being subjected to groundfire, as they flew low-level to ascertain the position of German troops. No. 26 Squadron, acting directly for GHQ, were operating from the landing ground at Arras and during the day had two Lysanders that failed to return. In the same period Nos. 2, 4 and 13 Squadrons moved up to advanced landing grounds in Belgium, with No. 4 Squadron providing valuable information for the ground forces, but they lost two of their Lysanders to enemy fighters.

The No. 59 Squadron Blenheim detachment were also flying low-level sorties to check the position of German forces and supply lines. Under Air Marshal Barratt's instruction a Blenheim was sent to check the situation in the north, with two Hurricanes as escort. The Hurricane pilots did not have maps for the area to be reconnoitred and so failed to take off with the Blenheim, which left on schedule . . . and failed to return.

Air Component fighter squadrons during the day flew 168 sorties. Nine Hurricanes of No. 3 Squadron engaged two waves of approximately fifty Ju87s, with each wave escorted by twenty Bf109s or Bf110s. Although one of the Hurricanes was hit and the pilot forced to bale out, the remainder continued tangling with the enemy formations, and claimed nine Ju87s, six Bf109s and one Bf110 destroyed, with others damaged.

By 15th May the Dutch and Belgian Air Forces had, to all intents and purposes, ceased to exist, their airfields forming graveyards for many of their aircraft. For whereas in the years prior to 1939 the British people had been pacifist or apathetic, the Belgian and Dutch had placed their faith in their neutrality, all of it to be swept aside by a competent and ruthless enemy. In spite of valour and bravery in many instances, the Dutch and Belgian Air Forces were partly destroyed on

He111s of KG26.

the ground in pre-emptive strikes; the Belgians lost all their twelve Hurricanes on the ground over the first two days . . . thus negating General Galland's subsequent claim to have shot down Belgian Hurricanes.

By 15th May, No. 4 Squadron had moved to Lille-Ronchin with one flight based at the forward landing ground of Aspelaere. Two more Lysanders failed to return from a tactical reconnaissance during the day. No. 2 Squadron, likewise, had been on the move. Having first reconnoitered Ledegham as a forward landing ground, they moved there from Bethune on the 15th. Later they sent four Lysanders to report to 'MacForce', which was moving to the Cambrai area. One Lysander, crewed by Pilot Officer Dearden and AC. Patterson, was attacked by no less than nine Bf109s whilst on reconnaissance. Dearden dived to ground level, Patterson wielding his solitary 'K' gun at the fighters; a fuel tank was holed, bullets and shells carved up various parts of the airframe, but by using every bit of ground cover the damaged Lysander escaped, landing at Douai in an unairworthy condition. Dearden returned to the squadron and left Patterson to guard the aircraft, with the possibility of salvage. However, before a squadron party could reach the Lysander the enemy troops had advanced too close, so Patterson was ordered to destroy the aircraft and get out.

Chapter Three
Retirement Behind the Marne

The line of German advance was now placing the AASF airfields in jeopardy, so Barratt advised Playfair to prepare plans for an evacuation of the squadrons to new airfields in southern Champagne, around Troyes. During the period of the 'Phoney War' the French had constructed new airfields in this area to allow the movement to France of more RAF squadrons. These were now to prove of use to the original AASF squadrons. By 15th May, the Luftwaffe II and V Fliegerkorp were concentrating their attacks on centres of communication, cross-roads and main roads in the area of Metz, Verdun, Reims, Soissons-et-Langres, Troyes and Mareuil-sur-Ourcq. During the day, came orders from AASF Headquarters that the Battle squadrons were to be restricted to night operations, until further notice anyway. It had been found that from the 10th May to 14th May inclusive, from 130 sorties between 60 to 70 aircraft had been lost . . . or approximately 50%. At this suicidal rate it would have been impossible for the Battle squadrons to continue to operate; for as well as the lost aircraft, there were also the damaged ones waiting repair. This, combined with the retirement behind the line of the Marne on 16th May, made them unable to operate for at least four days. It must be understood that the Battle squadrons were day bombers, and their aircrews had no intensive flying training at night, being restricted to night take-offs and landings. The restriction probably preserved the remaining aircrew lives for a few more days.

With the 7th Panzer Division having created a pocket west of Dinant and with Guderian's Panzers on the flank of the 9th French Army, the decision was made to evacuate the Meuse Line. General d'Astier was requested to give air support and called on the RAF for support. At 08.00 hours the Luftwaffe threw in their support to the Panzers again, and Ju87s began their attacks on points of resistance. Meanwhile, the French 1st Divisions Cuirassées* had concentrated their armoured column near Flavion, but without fuel tankers. Just as they were refuelling they were attacked by Rommel's 7th Panzer Division. The French put up defensive fire and counter-attacked with their remaining tanks, but all this failed and by the end of the day there were only four servicable French tanks able to retire from the fray.

---

*French armoured force (Divisions Cuirassées), intended to be a breakthough force in attack. Unfortunately, these had been hastily formed in late 1939, and were deficient in equipment.

'Blitzed'

Flying Officer N. Orton of No. 73
Squadron climbs into his Hurricane at
Rouvres for a patrol. (S/Ldr. C. Campbell
DFC)

Unlike the Germans, neither the French nor the British had learnt that tanks needed infantry and anti-tank guns to be successful.

On 15th May, No. 60 Wing complained to GHQ that their Hurricanes were now meeting waves of at least 30 enemy bombers protected by large formations of enemy fighters. This resulted in the Wing losing fighters without shooting down bombers. Unfortunately no more fighters or squadrons could be spared. During the day Nos. 3 and 615 Squadrons engaged numerous enemy aircraft that resulted in No. 3 Squadron claiming two Do17s and one Bf109 for the loss of three Hurricanes. No. 615 Squadron claimed two Bf110s for the loss of one Hurricane. The day finished with the Air Component fighters flying 164 sorties, in which 33 enemy aircraft were destroyed for the loss of 13 Hurricanes.

The AASF fighters in this period started the day unsuccessfully, with No. 73 Squadron failing to intercept a raid of five enemy aircraft near Reims. Then six Hurricanes of No. 1 Squadron engaged twenty-five Bf110s southeast of Reims and destroyed five. This was followed by twelve of No. 501 Squadron's Hurricanes intercepting six Do17 bombers attacking Auberne and claiming two destroyed. Two Hurricanes force landed and two more were unserviceable.

At midday six Hurricanes of No. 1 Squadron intercepted four Bf110s northwest of Verdun, and in the combat claimed two destroyed for the loss of one Hurricane. This was only one of many raids that were intercepted. However many more raids got through as there were not enough fighters to cover all the air space and provide fighter cover for Allied bomber targets. Many French fighter squadrons were overwhelmed as they flew fighters that could not even catch the enemy bombers and were thus incapable of fighting the Bf109.

Then, at 13.45 hours, six Hurricanes of No. 73 Squadron pursued a formation of enemy aircraft but met eight Bf110s flying at 12,000ft and went into the attack. Out manoeuvring the Bf110s was no problem, but catching them was different, just the same the destruction of three was claimed for the loss of one Hurricane. The RAF fighters were by now flying so many sorties daily that fatigue was starting to prove a problem which would only increase as the days went by.

At this stage in the battle the 9th French Army were breaking up under repeated Luftwaffe attacks. Both military personnel and civilians were being machinegunned on the roads; some French units were outflanked and their 'soft' transport destroyed. At Stonne, near Sedan, the Grossdeutchland Regiment, backed by anti-tank guns, came up against the French 3rd Divisions Cuirassées and received a bloody nose; so fresh reinforcements were brought up and more armour sent to break up a French armoured thrust to Chémery. The Luftwaffe, meanwhile, concentrated their attacks on targets behind the front lines, one of the their victims being the French 2nd Divisions Cuirassées DC R, who were caught loading their tanks at Chalons.

Up in Belgium the French 1st Army were taking the brunt of the attacks from the 5th and 7th Panzer Divisions, the BEF being not quite so hard pressed. But with the collapse of the French 9th Army it was decided to retire the whole Allied front back to the Escaut. General d'Astier had by then been ordered to switch air priority from the 2nd Army Front to the 9th Army Front to relieve the pressure there; but no more than 237 single-seat fighters, 38 night fighters and 38 bombers were available. By midday half of the fighter strength had been wiped out during bombing attacks. Against the 250 Allied fighters that were available, Loerzer and Richthofen could muster 814 aircraft on this date. With the flak batteries that Guderian had rushed forward to guard the bridgeheads over the Meuse, the area became like 'Death Valley' to Allied aircraft. By the end of the day the Germans had claimed 200 Allied aircraft shot down by the Luftwaffe, plus a further 112 by flak. The actual losses were less than 100, although many more were damaged.

2 Group Blenheims were again ordered out, with No. 15 Squadron's last three serviceable aircraft joining up with nine of No. 40 Squadron in an attack on the Dinant-Celles road. The attack was carried out from 10,000ft. with dives to 5,000ft. Due to stiff opposition the attack was not a success and Wing Commander Barlow of No. 40 Squadron failed to return, as did another No. 40 Squadron aircraft. Pilot Officer Harrison of No. 15 Squadron force landed in Belgium. Another attack was made by twelve Blenheims of No. 82 Squadron, which were escorted by French Hawk 75s. The target was troop

concentrations at Montherme, so the squadron decided to bomb in line astern. No losses were incurred as the Hawk 75s gave the enemy fighters sufficient opposition. French fighters also provided patrols over target areas. Unfortunately, there were still not enough fighter escorts.

Nos. 15 and 40 Squadrons were now at Wyton in 2 Group, and a member of the latter squadron was Jack Wey. For the aircrew the chances of a 'tomorrow' were slight, and for the groundcrew there was only work, losing their aircraft and crew, new aircraft to be modified, others to be repaired:

> "The main thoughts were of working hours that would give a Trades Unionist apoplexy! The continuous work necessary to keep sufficient Blenheims available for the sorties. Things like doing repair or servicing for 48 hours or more at a stint and eating meals cooked on a hotplate in the hangar . . . if one could find the time. Things like falling asleep while waiting for an oil tank to drain into a waste drum, only to wake and find the drum had only room for five gallons and the tank had held 8 gallons . . . then three gallons or so had to be mopped and scraped off the hangar floor, making my tiredness even more unbearable."

Air Component Blenheims were, due to faulty aircraft recognition by the fighter pilots, receiving the attention of Hurricanes as well as Bf109s. This resulted on 15th May with L9399, flown by Pilot Officer Bone on a photo' sortie over Tornai, being shot down by a Hurricane. The following day L4852, flown by Flight Lieutenant Daly, was going in to land at Glisy airfield when it was shot down by a Hurricane, in spite of recognition signals being fired. The aircraft caught fire and the crew were badly burnt. This was the second time in a week that the crew had been shot down by a Hurricane. To be fair, the fighter pilots were out numbered, fatigued, and often fighting at odds of 20 to 1; not that the above can excuse such negligence.

On 15th May, Sergeant Allard of No. 85 Squadron knocked down a lone He111 about 1½ miles from his airfield, a solitary enemy aircraft was considered rare. During the day the Squadron claimed four enemy aircraft but three Hurricanes failed to return from a patrol over Belgium. Fortunately, the following day, two of the pilots turned up on foot at the squadron, the third was in hospital, injured.

No. 103 Squadron had in the meantime started to evacuate from Betheniville, a volunteer rear party staying behind until the 16th to collect and salvage as much equipment as possible. They not only did that, but made four out of seven abandoned Hurricanes serviceable. These were collected by No. 103 (Battle) Squadron pilots and flown to their new airfield at Rheges. No. 226 Squadron moved to their new airfield at Faux-Villecerf, having to destroy seven severely damaged Battles and non-removable stores.

Battle K9264 of No. 103 Squadron. Note the unapproved method of marking.

No. 4 Squadron had moved to Lille-Ronchin with fourteen serviceable Lysanders and were using Aspelaere as an advanced landing ground; while 'C' Flight of No. 2 Squadron had moved from Bethune to Ledegham. This was not to be for long due to GHQs decision to retire the troops from the Dyle Line. No. 4 Squadron lost one Lysander, and another was attacked by six Bf109s, the Lysander air gunner putting one into the 'deck'.

By 16th May the evacuation of the AASF squadrons and Wing HQs commenced, moving to their new bases in southern Champagne around Troyes. Nos. 114 and 139 Squadron had between them only nine Blenheims, so the decision was made to amalgamate these with the Air Component reconnaissance squadrons – yet moral was still high. Wireless-operator air-gunner John Parry:

> "Morale on the squadron was excellent throughout this time, no shortage of volunteer aircrew . . . aircraft might go missing, but it couldn't happen to us."

No. 1 Squadron had been operating from Berry-au-Bac up to 15th May, but with the Germans approaching Rethel, and also a loss of communication with HQ at Reims on the 16th, the commanding officer, Wing Commander Halahan*, ordered a move to Vraux. Hardly had the last lorry of the main road party crossed the bridge spanning the Marne-Aisne Canal at Berry-au-Bac, when it was blown by French engineers. Within a short space of time French machine-gunners on the canal bank were engaging a motorcycle unit of a Panzer outfit.

---

*Served later in Malta during the siege days.

Naturally the personnel of No. 114 Squadron were pleased to have fighters stationed with them, and accommodation and food were soon found. Late in the morning of the following day, five Hurricanes took-off heading towards an attack. About one-and-a-quarter hours later the first of four Hurricanes landed, so shot-up that it was a write-off, but the pilot had sent two Bf110s down in flames. The other three also got Bf110s, but the fifth member was missing; he later turned up safely, having been shot down in flames after shooting down a Bf110. Baling out of his aircraft he had then become the target for some French infantry, who were fortunately bad shots, and he was able to give them a blistering in their own language, in which he was proficient.

On the 16th, No. 73 Squadron moved to Villeneuve Airfield. The following day, Flying Officer 'Cobber' Kain took off and attacked a formation of fifteen Bf110s, but in the melée only damaged one. Later on, still on his own, he attacked a solitary Ju88, but was pounced on by ten Bf109s. Seeing them coming down, Kain turned into the attack, shooting one down and making good his escape.

Within 24 hours, orders were given to No. 114 Squadron to proceed to Nantes. Its last three remaining Blenheims were to be handed over to No. 18 Squadron at Meharicourt. From numerous accounts it would appear that the safe arrival of the squadron ground party at Nantes, as a cohesive unit, was in no small part due to the direction and control of their CO, Wing Commander P. Wright.*

Of the departure from Vraux, Reg Stride had this to say:

"We were lucky to be under the control of Wing Commander Wright, he was the perfect CO to take charge when we were literally depressed with the situation. He told us bluntly what the situation was; he organised our convoy, petrol, oil and water supplies, rations etc, including a lorry-load of NAAFI 'goodies'. He briefed all the SNCOs and gave instructions for everybody to conserve ammunition, if the convoy was strafed to get well clear of the vehicles, and a 'loose' vehicle convoy formation.

"We had every faith in our new CO. He was a thorough gentleman and we all respected him. He, however, admitted that he could not achieve his aim of getting us back to England without the help of each and everyone in the unit, SNCOs, corporals, and airmen."

"He not only got the unit back but he also completed an operational tour himself flying with the squadron on Blenheims."

The 16th May would find No. 139 Squadron flying their last operational sorties in France, 71 Wing HQ already having warned the squadron that they were to move to Lannoy. At first light three aircraft were airborne to carry out an attack on Montherme, but one had to return with engine trouble. The other two, L8760 flown by Flying

*Resigned the RAF in 1946 as Air Commodore P. Wright OBE, DFC.

No. 144 Squadron officers: L to R: S/Ldr. Outram, 'A' Flight; W/Cmd. P. Wright, CO; S/Ldr. Kitley, 'B' Flight. (T. Davies)

Officer Walsh, Sergeant Paine and AC. Parry, and L4977, flown by Pilot Officer King, Sergeant Woods and Corporal Arrowsmith, set course for the target area. However, early morning mist obscured the ground and the two aircraft were forced to return, being first fired at by enemy fighters and then French ack-ack, resulting in L8760 being damaged beyond squadron repair. Further reconnaissance flights were flown during the day until, at 19.40 hours, a last reconnaissance was called for.

By this time HQ Reims and the Army Command had lost track of the German advance. Hampered by the flak and fighters in the area, the reconnaissance aircraft found little to report. John Parry's pilot was jokingly told to fly east until he was fired at – that would be the German line! John, who had already survived one shooting up, was to go out again:

> "By now the phone from HQ was red-hot, more info' required. So took-off at 19.30 hours with Flying Officer Turnbull and Sergeant Paine in L8756 on what was to be the last op' of 139 in France. It happened to be a lovely evening, and we saw the 6th Panzer making their way through Hirson and the 8th Panzer around Montmedy and Rocroi. Of course there was lots of flak, my radio was damaged, the aerial mast flew past my turret and disappeared but no fighters came up, so again we got away with it."

81

Due to darkness closing in the pilot landed at Romilly.

The following day No. 1 Squadron was also on the move again. Under orders from HQ, the squadron moved to Anglure, the advance-guard moving off during the night. At Anglure the squadron settled down alongside the Hurricanes of No. 501 Squadron.

The movement of the AASF squadrons to the Troyes area resulted in the cessation of AASF operations for the period of 16th to 18th May, inclusive. Further to this some of the MT vehicles that were provided for the move were minus starting handles and spares. It was later found that these had all been loaded onto a solitary lorry, which was sent to Base! A report would later be raised on the MT problem and organisation, or lack of it, which criticised the motor transport action and made the point that the lesson of the move was " . . . a need for 100% mobility".

The reported impregnability of the Maginot Line had fostered a false sense of security, not only in the French but in the AASF also. They all failed to remember that there was no Maginot Line as such through the Ardennes and northwards. The AASF squadrons had very little mobility and had become static, the motor transport establishment and the actual amount of motor transport available bore no relationship to that which was necessary. There have been claims that the AASF were 600 vehicles below establishment so that when orders came to be issued for the move to the Troyes area, problems with motor transport appeared. Fortunately, the Air Attache at the British Embassy in Paris worked wonders and managed to persuade the French to loan to the RAF three hundred new American 'White' and 'Dodge' lorries. These vehicles were retained until the final evacuation from France, in spite of protests from the French.

The unfortunate part of the whole campaign was that there was a great deal of war material in France, both British and French, which was not made available to front line forces. Maybe this was due to maladministration, maybe Fifth Column work, or maybe sheer bloodymindedness. One thing that stands out above all this, was the close relationship between the French villagers in the Reims area and the RAF personnel. With the withdrawal of the AASF squadrons a certain amount of despondency was seen, for large numbers of the older French generation despised or hated the Germans.

On the subject of the Fifth Column, naturally a lot of this was just rumour, which could be just as bad as direct action, destroying morale and creating panic. Fifth Column work did take place, as did the sniping at our troops during the retreat; whilst rumours of German paratroops being dropped disguised as nuns etc. did not help the moral of troops detailed for night-guard duties. The possibility of paratroops being dropped increased after May 10, 1940, with the Luftwaffe dropping paratroops at key points, and also Fiesler Storch aircraft landing special squads to isolate certain cross-roads.

At 02.30 hours on 17th May, 71 Wing HQ issued their last instructions before the Wing moved. These were issued to No. 114 Squadron and called for the reconnaissance of the roads between Reims, Rethel and Vouzieres, the road from Suippes to Attigny, and the road from Vouzieres to St Menehoul. At 05.50 hours Blenheim L9466, crewed by Flying Officer Kennedy, observer Sergeant Lutwych and air gunner AC. White took-off. Their luck was in and the mission was flown without incident, the aircraft landing at base at 08.15 hours.

From the 17th until 19th May inclusive, there were seven home based squadrons of 11 Group operating in support of the fighter squadrons of the BAFF. There were also three composite squadrons, 56/213, 111/253 and 145/601 Squadrons, who operated daily from refuelling points in France, employed singly or in flights, on escort and offensive duties then returning at night for servicing at forward bases in Kent.

From 11th to 15th May there had been thirty-two air raids in the Reims area, some damage being inflicted on the AASF HQ MT section, Reims railway station and to units at Reims aerodrome. Arthur Phipps was working the best part of 24 hours on the 15th, getting movement orders out to the squadrons. Then on the 16th came orders to move, so the HQ unit packed everything into lorries and joined the evacuation to Troyes, being delayed by the refugees and diversions through side roads. Phipps remembers:

"My first insight into the side-effects of warfare was of the road from Reims to Troyes, where we encountered endless streams of pathetic refugees from the north, pulling handcarts with the old people sitting on small piles of personal possessions – they were hungry and absolutely exhausted. Sometimes, despite our efforts to keep clear, we were jammed in their midst and could do nothing apart from hand out a few bars of chocolate to the children and cigarettes to the adults."

Among the units moving to new airfields was No. 88 Squadron with their Battles. Telephone communications with the Wing HQ had already been severed, so an advance party left early in the morning for the airfield at Les Grandes Chappeles. Due to a shortage of vehicles it was necessary for the vehicles to return to Mourmelon-le-Grand to collect oil, fuel and bombs, and to destroy all stores that could not be moved. A similar situation faced No. 150 Squadron, who were moving to Pouan from Ecury-sur-Coole. Wing HQ had alerted the squadron to the possibility of German paratroops being dropped in the

Chalons area, instead, the following day a heavy bombing attack was made on Chalons by fourteen enemy bombers.

The evacuation of the AASF squadrons to the Troyes area placed both the Rivers Marne and Aisne between the AASF and the German advance. At this stage of the German attack they made no attempt to cross the Aisne, but used it to cover their left flank in their advance to the Channel coast.

On 17th May, with the withdrawal of the AASF squadrons south, 2 Group was called on to attempt to block the German passage from Gembloux. No. 82 Squadron despatched twelve Blenheims with fighters of the BAFF to provide cover in the target area. The plan called for the Blenheims to approach the target at 5,000ft. from the southeast, then to dive to 2,000ft. for bomb release. Although the fighters were in the target area on time, the Blenheims were intercepted before the target by at least fifteen Bf109s. The Blenheims who were flying in two boxes of six, were bracketed by heavy flak concentration and forced to open out their formation, one aircraft (P8830) on the right wing was hit and dived away. The Bf109s attacked before the Blenheims could close up their formation; Sergeant Morrison and crew (P8858) were the only survivors. Their aircraft damaged by flak and fighters, they reported seeing three Blenheims shot down in flames by the Bf109s. One of these Blenheims, P9210, was seen to be hit in the mainplaine, which burst into flames.

Three Hurricane squadrons were detailed on the 18th to patrol over the Aisne bridges, but not to patrol simultaneously. No. 73 Squadron were to patrol first, followed by No. 501 and then No. 1 Squadron. After their allotted time on patrol No. 1 Squadron started to lose height for their return to base, when they saw a formation of twenty-five Blenheims below them. Closing in with the intention of escorting them back, someone shouted "They're bloody Heinkels". The squadron then went into formation attack, the enemy maintained good formation descipline and fire control. In spite of this, within minutes the Heinkel formation broke with five enemy aircraft going down out of control or with Hurricanes about to execute a kill.

Further attacks by 2 Group Blenheims were still called for, although the number of Blenheims available were much reduced by losses and damage. No. 15 Squadron for instance could only put up six aircraft. The plan called for the Blenheims to fly from England and land at designated French airfields to pick up French escorts then, after the first attack they would land, rearm and refuel and carry out a further attack. Things could go wrong, and did.

No. 40 Squadron operated from Abbeville and bombed German troops at Longacres before landing at Poix. No. 21 Squadron flew to

Blenheim IV L8852 of No. 15 Squadron at Wyton. Failed to return on 18 May 1940.

Poix to pick up their escort, but when none arrived the squadron returned to base. No. 107 Squadron and No. 110 Squadron Blenheims also flew to Poix, only to find German troops on the village outskirts, so they quickly vacated the airfield. No. 110 Squardon were to lose L9241, N6208 and N6210 during the day. Poix airfield had already been bombed early on by eighteen He111s and with the advanced units of the enemy approaching, Nos. 53 and 59 squadrons were ordered to evacuate Poix. Unserviceable aircraft and non-removable equipment was to be destroyed, and the squadrons move on to Crecy.

No. 15 Squadron were supposed to rendezvous with French fighter squadrons over Douai, but when none appeared the decision was made to press on with their attack on enemy troops near Le Cateaux. The squadron met a screen of murderous flak and, as the Blenheims pulled out of their dives, they were jumped by Bf109s. P6917, L8853 and L8852 were shot down over the target area, while the three remaining aircraft, all badly damaged, succeeded in landing at Poix. L9030, flown by Pilot Officer Robinson, was beyond repair and had to be abandoned. L8848, flown by Flying Officer George, was damaged with all guns out of action. George refuelled and tagged on to the remainder of No. 40 Squadron for the return to Wyton. Flying Officer Trent's* P6913 had a badly damaged rear spar and other damage. Upon landing at Poix it was immediately grounded by the Engineering Officer. During the night, with the approach of the enemy, and in spite of threats from the Engineering Officer, Trent decided to press

*Retired as Group Captain Trent VC, DFC. Died at his home in New Zealand 1986.

on to the UK, and in spite of being shot at by Allied ack-ack on the way back, made a safe landing at Martlesham.

Of the attack on Le Chateaux, Hugh George wrote:

> "We attacked individually, first in a dive with 250 pounders and then did a second run at low level hitting the German troops (and there were thousands of them) with 40 pounders. The assorted AA fire was very intense and then we were jumped by 109s. The sky suddenly seemed to be full of them and I remember being involved in an almighty dogfight. My gunner (O'Donnell) first opened up at close range, but his gun packed up after firing I think 5 rounds. Split cartridge cases. Then my observer (Box) had a go with the backward firing gun, but the tortuous feed seized up after 1 or perhaps 2 rounds. then I succeeded in getting on the tail of the 109 which was attacking us and closed to point blank range and let him have it with my front gun. Except that the gun failed to fire. So it turned into a hell for leather chase across France at nought feet, finishing up down somebody's main street from which the 109 did not seem to emerge."*

From the three aircraft shot down in the target area only one man escaped. He was the air gunner of L8853, LAC. Thomas, who was taken prisoner. Meanwhile, No. 139 Squadron in France had destroyed their three unserviceable aircraft (including L8760, which had been severely damaged on the 16th), the fuel dump and bomb dump. The four remaining serviceable aircraft then took off at 15.30 hours to join No. 57 Squadron, which had eventually been traced to Abbeville. Air gunner John Parry recorded:

> "Took off in L8756 to deliver it to RAF Air Component at Rosiere, everyone had moved out when we got there, aerodrome deserted as the Germans were getting near to Amiens. Took off again and landed at Poix, deserted. Then to Poix satellite once more, everyone was moving out. Eventually landed at Abbeville, where the Air Component were glad to take over our aircraft."

Some of the crews hitched a lift from there to Paris, where they were promptly arrested as Fifth Columnists! They were released after being vouched for by HQ, the Railway Transport Officer soon had them on the first train to Nantes.

Another member of No. 139 Squadron was 'Doc' Walls, a Fitter II:

> "The squadron's activities become centred on attacking roads and bridges near the Belgian frontier. We lost many aircraft in those early operations and many staggered back badly damaged."

It was quite often necessary to canabalise unserviceable aircraft to make other aircraft serviceable, and the doping of fabric patches over minor damage in the aircraft skin was accepted as the speediest

*Retired as Wing Commander H. George DFC and presently Chairman of the Blenheim Society.

method of repair. Such expedients were necessary to get aircraft back into the air., yet the groundcrews appreciated the aircrews' dangerous job, and were concerned and anxious whilst 'their crew' was on a raid. They could see how physically exhausted 'their crew' were, if they returned.

Exhaustion was affecting the fighter squadrons as well, so that around this period it became necessary for the Air Officer Commanding in Chief to signal to the DCAS Air Ministry for reliefs, stating:

> "Those in this country are absolutely whacked. It is absolutely essential they should be replaced. 40 required, 20 replacements and 20 reinforcements, including 4 Flight Commanders."

No 607 Squadron were still at Vitry-en-Artois, and serving with them was Sergeant D. Brown,* a Fitter A & E.:

> "On the 18th May, in the afternoon, our aircraft were busy scrapping with a flock of Me109s and 110s over Arras (we had a grandstand view) when a formation of twin-engine bombers appeared out of the mist, in the circuit. As we were designated as an 'Advanced Landing Ground for Blenheims' we paid little attention, apart from criticising their lousey formation. However, on their final approach they came in line abreast at about 100 feet. When tracer bullets began coming from their nose guns, we realised that what we thought were Blenheims were very unfriendly Dorniers with bomb doors open. We scattered like rabbits as they flew over and dropped bombs (delayed action) at intervals over the whole airfield. When they went off, the field was like a potato patch. Fuel and bomb dumps went up and they left us in a hell of a mess, but no lives were lost. The Dorniers did not live to tell the tale, Hurricanes from Douai were airbourne and waiting for them, and we were avenged.

> "When our Hurricanes returned they were able to land between the rows of bomb craters, and we were able to re-arm and refuel ready for the next raid, which was a low level shoot-up by Me109s. Apart from scaring the pants off us, little damage was done. By now we were down to six Hurricanes which were still serviceable."

The following day the squadron were moving out, breaking their journey at a small grass airfield, but as dawn broke a number of Stukas appeared and reduced the serviceable Hurricanes down to three. And so the squadron was evacuated, but as Brown said, "We were defeated but not demoralised."

The combat over Arras mentioned above resulted in a number of claimed 'kills', but this was not without British casualties. As the squadron sailed home it had the satisfaction of knowing that their pilots had over a period of approximately ten days claimed the destruction of 72 German aircraft. Even if some of these may have

*Retired from the RAF as Squadron Leader D. R. Brown.

turned out to have been damaged instead of destroyed, it was still a good record.

The attack on Vitry-en-Artois, previously mentioned, was well executed, for three of No. 56 Squadron's Hurricanes were on patrol over the airfield, when approximately ten Bf110s were seen approaching. The three Hurricanes went to head them off, moving away from the airfield area and catching the enemy ten miles south of Vitry and a combat ensued in which four of the Bf110s were shot down. As the combat moved away from the airfield a formation of nine Do17s escorted by Bf110s swept across the airfield at about 50 feet, dropping small calibre bombs, and with the air gunners attacking the RAF aircraft. This left eight Hurricanes, one Blenheim, a petrol bowser and an ammunition dump destroyed. Flight Lieutenant Soden bravely took off, ignoring the unexploded bombs, bomb craters and groundfire, to chase the raiders. However, a Hurricane was seen to be shot down in flames a few miles from Vitry, and Soden did not return. The squadron gained the impression that the initial approach by the Bf110s was a decoy to lure the Hurricane defence away.

On 19th May, ten aircraft of the No. 145/601 composite Squadron led by Squadron Leader Miller were on an offensive patrol in the Arras region, when a large formation of enemy bombers escorted by Bf110s were sighted. While Flight Lieutenant R. Dutton engaged the fighters, the remainder of the squadron went in to attack the bombers, who were flying at 15–16,000 feet south of Arras. Six enemy aircraft were claimed as shot down, but the British fighter unit lost three Hurricanes.

Squadron Leader Miller's combat report of his combat reads thus:

"While on patrol at 20,000 feet sighted successive formations of enemy bombers approaching from north east. Dived on the last formation of about seven aircraft with Blue Section leader in line abreast. Red Section broke up and attacked Me110s, which dived from above and astern. Green Leader attacked rear formation, but Green 2 and 3 broke away and attacked aircraft in forward section. I attacked outside aircraft on side of formation, which gave out clouds of black smoke and was seen to go down."

No. 253 Squadron were also engaged in combat on the same day, being part of composite unit No. 111/253 Squadron. Taking off to intercept enemy aircraft, the squadron was involved with a group of Bf109s. This resulted in two Hurricanes failing to return, one being seen to go down in flames. Pilot Officer Greenwood shot down a Bf109 and Pilot Officer Clifton claimed a possible. The skies were full of whirling Bf109s, tracer shooting across space, yawing and turning . . . then an empty sky.

Pilots of No. 87 Squadron in August, 1939. Clockwise: P/O Mackworth (killed May 14th); P/O Joyce (injured May 14th); Sgt. Penikett; Sgt. Thurgar (killed February 12th); F/O Vose-Jeff (killed August 11th); P/O Cock (injured August 11th).

No. 87 Squadron were still at Lille-Marq on 19th May, and after another night punctuated by a cacaphony of noise from enemy action, ack-ack fire and air raid sirens, were ready to respond to the next call for action. This was not long in coming and the squadron were soon in the air and heading in the direction of ack-ack fire. The enemy aircraft turned out to be nine Bf109s, with which the Hurricanes quickly engaged. One Bf109 left the combat, descending with smoke pouring from its engine, followed by Flying Officer Dunn's aircraft being hit and going down in flames, but he survived.

Later on in the day two No. 4 Squadron Lysanders were carrying out practice landings at Lille-Marq, when five Bf109s came in fast and low and shot both down, killing all four crew. A number of Hurricanes took off in pursuit, one flown by Flying Officer 'Widge' Gleed of No. 87 Squadron. The enemy aircraft headed back homewards and appeared not to notice that they were being pursued, but Gleed with his throttle through the gate closed up enough to pour in a burst on one, which broke away from the formation and was last seen at ground level, with smoke pouring from it. Two other Bf109s were claimed by other pilots.

During the day No. 85 Squadron, operating from Mons-en-Chaussee, knocked down seven enemy aircraft, but were to lose three Hurricanes during the day's operations. Surprisingly, a number of the pilots were 'hoofing' it back to the squadrons through enemy lines.

No. 57 Squadron had, on 18th May, sent six of their Blenheims to make an attack on La Cateaux. Making their attack through a sky that appeared to be erupting with intense and accurate flak, three of the aircraft were badly damaged. Landing back at Poix the crews found themselves on their own, for the squadron had in the meantime been ordered to move to Crecy. With the enemy at Amiens, the six crews spent the night warming-up their engines in case of a panic take-off. Now on the 19th, they had rejoined their squadron at Crecy. On this day both Nos. 57 and 59 Squadrons were ordered back to the UK.

General Franklyne, on the 19th, made his final plans for an armoured thrust at Arras. The move commenced at 14.00 hours and caught Rommel's infantry separated from its armour. Within minutes the German 'soft' vehicles and anti-tank guns were destroyed by the British Matildas, and casualties inflicted on the enemy infantry. Then the Matildas came up against the 88mm anti-aircraft guns, which, firing over open sights, put an end to Franklyn's thrust . . . and the Matildas.

Nevertheless, it gave Rommel a few nasty shocks and something to worry about, for his casualties were in excess of the British.

General Frere of the French Army was at the same time attempting to hold a defence line on the Somme with insufficient forces. He could not stop the Germans infiltrating and slipping across the Ouse, and then driving on to Peronne. There they successfully bridged the Somme and drove on to Amiens with their armour. In the Amiens area the Royal Sussex and some French units attempted to bar the way, but the 1st Panzer Division threw them aside and raced on south of the city. The 2nd Panzer Division were also moving fast and racing for Abbeville. Cutting through the British 35th Brigade they captured the river crossings at St Valery-sur-Somme.

67 Wing, on 19th May, were detailed for escort duties to French and British bombers in attacks on the German spearheads, all of which was to have little effect on the battle outcome. The enemy columns were well protected by both medium and light flak, expert at their job and well backed up by infantry trained in anti-aircraft defence.

During the day No. 73 Squadron were in the air with twelve Hurricanes and saw two formations of He111s with five Ju88s, all escorted by three layers of Bf110s stacked above. The Hurricanes attacked and broke the He111 formation, while the Bf110s flew steadily on. The leader of one flight, Flight Lieutenent Scoular, saw the first enemy aircraft he attacked dive away with pieces falling off. Then he got in three short bursts into another He111, which went down out of control. During this time three other Hurricanes put another He111 down before the Bf110s intervened. The other flight led by Kain, shot down a Ju88 in a head-on attack and put down a

Squadron Leader 'Hank' More of No. 73 Squadron discussing a 'dogfight' with his pilots. 'Cobber' Kain with white pullover. (S/Ldr. C. Campbell DFC)

Bf110 which attempted to intervene. The day concluded with No. 73 Squadron claiming one Bf110, seven Ju88s and three He111s for the loss of three Hurricanes.

In another combat an interception was carried out against an He111, which was flying at 5,000 feet. This was carried out by Flight Lieutenant I. Gleed and Flying Officer R. Rayner, the latter's combat report read:

"Flight Lieutenant Gleed and myself, operating from Lille-Marq, after a panic take-off, encountered one He111K over Orchies. I attacked from starboard quarter and Flight Lieutenant Gleed from astern simultaneously. Aircraft dived into ground and blew up."

The last No. 114 Squadron Blenheim was flown away to Meharicourt by Sergeant Pilot G. Potter and crew. Unaware that No. 18 Squadron had evacuated to Crecy, the crew landed to find the place deserted, so went in search of any locals. Finding only some old folk, these told them that the Germans had passed through the day before! Hurrying back to their aircraft, they got the engines started; just as the second engine fired up, a German motorcyclist appeared on the edge of the airfield. A getaway was quickly made and Potter headed for Glisy, where again there was no trace of No. 18 Squadron. Eventually the squadron was traced to Crecy, the aircraft handed over, and the crew then started hitching lifts to Nancy to rejoin their own squadron. Gillie Potter is not a man for overstating things, but remarked:

Hurricanes of No. 85 Squadron on 'Readiness'. The strong construction of the Hurricane made it suitable for rough French airfields.

Flight Lieutenant Ian Scoular. 'B' Flight Commander of No. 73 Squadron. (S/Ldr. C. Campbell DFC)

''Landed at Meharicourt where I had a close encounter with a German motorcyclist.''

On this day No. 142 Squadron had only three serviceable Battles left, which were despatched on a daylight attack on enemy troops west of Laon. The result was almost a foregone conclusion.

K7696 P/O. Taylor   Sgt. Lang   LAC. Long
Failed to return and the crew became PoWs
L5226 Sgt. Godsall   Sgt. Hopgood   LAC. Boyle
Failed to return.
The third aircraft force-landed ten miles south of Epernay.

Evacuation of the Air Component squadrons had by now been ordered, so No. 3, 32 and 79 Squadrons got ready for evacuation, followed by the evacuation of No. 85, 87, 607 and 615 Squadrons. Of the 261 Hurricanes originally committed to the battle in France only 66 were evacuated. Only 74 Hurricanes were lost in combat, the remainder were either destroyed on the ground during the air attacks, or had to be abandoned due to unserviceability or shortage of pilots. (The latter is amazing when one considers the request by the French to the RAF DCAS in early June, see page 128.)

As well as the squadrons evacuating and destroying equipment and materials that they were unable to take with them, similar action was taking place at aircraft storage parks. L. Lineker at an Air Stores Park at Glisy airfield, says of the day of evacuation:

''The day we left we burnt quite a number of new Hurricanes, as there weren't any pilots to fly them away. They were manhandled in threes nose-to-nose and a petrol soaked rag was lighted and thrown under them.''

Typex W/T Section at Nancy HQ. Back row L to R: Norton, Sgt. Gamblin, McMinn, unknown, Edwards; front row L to R: H. Cooper, unknown, Simpson. (F/Lt. H. Cooper)

At the Typex section at Nancy HQ, Wing Commander Cleveland, the Officer Commanding the RAF HQ there, advised the staff to make their way north. Having piled their kit etc. into an American 'White' lorry and the Typex into a Renault van, the section started moving off, driving first northwest and then west. At one bridge a French Army officer with red tabs and Colonel's insignia tried to direct them to the east. The drivers ignored his directions as it was considered that in directing them in that direction they would be going into the arms of the Hun, and there was the possibility that he was Fifth Column. H. Cooper of the Typex Section remembers the refugees that they saw:

> "It was really grim to see these people with all their possessions, just drifting along, with the same expression on all their faces, of sheer and utter fear and hopelessness."

Whether to Troyes or Nantes, the same grim scenes were repeated, with frightened refugees fleeing from the hated Hun; military traffic trying to get to airfields or ports, always the possibility of being bombed or machinegunned on the roads; shortage of food, fuel and rest. Chaos was the order of the day, among troops and civilians alike. No one any longer was sure of orders or instructions, rumour bred rumour and suspicion. When aircraft appeared and the refugees sought the supposed safety of the ditches, the military drivers put their foot down, hoping to get further along the road without being shot-up. Many times it worked, but not always; Owen Baum recalls:

> "Amongst the debris of war I was saddened to see, lying on its side in a ditch, a Leyland single-decker bus, once part of a fleet run by the late Charles Allen of Mountsorrel."

During 19th May at No. 615 Squadron's advance base in Belgium, a Belgian Army officer arrived with orders to blow up the airfield immediately. Evenutally, after a great deal of arguing, he agreed to mine the airfield, leaving a clear path for the Hurricanes to take-off, and to explode the mines after 615's departure. While starting some of

A Bf109E-1 of II/JG53.

the aircraft was no problem, others had flattish batteries, so the departure was prolonged. Never-the-less, they all got away and joined No. 607 Squadron and another squadron at Abbeville, where the AOC had also moved his residence.

A request was received from the BEF for aircraft to straff German Army transport on the main road from Cambrai to Arras, Joe Kayll takes up the story:

> "From the three squadrons we managed to assemble twelve serviceable aircraft, which I led to the main road east of Arras. The German Army were well deployed with anti-aircraft guns in fields each side of the road. Several German transports were damaged but we lost three aircraft to ground fire."

Authority for withdrawal of all Air Component squadrons was given on 19th May, and some squadrons were re-established in the area north-west of Paris. The next move for the Air Component squadrons, mainly Lysanders, was to the south of England, leaving just four Lysanders of No. 4 Squadron attached to GHQ. Sergeant W. Fenton* of No. 2 Squadron was told, along with others of the squadron, to get out quick. Having in his charge a six-wheeled Crossley workshop lorry loaded with engineering spares and a lathe, Fenton decided no German was going to get this if he could help it so he loaded up with fuel at the airfield. Then with a personal set of maps and a Sergeant Pepper as mate, he set off for Dunkirk. Bombed several times, mixed up with refugees and nearly captured by the Germans, Fenton managed to bypass some areas by driving the Crossley across fields. From roadside enquiries Fenton found that to get to Dunkirk he would probably run into the German lines of advance, so revised his plans and decided on a night drive via Rouen to Cherbourg. After wards it was found that other No. 2 Squadron personnel had also been given the same advice and had also made for Cherbourg.

*Joined the RAF Servicing Commandos and retired as Squadron Leader.

AW27 "Ettrick" of Imperial Airways (National Air Communications) at Abbeville. Due to shortage of washing facilities, airmen are washing in puddles on the airfield.

No. 87 Squadron were also operating at a forward airfield when the German breakthrough put the airfield in danger. The CO called all the squadron together to give instructions. Stan Cain remembers the gist of what he said:

"Well chaps I think we had better go back to Lille-Marcq, as one of the 'brown jobs',* with a red hat, has just told me that the Germans have broken through and are heading our way with some bloody big tanks; so we'll get the aircraft off, have a go at them and land back with the squadron. The rest, break camp, take what you can get on the transport, leave what you can't but destroy it, be gone by lunchtime, good-luck and we will see you back at Lille-Marcq.

"We packed up a bit on the quick side and all we left were our tents, which we gave to some French refugees. We duly arrived back at Lille-Marcq in a couple of days, only to find that the squadron had moved back to Merville, so away we went again and joined them there."

No. 615 Squadron was one of the Air Component units evacuated to the UK. Squadron Leader Joe Kayll DSO, DFC. the squadron Commanding Officer had this to say of morale at the time:

"The morale and efficiency of the groundcrews was remarkable, considering the squadron occupied four aerodromes during 11 days, moving all equipment and arranging new billets all over Belgium. Pilot morale was equally good and nearly every patrol was eventful. We did feel rather out on a limb in Belgium and it was difficult to find out what was really happening."

* British Army Personnel.

Another unit on the road was the Wing HQ at Poix, one of the members was Harry Fenwick. He was driving a staff car, loaded with HQ officers, to Boulogne. Near to the port he found the place in panic and chaos. Having seen the officers leave for the ship with no attempt made to load him and the car and after waiting around for a few hours, with no instructions having been given and the chaos getting worse, Fenwick decided that he had been forgotten in the panic. Not wanting to have the staff car or himself taken over by the Germans, Fenwick set out for Cherbourg. Although the roads were blocked by French and British troops as well as civilians, bombs did clear the roads at times. That was when Fenwick kept driving.

> "Now after travelling for a time, I saw sitting at the side of the road a complete RAF aircrew. They had done their job, lost their aircraft and were hoping someone would pick them up. The pilot was in good shape but the rest of the crew were in a state of shock. They were in for a bigger shock for I was running out of petrol. Then a chance in a million; a Queen Mary truck appeared from nowhere with many tins of petrol and I was not only able to fill up but obtained some spare."

The Queen Mary was from the same squadron as the aircrew, so the aircrew transferred to that with thanks to Fenwick.

No. 4 Squadron had evacuated to the airfield at Clairmarais on 20th May, where 'A' Flight of No. 13 Squadron joined them. This Flight was commanded by Flight Lieutenant Graham, who had no instructions where to move to. Graham took off later on reconnaissance and his Lysander was attacked by three Do17s which shot him down, killing both crew members. Two days later the squadron moved off to Dunkirk, the aircraft flying back to the UK. The squadron's first sight of Dunkirk was of the oil tanks burning from a previous raid and during the day six further bombing attacks were made. Although the squadron boarded the *SS. St Helier*, they were forced to leave their motor transport behind.

Another Crossley lorry with trailer was from No. 607 Squadron. This carried the Engineer Officer, twenty airmen and D. R. Brown. Its eventual destination was Cherbourg. On the way they tried all the ports, but most were blocked with bombed ships. At Le Havre they found fuel and food with an RAF Maintenance and Stores Unit, then headed for the River Seine and the ferry. Says D. R. Brown:

> "The ferry was at the other side, and refused to come over for us. However, three of us 'borrowed' a motor boat and went over for it. The Ferry Master had to be 'persuaded' at pistol point to co-operate, which he did. Safely over, we headed for Cherbourg, via Caen. Twelve hours later we heard that Le Havre had been occupied by the Panzers. We had escaped the net."

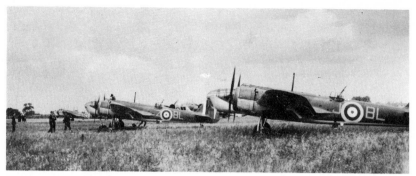

Blenheim IVs of No. 40 Squadron at Wyton in 1940, soon to start up and take-off. Light series bomb carriers are fitted under the fuselage.

The newspapers in Great Britain told of a 'strategic retreat' and the exploits of our fighter pilots, meanwhile our bombers were being slaughtered. Two Blenheims, N3552 and P4937, of No. 40 Squadron at Wyton were despatched in the early morning of 21st May, to carry out a reconnaissance of the Amiens and Audenarde area, then to land at Merville for interrogation. On preparing to land at Merville it was noticed that the airfield was deserted, so course was set for Wyton. The same day thirteen No. 57 Squadron Blenheims landed at Wyton, having evacuated from France. Most were quite heavily damaged, with one having a hole in its propeller the size of a fist. All aircraft were carrying squadron groundcrew as passengers.

Next, three No. 40 Squadron Blenheims and six No. 15 Squadron aircraft took-off to strike at vehicles at Montreuil. R3706, of No. 15 Squadron flown by Flight Lieutenant Webster, was hit in the wing and port engine. It crashed between Etaples and Boulogne, but the crew escaped and made their way back. The attack was carried out at low level against tanks. During the attack Flying Officer Clarke (L9024) was so low that when his aircraft was severely hit and he was injured, the port wingtip dug into a French field. It cut a furrow and smashed the outer four feet of wing, bending it up to approximately 25 degrees, with earth embedded inside. In spite of this, Clarke recovered from what appeared to be a fatal crash and brought his aircraft and crew safely back to base.

On 11th June the same officer lost his life. Coming out of cloud his wingman crashed into him. Clarke's aircraft was severely damaged, yet he managed to maintain some measure of control while heading back towards Allied territory. Then, with the aircraft disintegrating, Clarke ordered his crew to bale-out, but he was unable to do the same before the aircraft went out of control, and he was killed. For neither of these acts of gallantry was an award made.

A formation of No. 16 Squadron Lysanders with blue-red roundels. Light series carriers are on bomb 'wings'.

In the afternoon nine No. 21 Squadron and three No. 82 Squadron aircraft joined twelve of No. 107 Squadron. Flying first to Boulogne they commenced searching for tank and MT convoys. From there they went to the Etampes, Montreuil and Hesden area. Flak was light, but the targets difficult to locate due to the number of refugees. No. 82 Squadron carried out shallow dive-bombing, but No. 107 Squadron had to call off their attack as the road was packed with refugees. The squadrons were lucky to get away without casualties as too much time was wasted searching for the targets, there being no accurate information.

The Lysander squadrons of the Air Component, now based in England, were still operating in aid of the BEF, although operating at this distance from the combat area reducing the sortie time over the target. On 22nd May eleven Lysanders of Nos. 2, 16 and 26 Squadrons carried out attacks on enemy troops and vehicles on roads in the Boulogne, Samar and Montreuil area. From the attacks one aircraft failed to return, whilst another was blown apart and the crew killed, when a 'hung-up' bomb fell off on landing.

On the same day, Lysander KO-U of No. 2 Squadron flown by Flying Officer Doidge and LAC Webborn took-off at 15.55 hours from Bekesbourne to carry out a tactical reconnaissance in the Merville airfield area. An Hs126 was observed below, so Doidge made an attacking dive on it and saw it crash. During the return flight an encounter was made with a Ju87 and during the combat the air gunner shot it down.

The traffic was not all one way, for two days later, Flying Officer Scotter and LAC. Evans, crewing Lysander KO-X of No. 2 Squadron, on a tactical reconnaissance in the Boulogne area, was attacked for about twenty minutes by approximately fifteen Bf109s. Although the Lysander was badly damaged by cannon fire in the undercarriage, fuel tank, cockpit and port mainplane, Scotter managed to fly it back to Hawkinge.

A re-organisation was taking place with the withdrawal of some units. 71 Wing Headquarters had, on 19th May, left Fagnieres for Nantes, the personnel split into a fast and a slow convoy. Both convoys had arrived at Nantes on the 22nd and joined No. 2 Base Area. The AASF Headquarters were still at Troyes and in communication with the squadrons, although telephone connections sometimes broke down. The AASF now controlled the following units:

67 Wing Headquarters	at Saron-sur-Aube
No. 1 Squadron (Hurricanes)	at Allemanche
No. 73 Squadron (Hurricanes)	at Gaye
No. 501 Squadron (Hurricanes)	at Allemanche
75 Wing Headquarters	at Meny-sur-Seine
No. 88 Squadron (Battles)	at Les-Grandes-Chappelles
No. 103 Squadron (Battles)	at St Lucien Ferme
No. 150 Squadron (Battles)	at Pouan
76 Wing Headquarters	at Marigny-le-Chatel
No. 12 Squadron (Battles)	at Echimmines
No. 142 Squadron (Battles)	at Faux-Ville-Cerf
No. 24 (Communications) Squadron detachment	at Echimmines

On 22nd May, eighteen Dewoitine D520s of the French Groupe de Chasse II/3, on patrol in the Bapaume-Cambrai sector in support of a French armoured counter-attack, caught a formation of Ju87s carrying out a dive bombing attack. Whilst six D520s flew top cover against the Bf109 escort, twelve D520s followed the Ju87s into their dives. In as many minutes eleven Ju87s were shot down. One D520, whose pilot escaped safely by parachute, was shot down, this being the only success of the ten Bf109s.

With the Panzer thrust to Boulogne, No. 107 Squadron made an early reconnaissance, which was followed in the afternoon by Wing Commander Embry leading a squadron attack on enemy troops heading towards Boulogne; P4925 was so badly damaged that it was forced to ditch on the way back. This was followed by a further raid by No. 107 Squadron in the same area, which was followed by Embry leading No. 110 Squadron in a third attack, this time also striking at the German HQ at Ribeaucourt. No. 15 Squadron Blenheims struck at Montreuil, while Nos. 21 and 82 Squadrons carried out low-level attacks on the Samuar-Montreuil road and No. 40 Squadron Blenheims attacked armoured vehicles north of Abbeville. L8762 of No. 110 Squadron, flown by Squadron Leader G. Hall, failed to return. N6207 force-landed with its undercarriage up, and P4838 of No. 82 Squadron failed to return. These were some of the forty-four Blenheims of 2 Group that were lost over the preceding nine days; there were now only sixty serviceable aircraft left in the Group. Fortunately, some of the crews managed to get back to Allied Lines.

On 23rd May, the British at Arras were consolidating their position and awaiting the next enemy thrust, which, when it came, was preceded by a heavy artillery barrage, following which, tanks moved in. In the afternoon the right flank was turned and the French tanks and 75mm field guns had withdrawn. By midnight, under the attack, the British forces were forced to withdraw from Arras up the Douai road. Twelve Blenheims with an escort of No. 32 Squadron Hurricanes then tried to bomb the southern exits from Arras, but bad weather at the target prevented accurate bombing. No. 82 Squadron aircraft were also on the attack, shallow dive-bombing AFVs near Forte Creche, but the Navy, being as trigger-happy as usual, opened fire on them. The escorting Hurricanes beat off an attack by about thirty Bf109s and Bf110s, claiming three Bf109s for no loss.

The day was marked by the encirclement of Boulogne, and by midnight the rear guard had reached the harbour and embarked on destroyers. Some isolated groups fought on, one was the remains of the French 21st Division under General Lanquetet, who only surrendered the following day after a threat from the Germans to obliterate the town. A further group of French and British troops hung out in one part of the town until they ran of ammunition on the 25th.

2 Group Blenheims were out again during the 24th. No. 40 Squadron attacked troops in the Bois de Boulogne, and lost two aircraft to flak; P4909 crewed by Wing Commander J. Llewellyn, Sergeant J. Beattie and Pilot Officer W. Edwards, and L8832, crewed by Flying Officer R. Jackoby, Sergeant P. Burrell and LAC. P. Whittle. No. 21 Squadron attacked stationary vehicles on the approach to Calais, followed by a further attack during the evening in the same area.

Twelve Blenheims of No. 107 Squadron with a Hurricane escort attacked roads and bridges in the Marck area. They were subjected to heavy flak, which damaged a number, but all returned safely. Their escort was heavily engaged by Bf109s. Examination of the raid photographs proved that there were no troop concentrations in the target area so the same crews were sent off again to attack more reported troop concentrations, again all returning safely.

Blenheim IV R3614 of No. 15 Squadron which crashed on the edge of Wyton airfield 24 May, 1940. P/O Henderson, Sgt. Holmes and LAC Austin were killed.

GERMAN SPEARHEADS CLOSING THE TRAP 24 MAY 1940

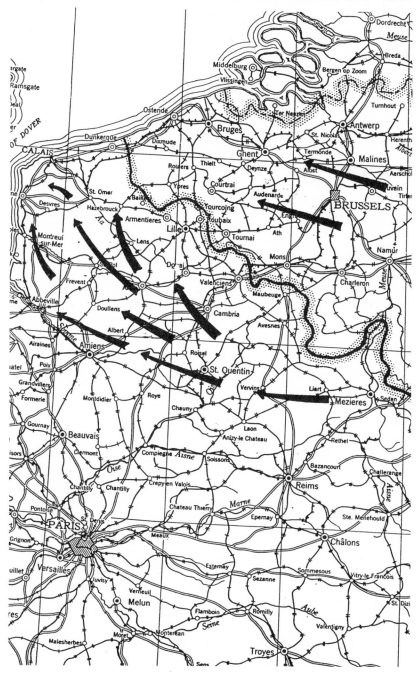

On 25th May 'Frankforce' under General Franklyn was ordered to hold the Ypres-Comines Canal against the German divisions advancing through Belgium, which were part of Richenau's 6th Army. Their first major attack against the British line commenced in the early morning of the 27th May. The British were forced back, but during the evening counter attacked and regained their earlier line on the canal, which they then held until the 28th. The officers were then told of the BEF evacuation and the part that 'Frankforce' had played in allowing the remainder of the BEF to start retiring. During this period the 7th Panzer Division was starting to encircle Lille, and although substantial numbers of British and French troops escaped the trap, approximately 35,000 men of the French 1st Army were encircled.

The Blenheims were out again on 25th May, and from 2 Group HQ was issued a message to the squadrons concerning the air operations. This message concluded with the sentence " . . . In view of the critical situation of the BEF, it is essential that all attacks are pressed home with vigour.'' Considering the aircrew losses and previous suicidal attacks, not to mention lack of contact with the AOC, the message was an insult to the crew concerned.

Aircraft of Nos. 15, 40, 107 and 110 Squadrons, escorted by two Hurricane squadrons, attacked pontoon bridges across the River Lys and enemy troop concentrations. No. 15 Squadron sent six aircraft to the Calais area, where just north of the town they were attacked by nine Bf109s, P6913 piloted by Pilot Officer Harrison being shot down. This was followed in the evening by 2 Group squadrons attacking Panzer units in the Bethune-Hazebrouk area. The next day the squadrons were out again, No. 40 Squadron bombing houses and roads at Harlebeke, with Nos. 21 and 82 Squadrons bombing bridges in the same area. Nos. 107 and 110 Squadrons flew an armed reconnaissance in the St Pol area, being escorted by three squadrons of Hurricanes. Bombs were dropped on AFVs in the Foret-de-Hesdin, and concentrated flak was encountered in the target area.

The siege of Calais had commenced on 22nd May. Why it was not evacuated is not known for sure, but its siege stretched RAF resources that much more. Supplies were parachuted in by Hectors and Lysanders, resulting in further aircraft and aircrew losses. The siege itself was as gallant an action as ever fought by the British Army, the units under Brigadier Nicholson only surrendering on 26th May after all ammunition and supplies had been exhausted. On this day General von Richthofen's VIII Fliegerkorp had ordered the Stuka units StG2 and StG77, escorted by Bf109s, to divebomb Calais and its exhausted, battered troops. Even concentrated attacks by RAF fighters failed to break through the escort. So drawing onto themselves the Panzers of

A Ju87 B-2 'Stuka' of I/StG1.

Guderian, the British troops at Calais contributed to the success of the evacuation from Dunkirk.

26th May saw two sections of No. 21 Squadron and two sections of No. 82 Squadron, escorted by Hurricane fighters, join up with two sections from Wyton. The target was the area along the River Lys from Menin to Cambrai. Troops, transports and pontoon bridges were shallow dive-bombed from 6,000 down to 2,000ft. In spite of a combination of heavy and light flak, the attack was successful; one bridge being hit as well as troops and roads. All aircraft returned successfully.

On 27th May Gort made the decision that the BEF would have to be withdrawn to Dunkirk, as the surrender of the Belgian Army left the BEF's left flank exposed. General Blanchard of the French 1st Army Group refused to retire to Dunkirk and General Priox's forces between Bethune and Lille were too exhausted to retire further. At Abbeville the enemy had prepared a well defended bridgehead, yet an attack was mounted by 2nd Armoured Brigade with the 2nd, 3rd and 5th Divisions Cuirassées. With a major concentration of anti-tank artillery the Germans took a toll of the Allied tanks. On completion of the operation, nothing had been gained, with 65 Allied tanks lost and 55 tanks worn out.

On 27th May, an outstanding crew of No. 103 Squadron, Sergeant Beardesley and LAC. Lewis, walked back to the squadron, having been shot down during a day operation on 25th May. This was the second time that they had walked back to the squadron after being shot down, the first time being on 14th May.

Early in the morning 2 Group squadrons were called out on further attacks on enemy targets in France; this affected Nos. 15, 21, 40, 82 and 107 Squadrons. Six Blenheims from Watton were detailed to attack a square of houses at Belle, where an 'intercept' had established that an enemy headquarters was established. Six Blenheims from Wyton were to carry out an armed reconnaissance against enemy forces advancing through the forest of Clairmarais, and Wattisham aircraft were detailed to make an attack on an MT column and AFVs on the road to St Omer. The trouble with this type of target was the time that passed between the determining of the target and the position of the mobile column by the time that the aircraft had arrived. This meant a search for the target, receiving the attention of enemy flak and fighters all the while. In the afternoon, No. 110 Squadron was called in to the same target at St Omer.

At approximately 16.00 hours No. 107 Squadron was again called on. Twelve Blenheims led by Wing Commander B. Embry took off to attack the same enemy column at St Omer, with instructions to press home their attack. What did Group Headquarters think the squadrons were doing? The formation arrived over the target at 6,000ft, to be met by accurate and moderately intense flak. Embry's aircraft was hit on the approach and Embry wounded in the leg. Having dropped his bombs, Embry's aircraft was again hit and severely damaged. The elevator controls had failed and the rudder was partly inoperative, so Embry warned the crew to stand by to bale out. In the meantime he tried using the engines to maintain directional control, but the aircraft slowly went out of control. Embry gave the order to bale out. The observer, Pilot Officer Whiting, successfully baled out, but although Embry again told the gunner, Corporal Lang, to bale out, there was no response. Looking back Embry could see Lang slumped in the turret, so reluctantly, as the aircraft was getting low, Embry baled out. After 27 days in enemy territory and in spite of being arrested three times, Embry arrived in Plymouth on 2nd August via Gibraltar.

The Luftwaffe was not escaping punishment either, when III/KG51 sent twelve He111s to attack Allied troops at Dunkirk. One He111 was shot down, and all the others were found riddled with shrapnel and bullet holes after they had landed at Frankfurt-Rhine/Main airfield. By this date the I and II Gruppen of KG51 had re-equipped with Ju88s, which from KG51s pont of view was just as well, for the He111 was proving an easy target for the Hurricanes during daylight operations.

The French continued to attack the Abbeville bridge-head on the 28th but still without success. At Lille the French 4 and 5 Corps were now surrounded, and although being cut to pieces refused to surrender;

An RAF pilot being interrogated 'in the field' by German officers. French POWs in the background. (J. de Vos)

this continued until the 31st, when a few managed to escape to Dunkirk. British forces under General Franklyn, having moved forward to hold the Ypres-Comines line, dealt out punishment to the German forces. They were then forced to withdraw towards Popering, suffering heavy casualties from concentrated mortar and artillery fire. It was in this area that SS troops, having captured some British soldiers and injured troops, proceeded to murder them with shots and grenades. The German SS, with its peculiar mentality, would expand on this atrocity throughout the war.

On the south-west flank nine German Divisions, six of which were armoured, failed to breakthrough an emergency line put up by the French 42nd, 44th and 48th Divisions. Enemy troops in the Ouest-Mont area were bombed by No. 15 Squadron Blenheims. No. 21 Squadron attacked troop concentrations in the forest at Clairmarais, but the weather was so bad that the attack had to go in at 600ft, resulting in the loss of L8744. No. 40 Squadron were detailed to attack enemy troops advancing from St Omer, but again time was lost in locating the target. Then Nos. 82, 107 and 110 Squadrons were called on to attack troop concentrations approaching the BEF perimeter.

Flying Officer Drake of No. 1 Squadron was one of many Hurricane pilots trying to provide coverage for both bombers and troops. During one sortie, going in to attack three Do17s, just as he pulled up to the tail of one and started to fire, a Bf110 came down out of the sun and pumped cannon shells into the Hurricane. As his Hurricane burst into flames he saw the Do17 that he had attacked, catch fire and crash. Drake undid his straps and baled out, only to be shot at by the Bf110 as he descended by parachute. Trying to 'slip' his parachute out of the way of the Hun's shooting was not entirely successful, as his arm had been injured. Fortunately the Bf110 rejoined its formation and Drake came down in a field. The French picked him up and attended to him, taking him to hospital.

Nine Blenheims of No. 107 and six of No. 110 Squadron took-off at 1940 hours to attack an enemy column on the road to St Omer. As usual, time was lost in locating the target, which did not agree with target details given on briefing. That attack was made on the enemy troops and also on a road junction in the vicinity, all aircraft returning safely.

The BAFF fighters were flying six and seven sorties each a day, but Luftwaffe fighter and bomber formations were overwhelming in numbers. With the 'target rich' scenario due to the Allies being so outnumbered in the air, the kill ratio was in favour of the Allied air force fighters. No. 1 Squadron had by this date chalked up 140 enemy aircraft 'killed', but the pilots had given up keeping scores through sheer exhaustion and lack of time.

No. 604 Squadron Blenheim fighters were operating from England and patrolling the Pas de Calais area. The composite squadrons were operating from their UK bases against the enemy aircraft formations attacking the BEF, the Luftwaffe formations being brought to combat quite often away from the BEF areas.

On 28th May, No. 242 Squadron Hurricanes took off and, via Manston, headed once more for the Dunkirk area. As they approached their patrol line they sighted about eighty enemy aircraft in the vicinity east of Ostend, but before they could attack, they themselves were intercepted by enemy fighters. Although losing two Hurricanes, the pilot of one returning the following day, Pilot Officer W. McKnight and Pilot Officer P. Turner each claimed a Bf109.

On another patrol, a Ju88 was chased off from Dunkirk, when just east of Ostend a number of enemy aircraft were sighted. Flight Lieutenent D. Miller reported:

"I noticed a group of approximately twelve Me109s and immediately attacked the leading four. I singled out the leader and gave him a burst of approximately 5 seconds from slightly above and to his beam. He appeared to go out of control and I looked around to see the sky filled with Me109s."

The same squadron, along with the other squadrons, was out on the patrol line around Dunkirk the following day. One of the combats involved Pilot Officer R. D. Grassick of No. 242 Squadron:

"As we approached Dunkirk, enemy aircraft were seen and they dived and attacked. I turned right, and one of the enemy (Me109s) dived lower than myself and came into my sight. I fired three bursts, two short and one long, and soon the aircraft began to smoke and I followed him down until he went into sea."

By 28th May most of No. 139 Squadron had left Nantes for the UK, travelling in cattle trucks to Cherbourg, although others, including air gunner John Parry, did not get away until 1st June. Arriving at Nantes station and being interested in machinery, he says:

"I went to inspect the French engine, a very powerful looking machine, and was surprised to see a British Army Sergeant driver, with a couple of 'bods' for stoking. He said he was on his way to Cherbourg, so I climbed aboard a truck. Each truck had a box of rations, bully beef, biscuits, bottle of water, with a bucket for a loo, about 36 hours later we arrived at Cherbourg."

Another RAF party arriving at Cherbourg was Sergeant Fenton of No. 2 Squadron and his Crossley workshop lorry. Having got his lorry and valuable load on to the docks, after a great deal of persuasion he managed to get the port authorities to use a dockside crane to winch the Crossley onto a UK bound boat to Southampton. His memory of the time was:

"Morale badly shaken, had a good swear, then had to face the fact that the enemy had got superior equipment and large quantities of it; assuming he had won the first round . . . but ready to fight the B******* another day."

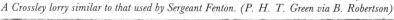

A Crossley lorry similar to that used by Sergeant Fenton. (P. H. T. Green via B. Robertson)

The Battle of France up to this point had been, from the BAFF's point of view, a struggle in support of the land armies. With the evacuation from Dunkirk in operation, the RAF's task now was to wrestle air supremacy from the Lufwaffe. So into the cauldron had been thrown not only 2 Group bombers, but more of the 11 Group fighter squadrons. Two of these were 'The Tigers', No. 74 Squadron and 'The Fighting Cocks', No. 43 Squadron. The latter squadron was lead by Squadron Leader C. G. Lott, and No. 74 Squadron was led by Squadron Leader F. L. White. Amongst the No. 74 Squadron personnel was a Flight Commander, Flight Lieutenant A. C. Malan, who would wreak havoc with his Spitfire. He was known in his flight for one sentence; after calling "Tally-ho" came "Let 'em have it, let 'em have it."

Flight Lieutenant A. 'Sailor' Malan,
Flight Commander with No. 74 Squadron
in May 1940.

With the evacuation fron Dunkirk and the necessity for inter-service co-operation, Dowding and Keith Park were to learn of the typical non-co-operative manner of the Royal Navy. On the one hand they complained of inadequate fighter defence over Boulogne, yet at the same time they informed Dowding that:

"Our destroyers fire at any aircraft that comes within range, whether they make our recognition signals or not."

The RAF were already fully aware of this stupidity, having been fired at and in some cases shot down, neither the RN nor the British Army appearing to be able to recognise aircraft or signals; fortunately, their gunnery in most cases was not up to the German flak standard.

By 28th May the Chief of Air Staff (Newall) was to off load further responsibility on to Dowding, informing him that the protection of Dunkirk was to be ensured from first light until darkness, by flying *continuous* fighter patrols in strength. This was an impossible order with only sixteen fighter squadrons available and the distance to be flown to Dunkirk before patrol. In the end it would become necessary to fly the patrols in squadron strength to counter the German attacks, as sections of fighters were suffering unnecessary losses to the large German formations. With the squadrons going out on patrols as a unit, this did of course mean that there were intervals when the defence of the area would have to depend solely on the anti-aircraft defence.

This anti-aircraft defence had been weakened on 27th May, when what was later claimed as an inarticulate message, led to the destruction of the BEF's 3.7 inch anti-aircraft gun batteries. This left the defence against German aircraft resting on the Bofors 40 mm guns and the light machine guns. On this day visibility was perfect and the Luftwaffe attacked Dunkirk continually, dropping an estimated 2,000 tons of HE bombs on the town.

The 31th May found a formation of Nos. 17, 145 and 245 Squadrons on an offensive patrol over Dunkirk and Furnes. During the approach three Bf109s were seen attacking an unescorted formation of Blenheims, so a section was detached to change the situation, which resulted in two Bf109s shot down and one wisely withdrawing. Another fighter formation consisted of Nos. 64, 229, 242 and 601 Squadrons patrolling over the same area, a bomber formation with fighter escort was sighted and the resulting combat was concluded with six enemy aircraft being put down.

Bf109E-3s of I/JG77.

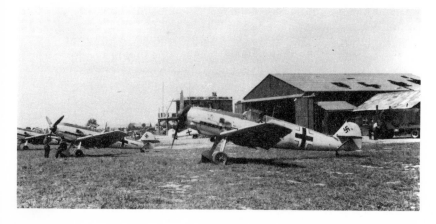

Hurricane P3878 'W' of No. 17 Squadron during the latter part of France campaign. It crashed in December 1940.

1st June found Nos. 43, 145 and 245 Squadrons briefed to patrol and protect the shipping coming out of Dunkirk. The first patrol was made without any incident or combat, and Nos. 43 and 145 Squadron returned to Hawkinge to refuel. At 11.00 hours the two squadrons were again airborne and twenty-five minutes later a formation of enemy bombers were sighted attacking shipping. While No. 43 Squadron remained on top, the nine No. 145 Squadron aircraft dived to the attack.

No. 43 Squadron were almost immediately involved in combat, for a large force of Bf109s appeared from inland, probably escort for the bombers, and at the same time Bf110s broke cloud cover in a dive on to the attacking No. 145 Squadron. The fight immediately broke up into individual combats. Squadron Leader Lott evading two Bf109s, got in a burst at a Bf110 from a deflection angle. It went into a dive and a burst from dead astern appeared to stoke up fires in the Bf110s engines, as they both poured out black smoke. Flying Officer Wilkinson, in a combat with two Bf109s, got in bursts at both and saw them lose interest. Flying Officer Edmunds had got bursts in at two separate Bf109s, then got behind a Bf109 attacking a Hurricane. His firing caused that to fall in pieces. He followed this by putting his remaining ammunition into a Bf110 that was attacking a Hurricane, this one went down in flames. Sergeant P. Ottewell closed on a Bf109 and from 100 yards fired two two-second bursts that caused the enemy to explode.

Hurricane 'A' of No. 145 Squadron shot down near Coxyde, Belgium during latter part of conflict. (J. De Vos)

Following that, Ottewell engaged two more Bf109s, but without causing visible damage. Then he got a burst into a Bf109 that crossed his sights, and that one went into the sea with smoke coming from its engine. He tried to engage a Bf 110 but this one pulled up into a climb and left the Hurricane behind. Turning from home Ottewell came down on a Bf110 and poured in a five second burst from dead astern, this one dived away with smoke and flame from the starboard engine.

Flight Sergeant Hallowes of No. 43 Squadron was to further improve the score, putting one Bf109 down in flames, knocking the mainplane of another, and then knocked the tail completely off a Bf110. However, the squadron had lost two aircraft. Meantime, No. 145 Squadron Hurricanes had mixed it with a large number of Bf109s and Bf110s, that resulted in Flight Lieutenant Dutton in P2770 shooting down a Bf110 and two Bf109s. Flight Lieutenant A. Boyd, showing no favouritism, shot down one of each, and Pilot Officers Yule, Newling and Weir got one Bf110 each. Pilot Officer L. Scott got hits in his radiator and force landed at Manston, while Pilot Officer H. Duncan in P3400 failed to return.

Nos. 17, 43, 145 and 245 Squadrons were detailed to patrol Dunkirk on the 2nd, but the patrol passed without incident or combat. Things were a little different for No. 111 Squadron, which was also out as part of a composite formation, for during the last part of their patrol an enemy formation was sighted and combat joined. This resulted in two Bf109s and one Bf110 being shot down with two possibly damaged.

Pilot Officer Wilson's aircraft crashed into the sea, but he baled out and returned to the squadron. Flight Lieutenant R. Powell of No. 111 Squadron was flying Hurricane N2429 and recorded in his combat report:

> "I was leading my section when I sighted a large Vic of Me110s flying north 2,000 feet below us. The leading section went into the attack, at the same time I saw a number of Me109s above, so I climbed with my Flight and engaged them. The Me109 climbed away. When I reached 25,000 feet I surprised one Me109 on its own and gave it a two second burst and it went down with black smoke pouring from its fuselage; remaining Me109s remained above me, and being short of fuel I returned to Manston."

Away from Dunkirk No. 73 Squadron were on offensive patrol and were flying over Malmaison airfield at 4,000 feet, being peppered by heavy and accurate flak. Pilot Officer Rutter saw nine Bf109s approaching, two of which fired at him. The squadron, having broken formation, were now circling the airfield. Rutter climbed into cloud cover, then on returning saw a Bf109 chasing a Hurricane. He closed on it and fired a short burst at close range, the Messerschmitt fell away with black smoke pouring from its fuselage and went rapidly earthwards. Sergeant Pilot Scott saw a Bf109 on the tail of a Hurricane, so caught up with the enemy and saw the Hurricane turn right, burst into flames and crash. As the Bf109 pulled up, Scott closed right up and opened fire. The enemy fell in pieces as it blew apart, the wreckage falling on a house in a village. Scott was forced to land near Paris, and two other Hurricanes failed to return.

During these latter days of the Dunkirk evacuation air fighting inland and off Dunkirk was fierce and deadly, yet quite often fighter formations returned without incident. During those hazardous days the fighter pilots of the regular air force squadrons and the auxiliary squadrons, pilots from Britain and the colonies and Commonwealth, proved a match for the experienced crews of the Luftwaffe. Notice had been served.

Coastal Command were also in the fighting at Dunkirk. On 1st June, three Hudsons headed towards the Dunkirk beaches on a fighting reconnaissance. The fighting part was soon in no doubt. Two packs of Ju87s, totalling about 40 aircraft, were positioning themselves for an attack on the cowering troops below, circling around like vultures over their prey. The three Hudsons hurtled into the fray. Whilst some of the Ju87s went into their dives, the others, like frightened sparrows under the attack of a sparrowhawk, scattered in disarray as the Hudsons, with all guns blazing, attacked. Within three or four minutes at least three Ju87s had been disposed of, the others routed with at least three others damaged.

112

Morane 406s lined up at Lille-Marcq Airfield in early 1940 . . . ideal for a straffing attack! The 406 proved a second rate fighter aircraft. (S. J. Cain)

On 3rd June the Luftwaffe made an all-out assault on airfields in the Paris area. The Armée de l'Air were in a state of total confusion. Some squadrons were warned and took off to meet the threat, whilst others received no warning and were caught in their messes. The first to meet the challenge were nine Morane 406s of Groupe de Chasse III/7, who took off from Coulommiers to attack a formation of Luftwaffe bombers. As some of the bombers were hit, the top escort of Bf109s swept into the attack, leaving the 406s to circle madly in the hope of escaping being shot down. Then the Bf109s broke off their attack and swept off to attack Dewoitine D520s of Groupe de Chasse of I/3, who had caught a formation of Do17s turning for home. As two of the bombers broke away smoking from the attack, the Bf109s hit the French fighters, who were forced to break left and right madly, each intent on looking after himself. For the loss of two D520s and three other pilots wounded, the French claimed one Bf109 and three Do17s possibly destroyed. All told the French defence was a spasmodic affair, in many cases a disaster, yet the Luftwaffe attack surprisingly enough achieved little outstanding success. Ground damage was minor and aircraft losses small in comparison with the effort the Luftwaffe put in.

The evacuation of Dunkirk (Dunkerque) was probably the first time that the majority of the British public woke up to the German threat. The evacuation was completed by 4th June and the RAF were at last able to total up its losses and claims. The claims of enemy aircraft shot down by the RAF were 262 having been revised from an original figure of 377. That this differed from the Luftwaffe loss records is nothing unusual, no more so than their score claims, compared with RAF losses in the air.

Although Dunkirk was a disaster for British ground forces, the Luftwaffe had been proved incapable of carrying out the allotted task given them by Göring. It also suffered losses necessitating re-equipment. KG51, for instance, had its I and II Gruppen equipped with Ju88s and its III Gruppen equipped with He111s, yet by the end of the Dunkirk period the strength of KG51 had fallen to less than half in terms of crews and machines. Some felt that leaders like Richthofen had too often forced the pace at the expense of casualties. As so often happens in warfare, the unit leaders were but the tools of politicians and the Service's chief. Who is to judge?

At Dunkirk, meanwhile, 40,000 troops were going into captivity. Most were troops of the French 1st Army who had valiantly fought a rearguard action on the perimeter to allow a successful evacuation, a point not exactly highlighted by the proponents of the British Army.

Chapter Four
The Final Days

The final evacuation from Dunkirk occurred on 4th June, 1940. The German offensive commenced again on the following day, with an attack across the Somme by Bock's Army Group on the right wing. French forces held the 'Weygand Line' behind the Somme and Aisne. It was the intention of the Allied Command to contain the enemy along this line, but the odds were against them and although the French fought with determination and desperation in the ruined villages, there was little hope of success. On this day the German fighter force had at its disposal 975 fighters assigned to the Western Front or facing France. The Allies could only muster 800 fighter aircraft, of which 300 were operating from Great Britain, 100 being night fighters or disposed protectively against any action by Italy. The bomber forces were at a greater difference, for whilst Germany could field 1700 long range bombers and 468 dive bombers, the RAF could only muster 550, of which 400 were based in great Britain. In the AASF things were even worse, for their fighter force could only muster eighteen serviceable aircraft! The Armée de l'Air was called upon to make an all out effort, flying any and every aircraft that was serviceable, which included even slow night bombers. In some cases there were fighter escorts, but in most instances there were no escorts available and the bomber losses were disastrous. In one case, twelve unescorted Breguet 693s were lost to Luftwaffe fighters as they went in on a low level attack on a German transport convoy.

By this date four AASF bomber squadrons had been withdrawn to Nantes, these were Nos. 105, 114, 139 and 218. These squadrons had been decimated in their attacks on the German spearheads and surviving aircraft had been turned over to the remaining operational squadrons. Their personnel would be in some cases posted to other squadrons, especially air gunners and armourers. This was a little demoralising as the squadrons had understood they were to be re-equipped. The remaining operational AASF squadrons were now disposed as follows:

No. 88 Squadron	(Battles)	at Harbouville,
No. 103 Squadron	(Battles)	at Harbouville,
No. 142 Squadron	(Battles)	at Houssay,
No. 150 Squadron	(Battles)	at Houssay,
No. 12 Squadron	(Battles)	at Souge,
No. 226 Squadron	(Battles)	at Souge,
No. 1 Squadron	(Hurricanes)	at Chateaudin,
No. 73 Squadron	(Hurricanes)	at Le Mans,
No. 501 Squadron	(Hurricanes)	at Le Mans.

On paper this represented a strength of 96 bomber aircraft and 48 fighters, but the actual strength was below this, as none of the squadrons were up to establishment.

Even though out performed so often, the French fighter pilots fought with elan and doggedness, which often finished with startling results as happened on 5th June. During the combat 2nd Lieutenant Pomier-Layraaues of the French Groupe de Chasse II/7, got on Luftwaffe Experten Werner Molders' tail and shot him down just west of Compiegne. Four other Bf109s then pounced on the Frenchman, but before he was shot down and killed he had shot down a further Bf109. Molders was more fortunate, being released after the Armistice he returned to the Luftwaffe, and continued flying until being killed in a transport aircraft accident.

The recommencement of the German attack towards Paris began, although Kleist's troops were stopped again by French troops south of Amiens and Peronne, with one Panzer unit losing 65% of its tanks. This was a rare occurrence and usually resulted in the Allied defenders being subjected to a combined shelling and dive-bombing attack. An attack between the Rivers Somme and Bresle forced the British 51st Division to give ground, a signal from them during the evening stated that their fighting efficiency was lowered due to the intense fighting.

During the 6th, German bomber formations attacked Beauvais, Compiegne and Soisson, as well as the battle areas; whilst from the Allied side, both British and French bombers attacked German mechanised forces in the Peronne loop of the Somme. One of the group of bombers was a force of twelve Blenheim IVs of No. 40 Squadron, who lost five of their number during the low level attacks. L8827, L9410 and P4927 failed to return; P4917 force landed in France with all the crew wounded and R3692 was shot down in 'No-Man's Land'. The pilot of the latter tried to get assistance for his wounded air gunner, but the enemy advance prevented this.

On the same day the last two original members of No. 73 Squadron, Scoular and 'Cobber' Kain, were ordered back to the UK for a rest. Before leaving on the following day Kain gave an aerobatic display, which unfortunately went wrong and his aircraft pancaked onto the ground. Kain was thrown clear but died of his injuries. The squadron ORB states that it was not in keeping with Kain's normal cool flying, could it have been fatigue?

On 6th June, Hurricanes of Nos. 43 and 601 Squadrons joined up with a flight of AASF Hurricanes to cover a raid by twenty-two Battles, whose target was a convoy and infantry in the Molliens-Vidame-Hornoy-Poix area. The formation was attacked by about thirty Bf109s, which resulted in the loss of three Battles. Then eighteen

'Cobber' Kain and colleagues of No. 73 Squadron reading a telegram about the award of his DFC. (S/Ldr. C. Campbell DFC)

Blenheim IV bombers of 2 Group, with an escort of twenty-four Fighter Command Hurricanes, attacked German troop concentrations in the Pont Remy-Oisemont-Poix-Picquicny area, the Hurricanes successfully taking on thirty-two Bf109s just south-west of Abbeville. This was followed at 17.30 to 18.00 hours with thirty-six Blenheims of 2 Group, with an escort of nineteen Hurricanes, making an attack on an enemy armoured column. The losses of Battles and Blenheims at this period amounted to about 9 and 7% respectively, many aircraft that did reach base were severely damaged or had crew members killed. There was an instance of one solitary bullet hitting a Blenheim and killing the air gunner. A Blenheim landed and started to taxi in, then stopped with engines still running. Groundcrew who ran out to it found all the crew injured and unconcious. Some aircraft that were badly damaged or returned on one engine stalled and crashed on the approach, some belly landed in with dead and injured crew members.

By the end of the day British forces were on the retreat from Neufchatel and Forges-les-Eaux, with the Panzer advance striking in the direction of Rouen and threatening the 51st Division, and also being in a position to link up with another thrust coming from Amiens. On 8th June the 51st Division was marching in retreat towards Le Havre, but they were too slow to escape the German advance. At the same time the British right flank was being endangered by another

Armourers of No. 15 Squadron bombing up a Blenheim IV with 250 lb GP bombs nose fused. One armourer is carrying a bomb hoist, used from inside the fuselage.

thrust and the armoured division was forced to retreat across the Seine as their rear was attacked. To the right of the Allied lines the Germans had exploited their crossing of the Aisne, and twelve German Infantry Divisions and Panzer units were twelve miles from Chateau Thierry on the Marne. The 6th Division was directed towards the river crossing at Les Andelys and the 46th Division towards that at Vernon, but by the following day Les Andelys was burning from a dive bomber attack and the bridge was 'blown'.

Fighter reinforcements in the form of two Hurricane squadrons, Nos. 17 and 242, had arrived at Chateaudin and Le Mans, while fighters in the UK were continuing to give fighter escort to 2 Group Blenheims. By now it was becoming apparent that if France should fall then the south of England would be exposed to the enemy. In spite of the fighter bases and satellites in the south, there would still be insufficient bases or landing grounds near to the south coast for defence purposes. While the battle against the German invaders continued in France, there was a panic situation in southern England as searches were made for suitable sites for conversion into airfields or advanced landing fields.

The 51st Division, with French units of the 9th Corps 10th Army, were by 9th June still retreating towards Le Havre. Their speed of retreat appeared to be too slow and the possibility of encirclement was becoming even greater. The Commanding Officer, Major-General Fortune of the 51st Division, was on this day to signal:

"Essential that air delay enemy movements mostly AFVs to south of St Saens-Bolbec road, also his infantry advance from east. Air support requested to prevent unrestrained bombing."

No. 1 Squadron Hurricanes patrolled this area to protect the 51st Division and reported no enemy air activity. No. 17 Squadron patrolled the Rouen to Le Havre area and again there was no enemy activity seen. A little further south seven No. 242 Squadron Hurricanes ran into a formation of ten to twenty Bf109s and a free-for-all developed.

Barratt had received a request from General Vuillemin by this date urging him to procure more fighters from England, so he forwarded this request to the CAS, complete with a covering letter reiterating his own predicament. Barratt stated that the fighter force at his disposal was completely inadequate for the tasks; the Armoured Division and the 51st Division had for days been requesting fighter protection, which he had been unable to supply continually due to the inadequacy of his resources. It must be pointed out that the fighter patrols that had operated over the unit's area of fighting, had not always found targets or enemy aircraft in the area indicated. Reconnaissance flights had determined that Rouen was evacuated, bridges demolished, with oil and fuel dumps burning. Meanwhile, in Paris, Staff at Ministeries

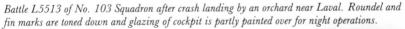

Battle L5513 of No. 103 Squadron after crash landing by an orchard near Laval. Roundel and fin marks are toned down and glazing of cockpit is partly painted over for night operations.

119

were burning documents and the Government was preparing to move to Tours. The battle was nearing its end.

Nos. 43 and 601 Squadrons joined up again on 7th June to patrol over France, the twenty Hurricanes of the two squadrons forming up over Tangmere, flying in sections of three. The first indication of trouble was when Flying Officer Edmonds' Hurricane burst into flames and dropped out of formation, followed within minutes by three more aircraft. They had been expertly 'bounced' by Bf109s. The remaining Hurricanes landed at Rouen (Boos) and prepared to patrol the line of the River Somme. From Boos aircraft of No. 43 Squadron along with three from No. 601 Squadron and six from No. 1 Squadron took-off led by Squadron leader Lott.

After about twenty minutes No. 1 Squadron aircraft broke away from the formation, and shortly afterwards twenty enemy bombers were sighted with an escort of approximately 60–70 Bf109s and Bf110s. The Hurricanes turned into them and engaged. Lott claimed a Bf109 destroyed, with Flight Lietuenant Simpson claiming a Bf109, which he set on fire and saw collide with a Bf110. Only these two pilots of No. 43 Squadron returned to Tangmere that evening. Things in the end did not turn out so badly for three missing pilots returned to the squadron within days. Three others were in hospital injured, but their kills had amounted to five, and one probable. For No. 43 squadron, it was the end of the French campaign, as it was withdrawn for rest and training.

It was certainly not the end of the line for the fighter squadrons of the BAFF, or for the other 11 Group fighter squadrons designated by

'T' of No. 56 Squadron, derelict on a beach near to Dunkirk. Possibly N2659 flown by P/O Dryden, which crash landed on 29 May, 1940. (J. De Vos)

Dowding and Park to attack the German forces along the French coast. A report that was issued covering the fighter operations stated:

> "German fighters were not met in small formation, but always in strength by 15 to 40 fighters. The Bf109s were usually supported by Bf110s, and their co-operation seemed to be good. The German A.A. batteries appeared to co-operate closely with their fighter patrols, in providing shell bursts to indicate the position of our formations."[*]

No. 56 Squadron, along with No. 151 Squadron operating from North Weald, were called on to provide fighter cover for the Blenheim bombers of 2 Group. During one of these sorties on 9th June, Sergeant Smythe of No. 56 Squadron got separated in the cloud cover. Seeing 24 Spitfires he decided to attach himself to those, but upon formatting he realised that the Spitfires wore black crosses and were Bf109s. So quickly selecting one he gave it a quick burst and departed, the remainder becoming decidedly angry.

On 7th June, three Blenheims of No. 107 Squadron were out on an early morning reconnaissance, from which R3686 failed to return. This was then followed by further 2 Group bomber attacks during the day, resulting in a number of aircraft receiving flak damage. At 17.00 hours nine Battles of No. 12 Squadron took off to attack AFVs in the Poix area, from which P2162 failed to return as the squadron ran into Bf109s.

A No. 12 Squadron crew. L to R: Sgts. G. Wheeldon and Shone with LAC J. Taylor. Shown after the battle having converted to Wellingtons. (G. R. Wheeldon)

One of the Battles was flown by Sergeant G. R. Wheeldon who, when the war hotted up, had left the Communications Flight and after a refresher on No. 98 Squadron Battles had arrived at No. 12 Squadron on 23rd May. Now on 7th June, with Sergeant J. Shone and LAC. J. Taylor, in L5415 he was out on a daylight operation, only to tangle with Bf109s . . .

---

[*]Air Vice-Marshal Keith Park's report on 11 Group units May–June 1940.

"I was caught by a Bf109 which came up from behind and below, and the first I knew about it was hearing an odd noise coming out to my left and seeing bright white lights shooting forwards from my left wing! Almost instantly the 109 whizzed over the top of our airccraft and as I thought about having a 'squirt' at it . . . my gun button was not on 'fire' . . . the Battle began to roll to the left and I had to turn my attention to see what was wrong. In fact, the attacker had blown away all the fabric from the port aileron causing loss of lift."

Being then in the target area Wheeldon dropped his bombs and returned to base.

On the following day the squadrons of 2 Group were out again in force, concentrating on hitting the troop formations in the area in which the 10th French Army had broken. Bomb loads for this type of target were usually two 250 lb GP bombs and twelve 40 lb GP bombs, the pilots being left to make their own decisions on the precise target. Unfortunately, by now communications had deteriorated so badly that targets had moved by the time that the squadrons took-off.

Amongst the squadrons sent out on 8th June were Nos. 15 and 40 Squadrons. The Blenheims of No. 15 Squadron were in two sections led by Squadron Leader Webster and Squadron Leader Burke, the target areas being AFVs at Liomer, Mellines, Vidame and Querauvilliers. Casualties were as follows: Squadron Leader Burke, Pilot Officer Moffatt and Sergeant Thompson in R3746 failed to return; N6177 flown by Pilot Officer Myland had to force land at Tangmere and was written-off; Flying Officer George in R3704 had his observer wounded during the attack.

Hugh George's account of the attack illustrated vividly the actions undertaken by the bomber crews of those days:

A No. 114 Squadron Blenheim, derelict at Vraux, being clambered over by German troops. (Gerard Faux)

"The raid on 8th June must rate pretty high, for I stopped amongst other things a 20mm shell which came in through the nose and exploded behind the instrument panel badly wounding my observer and doing the aircraft no good at all. To me the whole thing is still something of a mystery since I was going downhill steeply and at full bore using my front gun sight to dive bomb the AFVs, which hit me at the same moment as I hit them. My last recollection is of seeing my bombs cause three of them to do a sort of airborne Prince of Wales' feathers manoeuvre. I don't know exactly what height I was at, but it was as low as I dared without blowing myself up – and the airspeed would have been just off the clock. Which leads me to another mystery. My next conscious moment was when I found myself flying straight and level at an alarmingly low altitude and an even more alarmingly low airspeed of 100 mph . . . and nowhere near the scene of the attack, but where I knew not. I immediately tried (a) to get more knots on and (b) to climb a bit. But I was already at full throttle and the engines seemed to be OK. All I succeeded in doing was to lose another 10 mph and gain no height at all. It stayed that way for a long time till I eventually made the French coast, and then the aircraft seemed to pull itself together and pick up speed and altitude.''

The Blenheim had holes all over the place, so George naturally assumed that large pieces of Blenheim were dangling in the breeze creating drag.

"So what was going on? There was no doubt about the airspeed. The aircraft was wallowing about like a pregnant duck trying its damndest to stall. I remember that it was exceedingly difficult and exhausting keeping the thing in the air and that when I landed and got out my legs gave way.''

Nos. 107 and 110 Squadrons were also out bombing AFVs and troops, with No. 110 Squadron losing two aircraft, although the crews got back safely later. The following day the same two squadrons again dispatched eighteen Blenheims, but it was midday before they took off to bomb enemy troop columns in the Horney, Poix, Formerie, Forges-les-Eaux area. Although escorted by twelve Hurricanes, No. 107 Squadron had three aircraft that failed to return (L9323, R3739, R3685) and a number of others damaged.

On this same day Rundstedt started another attack, but this failed when the French 14th Division under General de Tassigny fought back and took 800 prisoners. On the following day a tank battle between the 1st Panzer Division and the French 3rd Armoured Division began. Again the Germans suffered heavy casualties, but insufficient infantry backing and shortage of fuel for the French resulted in the Panzers being over the Aisne by 11th June, with the capture of Chalons-sur-Marne on the following day.

123

10th June brought news of further disaster for the Allies, for the 51st Division and the French 9th Corps were fully enveloped, trapped by the German Army between Dieppe and St Valéry-en-Caen. The chance of fighting their way out was remote and there appeared little choice between evacuation and surrender, with little chance of evacuation. Further south the German troops, with skill and resourcefulness, had crossed the River Seine, in spite of the blown bridge.

An evacuation from Le Havre was also approaching and an Air Ministry notice issued on the 10th, ordered a series of special fighter patrols by BAFF Hurricanes to cover the evacuation of British and French troops under the cover of night. The operation orders stated that a patrol of squadron strength was to be mounted over Le Havre port and surrounding area, and maintained all day. Fact and fantasy was by now obviously getting a little jumbled, or were the Air Ministry passing the buck as had happened with Air Vice-Marshal Park; The army were evacuating and rightly expecting air cover to get them out of trouble and away from the German Army, yet airfields were being left undefended. The Air Ministry was ordering air cover with a fighter force inadequate to give sufficient cover over the battlefield or for escort duties. Someone, somewhere needed to do their sums and face facts.

No. 1 Squadron was, on 10th June, patrolling over Le Havre and Rouen, and six Blenheims of No. 107 and six of No. 110 Squadron took off from the UK to attack troops and MT around Formiers, Gourney, Fleury and Forges. The crews could see the oil tanks at Rouen still burning, and all the aircraft returned safely. Then at 12.30 hours six Blenheims of No. 40 Squadron took off from Wyton to attack AFVs on roads around Forges, Buchy and Rocien; again all the aircraft returned safely. Another unit attacking AFVs were three sections of No. 82 Squadron, whose target area was along the roads of Rouen and Les Andelys.

Although there was considerable low cloud the squadron dropped their bomb loads in dives from 5,000 feet down to 3,000 feet. Not only were hits observed on MT and roads, but Pilot Officer Percival in R3708 attacked and shot down an Hs126 with his forward gun. Again all our aircraft returned safely.

On the same day the AASF Battles were in the air again, with twelve of them attacking a bridge at Vernon, these taking-off at 10.45 hours. Then at 16.45 hours three No. 88 Squadron Battles made a raid in the Abbeville area, with a night raid to complete the day. Some of the targets attacked were Triers airfield, Loan, Foret-de-Gobein and various bridges.

124

GERMAN ARMY GROUP 'A' MOVEMENTS 9 JUNE 1940

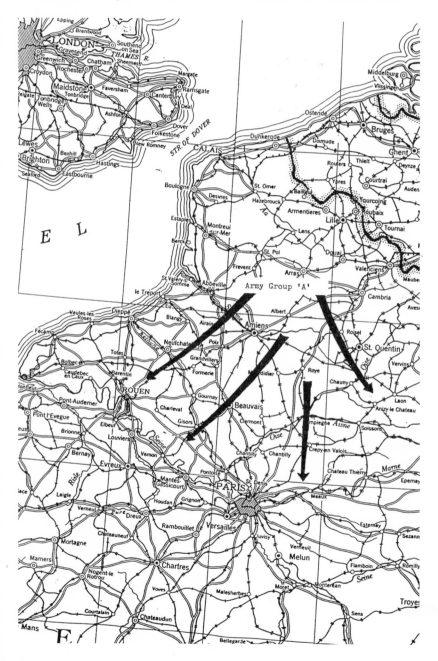

On 11th June, eleven aircraft of No. 111 Squadron joined up with No. 615 Squadron over Kenley, and flew over to patrol Lecamp-Dieppe and Le Treport area. Over Le Havre a formation of enemy fighters escorting bombers were encountered. The bombers were attacking Allied shipping leaving the port. The Yellow Section No. 111 Squadron was led by Sergeant Dymond, and was ordered into the attack. The general tactic was to break up the fighter formation and to get at the bombers. This was achieved and four Bf109s and two Dornier bombers claimed as shot down with others damaged.

Sergeant Dymond's combat report of the action reads:

"When approaching Le Havre I sighted enemy fighters and reported to Blue 1. I was ordered to take the lead and attack top fighters, which were Me109s. I led my section into an attack from astern, I fired a four second burst from dead astern at 350 yards closing to 300. Flames and smoke came from starboard wing and aircraft dived in flames. One Me109 followed formation to about 25 miles north of Le Havre, when I turned back, he dived and disappeared to east."

Another pilot in the No. 111 Squadron formation was Pilot Officer P. Simpson, flying Hurricane L1823:

"I was line astern with Green 1 who dived to attack. I saw one Me109 on my starboard side making a beam attack, I did a steep climbing turn and as I levelled out saw an enemy aircraft coming across my sight, I delivered a short burst and he immediately half rolled. I followed him down into a steep dive. I delivered a further attack from 150–100 yards astern. He dived vertically. As I was being attacked from astern I broke off and returned to Croydon."

With the Hurricanes and Spitfires of 11 Group covering the coastal areas as the Allied troops withdrew towards Brittany, the fighter squadrons of the BAFF were equally involved inland. No. 71 Squadron based at Le Mans was operating from Dreux as its advanced landing ground, and was gradually building up a score of enemy aircraft shot down. No. 1 Squadron were at Boos but preparing to move to Souge. In the end the groundcrew were moved without their aircraft and did not see their Hurricanes again until they met up at Angers two days later.

No. 73 Squadron had by this date moved to Le Mans, and would operate from there for another two days before moving to Nantes, still maintaining about ten of their Hurricanes serviceable.

The 'Y' intercept unit was in the area first hit by the Luftwaffe, and so was moved to Oysonville, near Paris. On 11th June it was on the move again towards Nantes and eventual evacuation, as LAC. Benjamin explains:

Hurricane L2124 'H' of No. 501 Squadron undergoing maintenance 'in the field', well illustrated by the conditions and gumboots!

"We were travelling in our unit MT trucks as fast as we could along the very congested roads. It was difficult to make speedy progress, what with the roads choked with refugees, many in horse-drawn carts, on bicycles, in all varieties of packed motor tranport, on foot and heavy laden, and all the roads being constantly machinegunned by the Luftwaffe.''

A similar story comes from L. Lineker, who was based with an Air Stores Park at Glisy. The unit's job was to check and refuel aircraft flying from the UK to the BAFF. Ground equipment was poor by modern standards and as with many other units refuelling was done from flimsy four gallon cans. One sentence explains what groundcrew suffered, as did lots of similar targets:

"We were bombed by night and day and ground strafed at very low level by Me109s. I was 21 years old at the time, and aged another ten years in as many minutes!''

To help prevent giving the Luftwaffe total air supremacy, Fighter Command diverted a number of their squadrons to fight over France and return to the UK at dusk. To refuel and re-arm these aircraft a refuelling and re-arming unit was hastily formed at Rouen. However, the facilities in the end proved inadequate and the airfields were subjected to bombing attacks, so these squadrons used forward airfields in Kent for servicing between sorties. The Hurricane squadrons suffered the greatest casualties in Fighter Command as they operated longer patrols and flew inland over the enemy flak defences, resulting on many occasions with the number of trained pilots in the

127

squadrons dropping below nine. This was not helped by the Air
Ministry policy of withdrawing pilots to replace wastage in Hurricane
squadrons of the BAFF.

By this date No. 103 Squadron and its Battles were at Ozouer-le-
Doyen, and had taken over No. 218 Squadron's aircraft. They were
now flying both day and night sorties, as were other Battle squadrons,
and as well as having their normal bomb load, were carrying four 25lb.
incendiary bombs loose in the rear cockpit to drop over the target. In a
day operation over Poix, a No. 103 Squadron Battle, flown by Pilot
Officer Thorogood, with observer Sergeant Anson and air-gunner
Pilot Officer Webster, saw about fifty Ju87s attacking a village. Thorogood put the Battle's nose down, diving into the middle of the Ju87s,
shooting one down before he was attacked by the escorting fighters.
Whether by good fortune, surprise or low flying the Battle got away,
with Webster claiming the shooting down of a Bf109. He was also
wounded, and all this on his first operational sortie with the squadron.

By this stage in the battle the French had a surplus of fighter pilots,
so Colonel Fournier of the Armée de l'Air approached the RAF
DCAS, Sholto Douglas, with a proposal that one hundred Hurricanes
be turned over to the French to form Hurricane squadrons in the
French Air Force, so as to utilise some of their 500 surplus pilots.
Though not *directly* rejected, the DCAS's opinion was that to accede to
this request would be a bad mistake; pointing out that if 100
Hurricanes were supplied, this would also require spares and
ammunition. At that period of time there were 240 Hurricanes in
Aircraft Servicing Units. The shortage was in experienced pilots and
operational squadrons. In the end the proposal was not accepted, so no
French Hurricane squadrons were formed.

Weygand had become the French Army Commander-in-Chief in
May, and by June was criticising Britain's contribution in France. He
said of Fighter Command:

> "We want them based on French airfields, we know it could mean the
> difference between victory and defeat."

Yet fighter strength in the RAF had been bled to the point (as
regards pilots) that Hugh Dowding, the Commander-in-Chief of
Fighter Command, had issued to Churchill and the Cabinet a warning
that Fighter Command strength had reached an all-time low, and that
if any more fighters were sent to France, then he could not be
responsible for the defence of Great Britain.

Fortunately Dowding's advice prevailed, against bitter criticism, so
that when Churchill met Prime Minster Reynaud at Briare on 11th
June, he followed Dowding's advice and fiercely refused to surrender

to the demands of Petain and Weygand. De Gaulle, now appointed as a Minister, attended this meeting and felt that at that moment strategic unity between the two countries was broken.

From the attitude of the two French Generals, De Gaulle sensed that they were already wearing the mantle of defeat, and at dinner that night icily rejected an invitation by Weygand to sit next to him, preferring Churchill's similar invitation. De Gaulle commented later that his conversation with Churchill strengthened his confidence in Churchill's determination to fight on.

By now battalions and detachments marched and staggered miles on the retreat, to escape the ever attacking and encircling grip of the Panzers. Sometimes they were without food, there was chaos, panic, and refugees blocked the roads. All this, in spite of huge depots and planned lines of communications. Now, lack of transport, bombing, and lack of direction meant that neither food nor ammunition was getting through.

Although Churchill's decision not to send any more fighter squadrons to France would ensure that Fighter Command would be in a position to expand to defend Great Britain, the fighter and bomber squadrons of the AASF were still fighting. They were still flying over the soil of France in a vain attempt to provide some cover for the BEF, even if the troops failed to understand air operations. This was backed up all the time by 2 Group Blenheims still making low attacks on any troop or AFV concentration.

Typical of this was an attack by No. 21 Squadron on 11th June. Three sections of the squadron had been detailed to carry out an attack on troops and AFVs in woods near La Mare, which was five miles WSW of Les Andelys. The formation crossed the coast at St Valery-en-Caux and were immediately set on by Luftwaffe fighters. During the combat two enemy aircraft were claimed shot down, but L8743, L8746 and R3674 were shot down. L8745 was so badly shot up that its pilot had to jettison its bombs and return to base, whilst another aircraft made a 'wheels-up' landing back at Watton. These were the casualties the BEF troops knew nothing about.

Air operations on 10th June started off with 2 Group Blenheims attacking enemy columns south of the Gournay to Rouen road, followed by twelve Battles of the AASF attacking an enemy column approaching Vernon. Two Battles failed to return (L5200 and P2328), while another was damaged by a Hurricane attack! This was followed by thirty-three 2 Group Blenheims, with escort provided by twenty Hurricanes, attacking MT and troop concentrations between Rouen and Les Andelys, and also on the Forges to Rouen road.

During this period of fighting, the Hurricanes of the AASF and

Blenheim IV of No. 107 Squadron 1940, fitted with Bristol BI. Mk. 4 turret, mounting twin Browning machine guns and belt feed.

Fighter Command were taking their toll of He111s and Dornier 17s, sufficient to cause the Luftwaffe to up gun these aircraft with more 7.92mm machineguns. This trade was not all onesided either, for the defensive armament of the Battle and Blenhiem was up gunned, both being fitted with a 'scatter' gun underneath of most doubtful use. The gun on the Blenheim was installed in a streamlined blister underneath the observer's position. Another modification on the Blenheim was the dorsal turret sprouting twin Browning 0.303in machineguns in place of the single Vickers 'K' gun. One of the first to introduce the Browning belt fed weapon as a local fitting, was No. 107 Squadron, whose Commanding Officer, Wing Commander Embry, encouraged the armourers to modify the Bristol turret.

Returning to the position of the 51st Division, the Allied intention was to hold a perimeter around St Valery-en-Caux and gradually withdraw into town, after destroying their vehicles. By 11th June the 51st were approaching the point of capture. German troops had penetrated the perimeter and by evening were in the town and in a position to shell the harbour and ships. The weather, which so often had saved Britain, was in this case to favour the enemy. Fog descended and most of the ships could not enter the harbour, so in the early hours of the morning the 51st Division was out of ammunition and forced to surrender, with 46,000 prisoners going into captivity. British fighter activities had in this period concentrated on the St Valery area in an endeavour to cover the evacuation. Although 147 aircraft were used only on four patrols were enemy aircraft seen and attacked.

Sgt. W/op. air gunner R. Pearce of No. 142 Squadron in a Battle rear cockpit illustrating use of the single Vickers 'K' gun. (R. Pearce)

Although St Valery and the 51st Division were captured, this information was not communicated to RAF Fighter Command, so that on 12th June there were 180 sorties laid on. At Le Havre the evacuation took place as planned and French and British troops were got away successfully, the operation being completed by the following day, with the Germans occupying the town on 14th June.

Also during 12th June Allied air reconnaissance had determined that not all the bridges, stated to have been demolished had in fact been 'blown'.* Battles were sent in to carry out attacks on bridgeheads and bridges, but early on this was hampered by mist (although it was also considered that it could possibly be smoke from fires, or even a smokescreen).

The Battle was often referred to by people as the 'Flying Coffin', for without self-sealing tanks, with or without the small fighter escorts, the aircraft was proving a deathtrap for its crews, as they were smashed or cremated in its metal case by light flak or hordes of Bf109s. By now a small sheet of armour plate was behind the gunner, and a sheet of armour plate laid on the floor to protect the observer when lying down. That a similar death was befalling Ju87 crews, then and in the following Battle of Britain, was no consolation to the Battle crews of the AASF. Yet without heroics they accepted their orders, climbed into their aircraft, knowing that for many of them this was a one-way ticket. The lucky ones would be those who were forced to crash land without their fuel tanks being hit.

Six Battles escorted by fighters attacked the bridge at Vezillon, but due to bad visibility there was no certainty of a hit. This was then followed by thirty-three Blenheims of 2 Group being dispatched to attack troop concentrations in woods north of the Seine. Their escort of twelve Hurricanes failed to materialise and three Blenheims failed to return – R3746, R3893 and R3810. At 15.15 hours twelve AASF Battles attacked the bridges and locality of Le Manoir, followed shortly afterwards by twelve Battles escorted by French fighters attacking the pontoon bridges at Verberie, Pontpoint and south of Chevrieres. One

---

*Reconnaissance also found a German spearhead twenty miles from Paris.

Battle was lost and another one force landed away from base. As well as the aircraft lost from these operations, four more of the Blenheims were damaged.

British forces were now south of the Seine, and the DCAS of the RAF sent a message to Barratt, detailing him in the event of a decisive breakthrough to retire the RAF units to Nantes and Bordeaux. Unfortunately, to do so would mean a complete break with the Armée de l'Air (who were now retiring south of Orleans) and operational airfields for the BAFF were extremely limited in the Nantes area. Barratt conferred with General d'Astier of the Armée de l'Air, which resulted in the BAFF being allocated airfields in the square formed by Rennes, Le Mans, Saumur and Nantes. From there the AASF could still give assistance to the remaining BEF and 10th Army.

During 13th June many Battle sorties were flown, amongst these were six sorties by No. 142 Squadron over the Vernon-Pacy-Evreux area; take-off being made at 05.00 hours and the bomb load dropped on MT in a wooded area. This was followed at 10.45 hours by three other No. 142 Squadron sorties to attack AFVs and troop concentrations on the Pacy, Vernon and Rouen roads. Bf109s attacked the Battles as they were bombing the targets, which resulted in the leader, Flight Lieutenant Hewson and crew being shot down, their aircraft force landing in flames. One of the others was shot down with the observer and air gunner injured by cannon shell splinters. The third aircraft, flown by Pilot Officer Franklin, returned to base badly damaged with the observer injured.

Further attacks by AASF Battles on German troops along the Seine, were prevented by bad weather. Five crews failed to find the target and four others failed to return. Twelve more Battles were then detailed to carry out attacks on a tank formation which had been reported by the French to be in the Marne area but HQ (North) BAFF had reported the information to AASF HQ as a concentration of about 1,000 tanks in the Foret-de Gault. The target was found in this area, where swarms of German MT could be seen, well protected by flak and fighters, yet somehow the Battles bombed and got away with just one No. 88 Squadron aircraft missing.

Still the Battles of the AASF had not finished, still more sacrifice was called for, still more action in a futile attempt to halt an army that Allied armies had retreated from. A further twenty-six Battles were dispatched to the area but this time there was to be no escape. Four went down shattered and in flames, shot down by Bf109s and flak before they had reached the target area. As the remainder pressed on to strike the target, six more went down as the formation was shattered and slaughtered.

Amongst those were aircraft from No. 142 Squadron, five aircraft from the squadron took off to attack AFVs reported refuelling in woods near Montmarial. As usual the Battles were not escorted and well short of the target twelve Bf109s dived out of the sun. One Battle, crewed by Sergeant Holiday, Sergeant Whiting and air gunner LAC. Joe Greenhall, attempted to take cover in some light cloud, but it was useless. Holiday put the Battle into a dive from 8,000ft, hoping to get to ground level, during which Holiday appears to have been wounded and lost conciousness. An account was written by Sergeant Observer Rudd:*

> "On the way down the Battle was set on fire by a cannon shell that exploded close to Joe's right leg. The dive continued . . . By now the starboard wing was well alight and Sergeant Whiting the observer crouched back towards Joe to escape the flames in the fuselage. Then the pilot regained conciousness and somehow managed to make a forced landing."

The observer and Greenall, who was bleeding profusely, got out of the rear cockpit and together went to help the pilot, who was hanging out of his cockpit with his uniform burning, and managed to get him clear. As they tried to get away the bombs exploded and all the crew received further injuries. The crew became PoWs and were taken to hospital, but after attempting to escape Greenall was kept under close surveillance. Asked afterwards how he felt diving to the ground in flames and wounded, Greenall replied: "I just kept firing and swearing at the B******'s". Like so many aircrew of the period, his courage and bravery received no recognition.

Even then the day was not over. Fifteen 2 Group Blenheims were next called in to attack in the same area, from which attack Blenheim R3616 failed to return.

During this retreat from their supposedly safe airfields, the squadron groundcrews of the AASF were carrying out repair and maintenance, subjected to bombing and strafing, realizing that little stood between them and the German advance. In some cases AASF convoys were pulling out of a town as the Germans entered at the opposite end. One RAF MT convoy, for instance, was heading to St Nazaire in the last few days, only to be diverted at the last minute to Brest. St Nazaire had fallen while they were travelling.

Being relatively small units, the squadron's morale and discipline was in general good, even though the groundcrews were physically exhausted trying to maintain their aircraft under appalling conditions. The aircrews were suffering mental and physical fatigue, the memory of being overwhelmed by masses of fighters and concentrated flak, yet

*Sergeant Observer with No. 142 Squadron, was wounded 6th June, 1940.

still they climbed into their aircraft and flew against impossible odds.

The action of 14th June opened with No. 88 Squadron Battles carrying out their last raid before returning to Houssay and then to the UK. Their targets were in the Evreux area. This was followed by an armed reconnaissance by four Battles of No. 142 Squadron, which bombed troops in woods south of the River Seine and south of Evreux. Following this, a further attack was put in by three grews of No. 142 Squadron, taking off at 13.00 hours. The three crews were:

Sergeant Spear, Sergeant Howard, LAC. Pearce.

Sergeant Ebert, Flight Sergeant Rex, LAC. Hogg.

Pilot Officer Edwards, Sergeant Green, LAC. Welsh.

They made an attack on Evreux Airfield and bombed Bf109s at their dispersal points, so paying them back for some of the punishment dealt out by them.

By now the squadron transport was loaded ready for the final move to Nantes, but No. 142 Squadron was to have one more fling, as was No. 12 Squadron. The latter squadron made an early morning raid and then returned to Souge, before their last eight Battles took-off for Abingdon. One of the pilots was Sergeant Wheeldon:

"On the 13th and 15th were were out again in daylight and on the 13th we were again attacked by a 109, but this time we saw him coming and as he dived I turned under him, which the Jerry pilot did not like, though I saw the smoke from his guns as he let-go a burst, which was far away from hitting us.

"The Op' on the 15th was an early morning one and on return to base, we were told to collect our small kit for a return to England. Having done what we were told we got back to the field and found the groundcrew still refuelling. Whilst waiting, I heard a sound of aero-engines and looking up saw a formation of, I think He111s, on a run up to our field. I yelled to the lads and they and my crew dashed over the railway line which ran along the field and flung ourselves down in the ditch just as the bombs hit the ground. After a short pause, I heard more engines, but this time it was some Hurricanes attacking the 111s; so we nipped back to the aircraft, told the groundcrew to close the tanks – the fuel was only a gallon or two short of full – and tried to start-up. Having a hot engine it was very reluctant to fire, and whilst the poor ground boys sweated away at turning the Merlin over on hand-starting, our Squadron Leader Flying, Squadron Leader Lowe, arrived on the field and went off, beckoning me to follow, which I did shortly afterwards when the engine finally fired!"

No. 142 Squadron put three Battles into the air, with each aircraft loaded with sixteen 40 lb. bombs, carrying out a dawn armed reconnaissance crewed by:

An He111 of KG1.

Sergeant Tweed, Sergeant Adams, LAC. Cave.
Sergeant Tremar, Sergeant Duffy, AC. Dunbar.
Pilot Officer Edwards, Sergeant Green, LAC. Welsh.
As no targets were seen during the reconnaissance the bombs were off loaded on a flak battery at Evreux and a return made back to Houssay. The squadron advance party had already left and the main ground party left at 13.00 hours. Three damaged Battles were destroyed to prevent them falling into enemy hands and the thirteen remaining aircraft took off for the UK. R. (Bob) Pearce* wrote of the time:

> "Those of us who returned home were indeed fortunate. Outnumbered and outgunned, the inadequacy of the Fairey Battle squadrons was all too manifest. The total loss of aircrew of the AASF in the period between the 10th May and our evacuation on the 15th June, exceeded 650 killed or missing and more than 230 prisoners of war.
>
> "While our contribution to the campaign was difficult to assess, we undoubtedly acted as guinea pigs to the new concept of modern air warfare. Hopefully, lessons were learnt from our endeavours which were of benefit to those that followed on."

For the Battle squadrons the nightmare in France was over, and nothing can give adequate credit to the aircrews of the Battle and Blenheim squadrons that operated over France in 1939–40. Now they were returning to the unconquered island kingdom of Britain, in the near future to fight again to retain what was theirs. Sergeant Pilot G. (Rex) Wheeldon writing of the return flight to Britain said:

> "I remember on the way in, we passed over Arundel School and looking down, saw a cricket match in progress, nice and peaceful in a lovely setting, as opposed to the chaos and turmoil we had left behind in France."

*Wireless operator air-gunner with No. 142 Squadron, commissioned 1942.

The fighter squadrons were also withdrawing towards Nantes, Dinant and Brest, having fought against overwhelming odds, without radar guidance, and with very little backing. They, like the other squadrons of BAFF had been asked to carry out tasks beyond human endeavour, had accepted those tasks and executed them, no service or country could ask more. Yet, like Rex Wheeldon, as they came back to Britain, the tranquil scenes and peaceful pastures raised the question, "For how long?" Before this question could be answered the RAF fighter squadrons of BAFF still had to provide cover for the remaining BEF to evacuate from the soil of France.

By 14th June, No. 103 Squadron was at Souge and under the control of 76 Wing. At 17.00 hours a low flying attack was made by enemy aircraft, which approached over a hill bordering the airfield. The surprise attack resulted in several Battles being hit and set on fire. On the following day the squadron was ordered to proceed to the UK, but an enemy attack coincided with the departure, and several aircraft were hit. No. 150 Squadron were at Houssay on that date, and the main party departed to the dispersal point near Nantes at first light, with the remaining twelve serviceable Battles departing direct to the UK. On the same day the BAFF HQ was proceeding to leave by convoy from Olivet, down by-ways south of the Loire, to Nantes. Arriving there on the 15th, Warrant Officer G. Jordan* remembers:

"Having destroyed all our furniture and vehicles, except one lorry which was loaded with filing cabinets to be sent to Brest and one for our own transport, we made our way north to an aerodrome under construction six miles outside St Nazaire. So we slept on the cobbles in the dockyard. Early on 17th June, we were one of the first parties on the jetty and there was a sea of khaki behind us. Not until 8 am were we allowed aboard a French tug which took us 4 miles out into the bay where, amongst other craft, the liner "Lancastria" was anchored. She embarked troops all day, airmen, pioneers, infantrymen, engineers, gunners, even 38 civilians, until 4 pm when she was bombed and sank in 17 minutes. Amongst the survivors were those from HQ BAFF, 67 Wing, 70 Wing, No. 73 Squadron, No. 98 Squadron, No 2 Air Mission and D Squadron. I was lucky enough to be picked up by HMS *Cambridgeshire* and transferred to S.S. *John Holt* with 1,008 others and taken to Devonport."

The AASF HQ, on 16th June, left Quince for St Nazaire, but on the road were redirected to Brest, arriving there on the 17th. Held at the roadside outside Brest with lorries taken away, the troops just had their small kit, Sergeant Phipps recorded:

"Early afternoon, we took our small kit from the lorries and were each issued with a rifle (no ammunition, of course – I felt we were merely acting as carriers). The lorries were then driven off with our kitbags, files etc."

*Retired postwar as Wing Commander and lives in New Zealand.

Interior of a damaged hangar at Mourmelon-le-Grand with Battles and a wrecked Magister. (Gerard Faux)

The RAF airmen were then marched to the harbour and embarked on SS *Bactria*, sailing at 17.00 hours for Plymouth. Whilst waiting outside Brest, Phipps heard a stream of rumours regarding both Canadian troops arriving and the Germans closing in, while at Plymouth ''nothing was more welcome to us than the cups of hot tea and 'wads' dispensed to us''.

The evacuation meant many things to many people; I am indebted to T. H. Davies, aircraft instrument maker with No. 114 Squadron, for his description:

> "Nantes was likened to a large market town, except that we were all military. Much of our equipment was taken from us and we were to attempt to reach the Channel ports. I am vague about the position, and once again rumours may seem to have become fact in our minds. It is my understanding that we split up. Some made for the port of Cherbourg; there was a rumour that a number of the squadron were on the ill-fated *Lancastria* that saw disaster at St Nazaire, when a bomb, by some trick of fate, went through the funnel. I think we were embarked higher up the coast at Boulogne – as I remember distinctly landing at dear old Folkstone – and was I relieved?"

The loss of the *Lancastria* was *possibly* the worst sea disaster of all time, for it has never been established how many people were on the vessel when it was hit by at least four bombs from an enemy aircraft, one of which set the vessel on fire, whilst the other three sank it. Trapped on board in the holds were thousands of civilians, soldiers and airmen; the Guinness Book of Records gives the figure as "about 4,000", but various unofficial sources have quoted figures higher than this.

Standing-off St Nazaire and in the Loire Estuary were a number of other liners and vessels as well as the *Lancastria*, one of which was the Polish ship, *Sobieske*. This was to escape from St Nazaire in an over-loaded condition crowded with all manner of servicemen and civilians, including the 'Y' unit and LAC. Benjamin. Having marched from Nantes to St Nazaire fully equipped and armed, the unit was then ordered to kick their kit into the water before boarding. Moving out of the Loire Estuary, the *Sobieske* was bombed and machinegunned. Fortunately this was unsuccessful, and the vessel docked at Falmouth on 18th June.

This episode was typical of hundreds, as personnel attempted to escape with their equipment, yet were forced to dump it on evacuation. Worse for latter day historians was the loss of squadron records, numerous squadrons losing these when handing them over to embarkation officers at the ports. Some equipment did not even get that far. Corporal Heslop from the direction finding unit recalls:

> "We went on to Nantes with the fighter squadrons, Nos. 1 and 73; but we were never again to erect the radio station. The 3 ton lorry and trailer served as our last transport, to St Nazaire (June 17th), where we handed it over to the demolition squads of the Royal Engineers."

The unit, along with others, then queued alongside the quayside wall and awaited evacuation. This came later on in the afternoon, when a Royal Navy destroyer performed what would be repeated many times, the transportation of personnel out to other ships, in this case the Canadian Pacific, *Duchess of York*. Two days later the personnel were disembarked at Liverpool amongst a cloud of rumours, for by then it was known that France had surrendered.

Rumours were certainly rife those days, especially amongst the civilians, but morale amongst the RAF personnel was in general good, even though self-preservation did become important at times. Jack Wey of No. 40 Squadron said of it:

"I don't think it ever crossed my mind that we could end up on the defeated side, then or at any other time throughout the duration of hostilities."

While L. Linekar said of those times:

"I was scared a few times but never lost any sleep over it. Looking back I would say that the morale was very high indeed, even during our exodus from France."

He came out at Cherbourg, after he and his colleagues had spent a night under their vehicle outside the port, the story of many at the time.

Amongst many parties heading for Nantes was the HQ Typex Section, which had followed a route from Nancy through Auxerre and Chateaurault, with H. Cooper* being told to guard the Typex machine with his life! So it was quite a shock, amidst visions of a court-martial, when, during a traffic holdup, he was relieving himself by the wayside only to see the lorry startup, gather speed and disappear. With the sight and sound of battle behind him Cooper set off after the lorry and was accompanied part of the journey by a British soldier, who appeared shell-shocked. As the hours seemed to drag by Cooper walked on, until to his relief a unit dispatch rider appeared. It appeared that when they found Cooper missing at a halt, the motorcyclist had volunteered to back towards the battle to look for him, which in the fluid state of the battle was extremely brave.

The dispatch rider and Cooper 'borrowed' another motorbike from a deserted Air Storage Park and put a few miles between them and the advancing German Army, in the meantime having a few escapades as they made their way to La Pallice to rejoin the Typex Section. On arrival at the port an Army officer ordered the Typex broken-up and thrown in the dock. When Cooper queried this a soldier was ordered to do it, and so the remains disappeared into the murky waters.

---

*Retired from the RAF as a Flight Lieutenant.

Another vehicle heading for Nantes or Cherbourg was the HQ staff car driven by Harry Fenwick, who says:

> "Remember I was young, in a strange country, and scared stiff of being caught by the Germans. Now I left the main road heading south on what might be termed a second class road."

This was to lead to trouble and a confrontation with a small German force, but scared as he was young Fenwick made it:

> "I kept driving until I saw the sign 'Cherbourg', and some place near the docks the chief of MPs took over. I was asked to wait in a field and late that night both my car and myself were put on a coal boat for Southampton."

No. 17 and 501 Squadrons were detailed to operate from Dinard to cover all Allied shipping into and out of St Malo and Cherbourg. From there, on 18th June, the two squadrons moved to the Channel Islands to fly defence sorties. They departed to England on the 19th, No. 17 Squadron flying to Tangmere to refuel before continuing on to Debden.

The last two squadrons to leave France, were Nos. 1 and 73 Squadrons, who had been the first two fighter squadrons to arrive in France. By this date No. 1 Squadron had chalked up a recorded 'kill' total of 155. Most of the ground personnel of the two squadrons were sent to either St Nazaire or Brest, to board ship for the UK, whilst the pilots and their aircraft remained at La Rochelle to maintain protective patrols over the ports. The airfield was littered with crashed, damaged and derelict aircraft, whilst there were rumours around of a possible armistice. The rumours were solid fact, but on 18th June came the orders for the two squadrons to depart for Tangmere.

The RAF squadrons had fought hard and defended to the end, the mobility of the squadrons had been outside their control, and in the end their ground personnel had gone home by sea. It was at the ports of departure where records, equipment and transport were lost.

Chaos had gradually undermined all ground organisations. At the French ports, equipment, stores and ammunition had been unloaded while similar material had been loaded for shipment back to the UK! The Army HQ stated that accurate information on German movements was not received, yet this statement is contradicted by the availability of RAF reconnaissance reports right up to 17th June. Some of the reconnaissance work was carried out by No. 55 Squadron, which had been evacuated from Boulogne to Gatwick, where it was commanded by Wing Commander E. Edwards.

By 15th June there was a force of 22,000 British troops in the Cherbourg area, plus five battalions of French infantry, as well as

French garrison troops with artillery. This was a force three times greater than Rommel's 7th Panzer Division, which was advancing on Cherbourg. However, lack of decision and initiative allowed the German advance to continue. Worst of all, stores and vehicles were left on the quayside, when there were empty holds on some of the ships. An exception to this was General Beauman's 'Beauforce' Division, whose troops had been on the march and in action for ten days. Arriving at Cherbourg on the evening of 16/17th June, they proceeded to load on to the ships all their remaining weapons: eight field guns, twenty anti-tank guns and four Bofors guns, out of an original complement of 36 guns. That there was time for other troops to do likewise is obvious because the French troops at Cherbourg fought tenaciously, and only surrendered 24 hours after the last British had left.

At Brest a further show of initiative took place, when the 1st Field Royal Canadian Horse Artillery were ordered to destroy all their vehicles and guns. Their Colonel refused to do this and argued over the telephone with his General until he was granted a concession of two hours for loading. By the deadline all their 24 guns had been loaded, plus 12 Bofors, seven predictors, 3 bren-gun carriers and some other vehicles. Unfortunately the deadline precluded the loading of the RCHA tractors and limbers, so these had to be abandoned. The absurdity and panic of the original order is highlighted by the fact that the French did not surrender Brest until 19th June, 48 hours later.

On 16th June the 2nd Armoured Brigade and some of the 3rd Armoured Brigade, loaded their tanks on a special train at Le Mans. The tank train then departed unescorted and the troops headed for Brest. The train and its load of tanks was never seen again.

At St Nazaire the troops of the 6th Royal Sussex were ordered to embark on the *SS. Floriston* and the *SS. Glenaffric*, when their commanding officer noticed loaded lorries on the quayside. Upon investigation it was found that they were loaded with brand-new Bren-guns, so on the CO's orders these guns and ammunition were acquired and then the troops embarked. On the way homeward the two ships were attacked by enemy aircraft, but the troops put up such a devastating volume of fire with their newly acquired weapons that the aircraft sheered off without doing any damage.

At some ports which had experienced heavy air-raids the dockside crane drivers had vacated their posts for safer refuges. Yet in many cases the Military made no attempt to use the dockside cranes, and few attempts were made to use the ships derricks to load vehicles or stores. This at a time when initiative and boldness could have paid a handsome bonus.

By now Guderian's armoured force was at St Dizier and von Kleist's similar force had taken Dijon, so completely isolating the Maginot Line, a defence line, which seems to have created a defence mentality. The isolation of the Line and the manning of its defences continued until the armistice, when senior French Generals ordered the men to surrender. By then a union between France and Great Britain had been proposed by Churchill. The emissary was Colonel General Charles de Gaulle*. On the evening of 16th June the Spanish Government were asked to intervene on behalf of the French Government, who wished to sue for peace. On 22nd June, 1940, an armistice was signed and Great Britain stood alone. Many French Air Force squadrons flew across to North African colonies, some opted to fight alongside the British in the Middle East.

Those that were left behind.

A few of the French forces along with Belgians, Dutch and Poles evacuated to Great Britain, including General de Gaulle. De Gaulle would in the end be the focal point of French resistance when other French Generals and politicians preferred the German yoke. The battle on French soil was over.

---

*General de Gaulle was tried and sentenced in his absence to death for desertion.

Chapter Five
Analysis of RAF Campaign

The operational aspects of the campaign and the overall effects must be taken against the backcloth of prewar planning, the economic strength of the United Kingdom and the aircraft specifications. As for the moral and courage of the RAF, there would not be enough ink in the country to write of the heroism and steadfastness of the RAF aircrew. One volume can never pay tribute to or cover all the actions carried out in the 1939–40 French Campaign, one can only skim the surface. This analysis will try to evaluate the hard facts, losses and equipment whilst the previous chapters pay tribute to RAF actions alongside the Armée de l'Air.

Whilst strict financial conditions in the inter-war formed some restriction on the amount of experimentation and development that could be carried out, some designs, projects and concepts were evaluated by the Air Ministery and Air Staff prior to the 1939–45 war. Unfortunately these were tempered by the economy, for in a democracy, the military strength of the nation is a product of the economic strength of the nation. Furthermore, it must be realized that sufficient numbers of the British public were still swayed, even as late as 1938, with the seductive propaganda of the socialist and pacifist members of the community. This was sufficient to frustrate popular agreement to re-arm on a large enough scale. But by 1938 it was already too late, the war was only twelve months away. Some of the projects evaluated, consolidated and brought to an operational state, were early warning radar, gun turrets and the Colt (Browning) 0.303in machinegun. Against this very little was done with regard to larger calibre weapons, bulletproof tanks or radio/radar navigational or bombing aids. In 1939 the RAF's navigational aids had hardly progressed since 1918 and the RAF aircraft went to France without rear armour. The aircraft specifications were quite often based on theories, or experience gained in the execution of duties defending the British Empire and Commonwealth. This in some cases resulted in misconceptions in the manner of defending bombers, the defence of bombers and fighter tactics, though the Luftwaffe were also to suffer misconceptions from their Spanish War experience.

With regard to losses, the British bomber losses were appallingly high. Between 10th to 14th May, 1940, AASF Battles flying 130 sorties lost 50% of their number, between 62 and 68 aircraft. As a consequence of these losses and the transfer of No. 1 Echelon beyond the Marne, they were unable to operate for four days, although on the night of 15/16th May an operation was carried out. When operations began again on day sorties on 19th May the losses were 18%. The movement of No. 1 Echelon to new bases indicated, as did the movement from the United Kingdom to France, that the RAF's interpretation of 'mobile' fell far short of the German Luftwaffe's. Whereas the latter service units were capable of moving immediately with the advance of the German Army, amply supported by transport aircraft ferrying in personnel, supplies and fuel, the RAF was tied mainly to the use of its own road transport, and that was in short supply as explained earlier.

From 20th May to 4th June, 1940, approximately 342 sorties were carried out by night and 57 by day. Whereas the day sorties saw a loss of 16%, the night losses were reduced to 0.6%. The night sorties by the Battles were considered by some experts as being of little value. In respect of accuracy this could of course be true, but in nuisance value it obviously contributed to the fatigue of the German troops, as expressed in some German Army diaries. The ten Battle Squadrons of the AASF could hardly accomplish the work that required at least ten times that number, as well as sufficient fighter escorts. Fighter escorts were to prove a sore point both to the AASF and No. 2 Group Blenheims. During the period 10th to 14th May, when British bombers' losses were at their highest, bomber sorties were flown mainly without a fighter escort. This was mainly because of the lack of fighter aircraft as there were only eight British fighter squadrons in France. These eight squadrons had to defend the BEF area as well as to provide a defence for the army co-operation and bomber squadrons, so the decision was made to fly standing patrols over the target area. This was to prove disastrously wrong at that period.

As the war progressed past 20th May to 4th June losses averaged 16% and from June 5th to 15th losses avaraged 9%. This was partly due to an increase in fighter coverage from the United Kingdom for 2 Group bombers, and as the German Army spread across France the anti-aircraft guns were spread wider; that is to say, that when the Panzerwaffe spearheads were at first striking across the borders of Belgium, France and Luxembourg, these concentrations were strongly protected by anti-aircraft guns and fighter aircraft. Likewise, with targets like the Meuse bridges there were heavy concentrations of anti-aircraft fire. A further factor contributing to these losses at the start of the campaign was the manner of attack that the Battle pilots made. This followed peacetime training exercises, attacking on a very low approach in formation. After a few days this method was abandoned in favour of individual attacks from a much higher altitude. Nevertheless,

No. 114 Squadron Blenheim N6145 wrecked on the ground at Vraux after the classic low-level attack. (R. Bright)

without a fighter escort high losses would, and did, continue as long as attacks were continued on targets where there were heavy defence concentrations.

The German attack on Conde-Vraux was a classic offensive strike that eliminated one AASF Blenheim Squadron on the ground. Unfortunately this was not to be emulated by the RAF during the French Campaign. With the elimination of one Blenheim squadron on the ground and the virtual extinction of the other in the air, the AASF Blenheims ceased to operate after 17th May. On this date out of twenty-five sorties 12 aircraft were lost. This was a loss of 48% and corresponded very closely to the Battle losses, caused in the same areas of attack and for the same reasons. During the whole of the campaign the 2 Group Blenheims operated by daylight. Over the period from 10th to 15th May they made 156 sorties for the loss of about 28 aircraft, a loss rate of 18%. Between 17th and 18th May they carried out 48 sorties for a loss of about 14 aircraft, a loss rate of 29%. During the latter part of the campaign the Blenheims operated 473 sorties and lost 34 aircraft, a loss rate of 7%, which was also the percentage loss rate over the whole campaign. On the whole this lower loss rate for 2 Group Blenheims as against the AASF Battles, was partly due to the more effective fighter escorts that were provided and also the fact that the Battles were slower and were subjected to hasty moves and enemy bombing of their bases.

Night sorties returned lower loss rates, so the security of night operations was apparent, but set against this was the reduced accuracy of night bombing. In the conditions appertaining to 1940 it appeared that this was the most economic method of bombing and would be exercised by Bomber Command through to 1944, except in special circumstances. It would be in the deserts of North Africa that the correct method of destroying the Panzerwaffe would be demonstrated, but the North African Army would have aircraft resources unknown to BAFF or the Armée de l'Air.

Studies and books by army survivors of the Battle of France clearly indicate a lack, on the part of the army, to understand air force operations. They also failed to supply sufficient anti-aircraft guns and effective anti-tank guns. The army supply problem, army trans-Channel organisation, allocation of troops and movements were, and are, open to criticism. Untrained troops were sent against German Panzer troop areas, units were split up, there was a shortage of ammunition for some weapons, but huge stocks of unused Bren machineguns in dumps in France which were not issued and were then captured by the Germans after the evacuation. There was the destruction of artillery and their tractors at ports when there was time to ship them back to the UK, stores being unloaded at French ports and similar stores being returned back to the UK. All this and much more.

Complaints from the army that AASF bombers were used strategically, opens the door to the fact that the army in many cases did not know anything about air operations. How could it be strategic bombing when the AASF Battles and Blenheims and 2 Group Blenheims were attacking troops, tanks and MT columns advancing against the Allied forces? With the Allied Armies in such array, it would have been hard to have distinguished in the fluid movement of the front line where to place bombs. Furthermore, target information when received was usually out of date due to the rate of retreat of the Allied ground forces and it is obvious from the same studies and books that ground communications at that period were in many cases almost non-existant. Another point of fact which appears to be ignored by both the Army and Navy, is the shortfall on financing of the RAF, both the other two services having greater budgets. When they talk of shortage of fighters in their vicinity, may they also remember the host of tasks that those few fighter squadrons were trying to perform, not least of which was trying to stop the best part of 1500 German aircraft attacking Allied troop and military installations.

The whole truth of the situation was that the British Army was in the main unprepared, under-equipped and under-trained for the job it was called on to do. There were individual and group instances of great heroism, but generally it was a period of retreat, chaos and confusion.

A full analysis of how many bomber raids were given fighter protection could not, and still cannot, be determined, because many of the records of the various units taking part in the campaign in France were lost. Differing degrees of fighter protection were obviously given over the whole period, for in the first period of confrontation and combat, during 10th to 14th May, the fighter squadrons of the BAFF were planned only to fly protective cover in the target area. In some cases French fighter units flew escort on some British raids, but from reports of aircrew survivors of these raids, close escorts were rare and bombers were in many cases intercepted by German fighters enroute to the target. As the Battle of France moved nearer to Northern France and the British coast, Fighter Command squadrons were able to provide close escort to the Blenheims. However, when the battle moved farther south, from about 5th June, the target areas were outside the range of Fighter Command squadrons. When this occurred the only fighter protection was that given by the overworked AASF fighter squadrons. It is only of academic interest to debate whether the bomber raids should have been reduced to allow for sufficient fighter protection from the five AASF fighter squadrons, for in the latter stages of the campaign the bomber raids were not against the main German armoured thrusts and the effect that the attacks had on the German attacking force was minimal. In spite of this, the aircrews of the British bomber squadrons were outstanding, and despite appalling losses never questioned their missions and fully lived up to the highest traditions of the RAF, performing acts of heroism daily, that would in later years have warranted the award of the highest decorations. The decision to fly target area fighter patrols instead of close escort was to cost the bomber squadrons dearly, and was a tragic mistake.

Battle N2150 of No. 12 Squadron alongside a wrecked Hurricane at Nantes-Bougenais Airfield being looked over by German personnel.

A collection of wrecked British aircraft at Nantes-Bougenais Airfield after take-over by the Germans.

In regard to the army co-operation squadrons there was nothing wrong with the concept of the Lysander or its use. If there was, then the same could be said against the Fieseler Storch and Hs126. The trouble lay in trying to operate these aircraft in an enemy controlled environment, without sufficient fighter cover and against an enemy well supplied with anit-aircraft weapons. The Germans were also well exercised in aircraft co-operation and anti-aircraft defence. Thirty-five Lysanders were lost in France, and the experience gained resulted in the formation of Army Co-operation Command before the end of 1940, using fighter type aircraft. As the Air Component aircraft were in general withdrawn to the south coast of England by 23rd May, damaged aircraft were not lost on evacuated airfields in France from that date. The Air Component was to lose a large amount of equipment due to the speed of the German advance in the BEF area, as well as some lost due to German interception which included aircraft being repaired.

The loss of equipment in France by the RAF, excluding aircraft, was estimated by the Air Officer Commanding Maintenance Command, to amount to the equivalent of four complete Aircraft Parks, or the value of £1,000,000 at that date. This *excluded* the equipment and spares held by the squadrons. Fortunately, machine tools and twenty tons of vital equipment, that were in short supply in Great Britain, were evacuated successfully. A large amount of AASF equipment and

A collection of wrecked RAF aircraft at an aircraft storage park in France. (J. De Vos)

squadron gear (including squadron records) were lost at the French west coast ports, due to lack of time and space in some cases, but in other cases due to failure on the part of port embarkation officers.

Aircraft lost as a direct result of the campaign in France amounted to a total of 959 although the official records do state that a number of the Fighter and Coastal Command losses were not strictly connected with the campaign. The losses from all causes amounted to:

AASF	Blenheim 37; Hurricane 55; Battle 137.
Air Component	Blenheim 41; Hurricane 203; Lysander 35.
Bomber Command	Blenheim 97; Hampden 17; Wellington 26; Whitley 26.
Fighter Command	Blenheim 11; Hurricane 128; Defiant 13; Spitfire 67.
Coastal Command	Blenheim 14; Anson 11; Beaufort 14; Hudson 10; Skua 4; Swordfish 11.

Personnel losses were high, with 915 flying personnel and 277 ground crew dead, missing or captured, of these 312 were pilots. A further 98 pilots and 86 other aircrew were injured. These air and groundcrew were the highly trained regular air force personnel who would in due course have formed the instructors and leaders of the RAF, so it is impossible to quantify their loss. For those who returned to fight again, the Blitzkrieg and the mobility of the Luftwaffe was an enlightening and awesome experience, the utter confusion of the evacuation was traumatic, yet morale was high enough in general that defeat was not even contemplated. As put by Flight Sergeant R. Stride,* chief of No. 114 Squadron's Radio Section:

"We (the RAF) were a cocky shower of B********s and even then, still thought we could not be beaten."

Maybe it took four more years, but he was right. Just after D Day in June 1944 he landed on the Normandy beaches with the Servicing Commandos of the Royal Air Force, then he went on to Burma until VJ Day.

A Bf109E-1 of II/JG53. A Burnt out French aircraft is in the foreground.

---

*Joined the RAF Servicing Commandos afterwards as a Warrant Officer.

Chapter Six
Aircraft of the British Air Forces France

The RAF was Trenchard's legacy, an independent air force and capable of independent air operations, not the distorted version that his opponents have publicised. The RAF were fortunate in many ways, for in most cases where mistaken policies or tactics were adopted, and experience had proved them incorrect, corrections were made. There was no Hermann Göring to ignore facts and insist on his point of view. Some specifications were wrong, some tactics were wrong, but most were correct and those that were not were corrected or modified. Specifications originated with the Air Staff asking for a specific financial sum being allocated from the Air Estimates for the aircraft in the experimental programme. Then during the following year the Air Staff would ask the Director of Operational Requirements to prepare for each aircraft type a statement covering its main operational features. These operational requirements were then handed to the Director of Technical Developments, whose purpose it was to ensure that the aircraft conformed to these specifications. To cover this the Director of Technical Developments prepared a technical specification to cover all engineering aspects, material to be used, testing etc. During this process the technical requirements would be commented on by the various specialists covering engines, electrics etc. All tender designs submitted against the specifications were analysed by the Director of Technical Developments staff, aided by the system specialists. This would then be followed by a conference convened and presided over by the Director of Technical Developments, which then analysed each design, placed them in order of merit and so decided which design(s) to proceed with. This normally resulted in two designs being chosen and a prototype of each being ordered, the final approval of course resting with the Chief of Air Staff.

Only four main types of aircraft were operationally based with the British Air Force France, two were built to a specification (Battle and Lysander), one was developed from a private venture twin-engined transport (Blenheim), while the fourth was initially built as a private venture based on two fighter specifications (Hurricane). While the Battle and Blenheim were adopted at the time as interim types, only the Hurricane stood any chance against the Luftwaffe that overwhelmed the BAFF and Armée de l'Air. A fifth aircraft was the Gloster Gladiator, which was flown by Nos. 607 and 615 Squadrons

151

These Squadrons had or were re-equipping with Hurricanes by May 1940 and flew some sorties with their biplanes.

The Battle, Blenheim and Lysander were roughly equivalent in type and performance to their opposite numbers in the Luftwaffe, the Ju87, Do17 and Hs 126. The Hurricane was inferior to both the Bf109 and Bf110 in performance at altitude, but could more than hold its own in speed and manoeuvrability at medium altitudes. In structural innovation the Hurricane was dated against the Bf109, yet its eight reliable Browning machineguns, wide track undercarriage and easily repaired structure produced a very viable fighter in the field. Unfortunately for Great Britain, France and the BAFF, there were not enough Hurricanes in the field. Likewise, the French equivalent, the Dewoitine D520, was insufficient in number to help.

1. Fairey Battle

When in 1932 the Air Ministry were considering a replacement day bomber for the Hawker Hart/Hind squadrons, they asked a number of firms to tender for an official preliminary requirement which covered the requirements for a fast, light day-bomber. Fairey Aviation, under their Head of Design, M. J. O. Lobelle, visualised this as a fast compact, two-seat low-wing monoplane powered by their Fairey P12 Prince engine. This engine was the result of an independent powerplant design team under the direction of Captain A. Graham Forsythe. The P12 Prince was a V12 liquid cooled engine, and was in direct competition with Rolls-Royce's PV12 engine (which became the Merlin). By the end of 1934 there were three P12 Prince engines that had completed 550 hours running under power, as well as having successfully completed a ten hour non-stop run at 520 hp, plus three one hour runs at the equivalent of 700 hp. At this particular date Rolls-Royce were not only having trouble with their PV12 engine, but were behind the P12 Prince in development.

In April 1933 the Air Ministry issued specification P27/32, in which the requirement for speed was to be comparable with that issued for the B9/32 twin engined bomber specification (for the Wellington). This P27/32 specification was more definitive, and to Fairey's surprise dictated a rather larger airframe than they had envisaged under the outline studies. With the increased equipment load required by the Air Ministry, it became obvious to Fairey Aviation that a larger airframe with a greater wingspan would be necessary. When tendering, Fairey sent a number of design studies to the Air Ministry to stress the need to change the specification, or the need for two engines if the speed and performance of the specification was to be met, otherwise an inferior performance would ensue. The basic design of all these P27/32

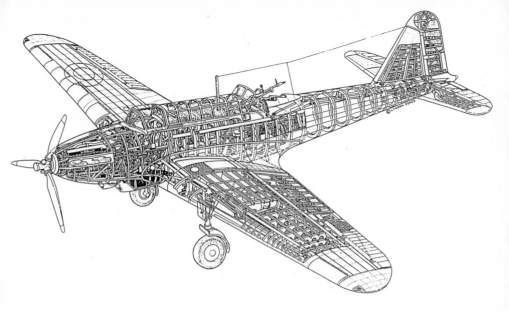

studies, right from its conception, was that the same structure would be suitable for all, whether single or twin engined. For instance, the single-leg retracting undercarriage was chosen, so that it could be almost fully retraced into a mainplane or into an engine nacelle.

On 24th October the Air Staff issued an amendment to the requirements, which increased the 'normal' and 'long range' requirements to bring them in line with the specification B9/32 for a twin engined bomber. The object of this was to make a direct comparison between the P27/32 and B9/32 bombers! Invitations to tender had been sent out to twelve manufacturers, but only seven submitted designs. These were Armstrong Whitworth, Bristol, Fairey, Gloster, Hawker, Vickers and Westland. The Fairey designs were nearest to the specification, and the Ministry accepted the single engine proposal. On 11th June, 1934, a contract for one prototype each from Fairey and Armstrong-Whitworth, was placed with the delivery to be within fifteen months (September 1935). Fairey was under the impression that their prototype would be powered with their Prince 12 engine, but no contract covered this. This had been deliberately done by the Ministry, so as to leave the way open for installation of the Merlin, when this became usable, although the original intention had been to use the Griffon engine.

Fairey, on 18th October, 1934, wrote to the Ministry asking for a postponement of the delivery date until December 1935, as having toured factories in the USA he wished to carry out a redesign based on knowledge acquired. This was followed the next day with performance calculations and general arrangement drawings of the redesign. These indicated a change from a semi-cantilever mainplane to a pure cantilever design, with bombs enclosed inside the wings. Also one long

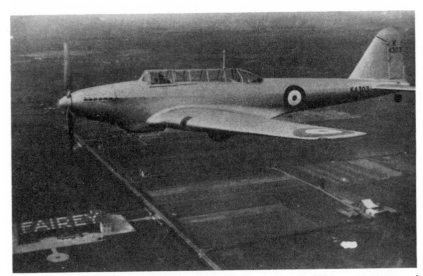

Fairey Battle prototype K4303 flying over the Hayes factory. Note the different crew canopy and Fairey-Reed two-blade metal propeller.

enclosed crew canopy was proposed instead of two separate ones, which improved the airflow, but the structural weight was higher and the performance lower. The Ministry accepted this revision on 19th January, 1935, and issued specification 23/35 to cover further development. This updated the aircraft and also added a further crew member, a wireless operator/air-gunner. Fairey opposed this as it would further increase the load and degrade the performance. The Ministry defended their decision, by insisting that the third crew member was necessary to man the rear gun, when the aircraft was on the bombing run and the observer engaged in bomb dropping. The Air Staff had by now reached the conclusion that the light bomber concept was dated and that the specification was not going to produce a high performance day bomber. Rather than cancel the contract because of the bad impression it would create they allowed the contract to continue. In 1935, when Scheme C was being discussed, the Sub-committee on Air Parity had recommended that an immediate order for 150 Battle aircraft should be placed. This was not acted on and it was not until 23rd May, 1936, that the first production order was placed.

Fairey opposed the whole concept of the light bomber specification as now postulated by the Air Ministry, but the Ministry was adamant and placed a contract with Fairey in which the maximum speed required was now to be not less than 195 mph! Having decided against the light bomber concept, it is all the more surprising that the Air Staff had now issued P4/34 for a light bomber with dive bombing capability.

A production Fairey Battle I under test at A&AEE Martlesham Heath, now fitted with three-blade propeller and non-standard spinner.

The delivery of the Battle prototype was behind even the amended schedule, and had its first flight on 10th March 1936, but it was as advanced as any similar light bomber anywhere. The test flying was carried out by Flight Lieutenant Chris Staniland, and the prototype was at this period powered by the Merlin I driving a fixed pitch Fairey-Reed propeller.

	Specification P27/32.	Prototype K4303.	Production K7558.
Bare weight	6,300 lb.	6,647 lb.	6,700 lb.
All up weight	not stated	10,770 lb.	10,898 lb.
Max speed at 15,000 ft.	not less than 195 mph.	252 mph.	253 mph.
Cruising speed	not stated	220 mph.	219 mph.
Maximum speed	not less than 195 mph.	257 mph.	252 mph.
Service ceiling	not less than 22,000 ft.	25,200 ft.	26,500 ft.
Take-off distance over 50 ft. barrier	500 yds.	445 yds.	690 yds.
Landing distance over 50 ft. barrier	200 yds	250 yds.	350 yds.
Range at 15,000 ft.	720 mile.	904 m at 200 mph.	1,050 mile 200 mph.

Figure 1. Comparison between specification and aircraft.

The Battle was one of the key types of the RAF expansion scheme and was the first service type to carry the 'Shadow Shading' camouflage of green and brown, known in the RAF as 'sand and spinach'. During the Munich crisis of 1938 the national markings were replaced with concentric rings of red and blue only.

Mixed

While the prototype was built at Fairey's Hayes factory, a new production line was set up at Heaton Chapel (Cheshire), and by 1938, a production line at Austin's shadow factory.

The defensive armament of the Battle consisted of one fixed forward firing 0.303in Browning machine gun mounted in the starboard mainplane between ribs 2 and 3 and a Vickers 'K' or Lewis 0.303in machine gun on a Fairey free mounting for the air gunner. During discussions at the Air Ministry early on in the design stage, they considered deleting the forward firing gun, but it was left for 'crew morale' reasons! The offensive armament was mounted on four bomb-carriers that were hydraulically raised and lowered from the interior of the wings, movement of the carriers operating the doors. These carriers held four 250 lb. bombs internally, or two 500 lb. bombs externally. One 250 lb. universal carrier could also be fitted under each wing outboard of the bomb doors. Regarding the internal carriers, before bombing the carriers were selected to 'lower' which lowered the carriers and opened the bomb-doors, thus placing the bombs clear of the wing structure for either level or dive bombing.

The Battle was, in its Mk I form, powered by the Merlin I which was rejected from the Hurricane production as this particular Merlin was not only unreliable but also down on power. Following Battles were powered by Merlin II and III engines, and in production form were fitted with DH two-position bracket type propellers. The aircraft was easy to fly, but being underpowered and late into service it was obsolete by the time that the war commenced. Yet no replacement for it was available, and so No. 1 Echelon went to war with an aircraft more suited to Empire policing.

Returning to the post-prototype period, trials were carried out at the Aircraft and Armament Experimental Establishment which resulted in a number of changes. Late in 1936 the production specificiation 14/36 was issued for the Battle I, and production trials determined that the all-up-weight was now 10,770 lbs. At this weight the aircraft met the requirements for a 1,000 mile range carrying 1,000 lb. of bombs at 200 mph. at 15,000 ft. By December, 1940, over 3,000 Battles had been produced, two and a half times the number originally intended to be ordered under Scheme F of 1936.

Contrary to numerous statements and articles, dive bombing was practiced pre-war as part of some squadrons' training. Operationally one section of No. 12 Squadron's attack on the Maastricht bridges carried out a dive bombing attack. However, when the enemy held air superiority, the conventional dive bomber was a 'dead turkey', even if proponents of the dive bomber closed their eyes to it. This lead to the development of the fighter-bomber.

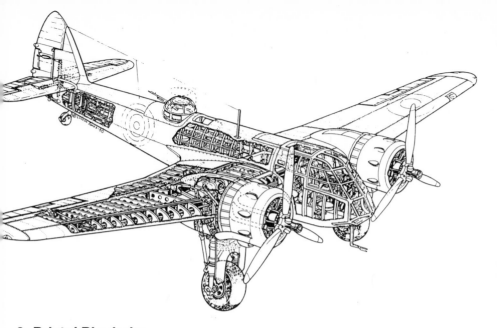

2. Bristol Blenheim

In 1933 at Bristols, Frank Barnwell and Roy Fedden discussed the possibility and potential of a small public transport aircraft. They reached the conclusion that such an aircraft, to be a viable proposition in the aircraft market, must have a cruising speed of at least 250 mph. From this Frank Barnwell, on 28th July sketched out a three-view drawing of a low-wing, twin-engined light transport monoplane, to seat six passengers. It was to be powered by Fedden's sleeve valve radial engine, the Aquila. This aircraft in the Bristol nomenclature was designated Type 135. It so transpired that Lord Rothermere at about this time declared his intention of combatting the American small monoplanes, by having built a British fast commercial aircraft. One of his staff, R. T. Lewis, the editor of the Bristol Evening News, being aware of the projects at Bristol and made known to Lord Rothermere the Type 135 development. On 26th March, 1934, Barnwell was informed that Lord Rothermere wanted the aircraft built for his private use. It was also his intention to bring its performance to the notice of the Government, to indicate that the RAF's existing fighters and bombers were dated. Being dependent on government contracts, the Directors of Bristol were a little apprehensive about this, but after a meeting with Lord Rothermere and the obtaining of his agreement to pay £18,000 for the aircraft, they agreed to proceed. The company then decided to build two aircraft, one for Lord Rothermere, powered by two Mercury engines, and a second one powered by Aquila engines. Revisions were made to the original 135 project and the capacity increased to eight passengers, being designated the Type 143. The Mercury powered aircraft was designated the Type 142 and had a slimmer fuselage than the Type 143.

Blenheim I prototype K7033 during its trials at A&AEE. Turret replaced with clear-view dome for trials. (RAE)

The Type 143 fuselage was shown at the Paris Show, where interest was shown by Finland, who wanted a similar sort of aircraft for both civil and military roles. So Bristols prepared a brochure on their aircraft, which they called the Type 143F, which was a convertable type with interchangeable nose and rear sections to allow its use in various rôles. The prototype (Construction number 7839) made its first flight on 20th January, 1936, and was civil registered G-ADEK. Unfortunately, there were no variable pitch propellers available to suit the Aquila and demonstrate its true potential, so the aircraft was stored. When the Aquila production (mainly hand built) was terminated after the outbreak of war the airframe was scrapped.

The Type 142 (construction number 7838) first flew on 12th April, 1935, and was civil registered G-ADCZ. It was powered by Mercury engines driving fixed-pitch four-blade propellers, which were later changed for three-blade Hamilton-Standard bracket type propellers. It then went to the A&AEE Martlesham Heath for its airworthiness trails, and it was at the A&AEE that damage was done when the undercarriage was accidentally retracted. At this period the Type 142 was faster than the fighter aircraft then in service with the RAF. During the performance and handling trials at A&AEE, it impressed the authorities sufficiently for the Air Ministry to request that they might be allowed to retain the Type 142 for full evaluation. It was agreed that work entailed by the evaluation would be charged to the Air Ministry, and not only was the request agreed to, but Lord Rothermere presented the aircraft to the Air Council and named the aircraft 'Britain First'.

The next step was taken by the Air Ministry, who requested from Bristol a design study of a light/medium bomber based on the Type 142. At a design conference called for by Air Commodore Verney of the Directorate of Technical Developments, held in July 1935, Barnwell presented the company's proposals for converting the Type 142 into a three crew mid-wing bomber, which they designated Type 142M. In this design study the wings were raised approximately 16 inches to allow for internal bomb stowage within the fuselage. The tailplane and elevators were to be raised approximately 8 inches and

158

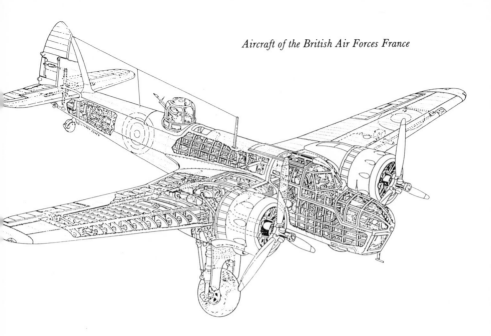

were to be of increased span, with the tailplane of the fixed type, as opposed to the 'variable' type on the Type 142. A Browning 0.303 machinegun and bomb-aimer's position was to be fitted in the nose, with a mid-upper turret of a partially retractable type to be installed on top of the fuselage just aft of the wings. With the removal of the passenger door and windows with the other alterations, Bristol stated in their proposal that the general stiffness and strength of the fuselage would be increased and cleanness of the outline improved. Officials were sceptical of the aircraft's strength because of the midwing position, which would entail cutting into a large section of the fuselage at its most highly stressed area, but the company's theoretical stiffness and stress calculations were to be proved correct by the final test results.

Consideration of the Type 142M by the Air Ministry was for its use as an interim medium bomber with which to re-equip the RAF, whilst the new aircraft types were being developed and tested. As an interim type there would be no restriction on it being sold to foreign powers acceptable to H.M. Government. In September, 1935, specification 28/35 was issued and a contract for 150 aircraft placed.

The Type 142M, Blenheim 1, was cleared for production in December 1936, and deliveries commenced in March 1937. Meanwhile an improved Mk 1 with increased fuel load and improved navigator's position was under development at Bristol. The prototype, K7072, made its first flight in September 1937, but the test pilot rejected the glazed nose because of distortion and glare. A period of development of this feature was embarked on, which resulted in the

Blenheim IV of No. 139 Squadron being maintained 'in the field'.

asymmetrical nose of the Mk IV Blenheim, which both satisfied the pilot's view and improved the navigator's position. The type was ordered into production against specification 11/36.

The finalised form of the Mk IV went into production in the summer of 1938. It had an extra tankage of 188 gallons of fuel, 94 gallons each side being added to the outer wings. Although the aircraft was strong enough to land fully loaded, this made the landing run excessive, so fuel jettison valves and underwing jettison pipes were installed outboard of the engine nacelles. The Mk IV was initially built in three forms, the difference being in fuel tankage:

Stage 1   500 – 900 miles with 280 gallons fuel,
Stage 2   750 – 1200 miles with 380 gallons fuel,
Stage 3   920 – 1500 miles with 468 gallons fuel.

The Blenheim 1 went into production with Bristol Mercury 8 engines and the Bristol Bl. Mk3 top turret; the Blenheim IV being powered by two Mercury 25 engines. The Blenheims were fitted with de Havilland two-pitch three-blade propellers and its bomb bay could accommodate four 250 lb. bombs, two 500 lb. bombs or Smoke Curtain installations. Small bombs or flares could be carried in the wing-centre-section racks.

The Bristol top turret was later upgunned with two Brownings and was then designated the Bl.Mk4 turret. Also fitted was a streamlined blister under the observer's position that mounted a rear firing 0.303 inch machinegun. Unfortunately, the Blenheims that went to France had neither of these modifications.

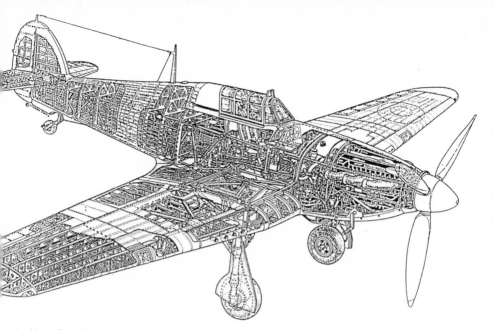

3. Hawker Hurricane

In 1931 the Air Staff issued specification F7/30 to the British aircraft industry, calling for a single-seat day and night fighter. The aircraft was to be powered by the Air Staff's choice of engine, the Rolls-Royce Goshawk, which was an evaporative cooled development of the Kestrel. Six companies tendered to the specification, amongst whom were Hawker with their PV3 and Supermarine with their Type 224. The contract in the end went to Glosters with their PV entry, the SS37.

Camm of Hawkers had meantime already commenced scheming out another new design using the Hawker Warren girder construction. This was the Fury Monoplane, powered by the Goshawk and in many ways based on the F7/30 specification. Its armament was intended to be four 0.303 inch Vickers machineguns, positioned two in the forward fuselage and two in the wing roots. Then came from Rolls-Royce the whisper of their PV.12 engine, with promise of 1,000 hp. This was sufficient for Camm to go ahead with a private venture redesign of his Fury Monoplane into the High Speed Monoplane. Stressing commenced in March 1934 with the detail drawings being started in the May. By the September of the same year Camm was in a position to submit to the Air Ministry the detail design and estimated performance, some of it in line with the F5/34 specification.

On 21st February, 1935, Hawkers received a contract for a 'High Speed Monoplane' K5083 against specification F36/34, carrying an armament of four machineguns. On the basis of an investigation by Squadron Leaders Sorley and Spreckley over the need to have increased armament, the Air Ministry decided to update their armament requirements to eight remote control machineguns. On

Hurricane prototype to specification F36/34. Features Watts wooden two-blade propeller and no ventral fin.

27th September an amendment to the F36/34 specification was issued calling for an armament of eight machineguns.

Camm was a jump ahead already, probably through the 'grapevine', and was investigating the 'levering in' of eight machineguns into his monoplane wing as well as in the redesigning of the wing to an all-metal type construction. Whilst the former presented little problem, Camm fortunately decided to treat the all-metal wing as a long-term project which allowed 490 Hurricanes to be produced by 3rd September, 1939. The stressed skin all-metal wing was eventually constructed and first flew in April 1939, which would have meant that very few Hurricanes would have been available for war in September if the design had waited for the all-metal wing.

The first flight of the prototype was made by P. Bulman on 6th November, 1935. As no Brownings were available, ballast was placed in the wings in lieu. The engine power was by the Merlin C, a version that was far from reliable and still required further development. Then on 3rd June, 1936, Hawkers received an Air Ministry contract for 100 Hurricanes to production specification 16/36 to be powered by the Merlin F. This was the Merlin I, but as this version was still having problems and was down in power, the Merlin II engines were substituted and the Merlin Is redirected to the Fairey Battle production.

The Hurricane's estimated design gross weight had been listed as 4,800 lb., but with the amended F36/34 the estimated gross weight grew to 5,200 lb., then when the prototype Hurricane was weighed it had risen to 5,416 lb.! The production Hurricane, however, with its various modifications and equipment changes, topped the scales at an average weight of 6,500 lb. This weight escalation was typical of most

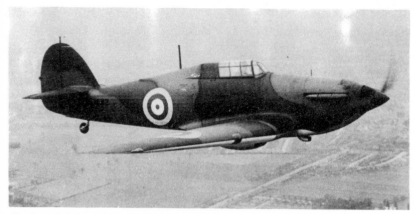

Hurricane L1582. Prior to its issue to a squadron and not fitted with ventral brake.

aircraft and was often related to the Air Staff's ever increasing call for equipment, armament or modifications. By August 1936 the Browning machineguns were available and fitted, and so allowed K5083 to go on armament trials.

These trials were satisfactory until carried out at higher altitudes, when the low outside air temperatures caused gun stoppages. This required some further redesign so as to channel hot air to the gun bays, but even this did not eliminate the problem entirely and stoppages at high altitudes or low temperatures still occurred in the early war years.

On the prototype the tailplane was strut-braced and the main undercarriage had hinged wheel doors at the bottom of the leg fairings, both of which were removed during the flight testing. Originally the tailwheel was also retractable, but during 1938, modification action taken for the production aircraft replaced this with a fixed tailwheel. This was followed by the addition of a small ventral fin to improve directional stability and spinning characteristics and faired in the tailwheel.

Between September 1938 and January 1939 the first production Hurricane Mk Is, L1547 and L1696, were at A&AEE on trials. The report from these trails established the speed at maximum power as 315 mph. (the F36/34 specification called for 320 mph. at 15,000 feet). The flying characteristics and controls were also reported on:

"... ailerons changed from light to heavy as the speed increased, although aileron response was rapid. In an eight turn spin there was 5,800 feet lost, but recovery posed no problems."

When the Hurricane was first introduced to the squadrons, the radiator had been enlarged and a ring and bead sight had been fitted. Even after the reflector gunsight was fitted the 'ring and bead' was kept as a back-up. The aircraft had the Watts two-blade, fixed-pitch wooden propeller fitted, and only during the Battle of France was a panic measure taken to introduce the three-blade variable pitch propeller. Some armour plate was fitted prior to war, but there was no armoured windscreen and no self sealing fuel tanks. These and more armour were only added in 1940.

The Hurricane entered service approximately eight months before the Spitfire, and with its wide track undercarriage was a more acceptable aircraft for the dirt and grass airfields at home and overseas than the Spitfire. Servicing and repair of the Hurricane was much easier than its companion aircraft and its deep wing offered more stowage for the grouping of guns and ammunition.

The Hurricanes that went to France in 1939–40 were the Mk I type powered by the Merlin II. Two Gladiator squadrons, Nos. 607 and 615, converted on to the Hurricane in France as the Blitzkrieg commenced. Wing Commander W. Blackadder of No. 607 Squadron had this to say of the changeover:

> ''There had been a lot of nonsense talked about the difficulties of flying a monoplane, but I don't think 607 pilots confirmed that view. We certainly found the Hurricane could absorb punishment and survive, while its big increase in speed over the Gladiator and its eight machineguns gave the pilot a better chance of catching and shooting down the Germans.''

	Hawker Hurricane I	Messerschmitt Bf109E
Wingspan	40 ft.	32 ft. 5½ in.
Wing area	258 sq. ft.	172.84 sq. ft.
Length (tail up)	31 ft. 4 in.	28 ft. 10½ in.
Aspect ratio	6.2	6.0
Empty weight	4,710/5,420 lb.	4,472/4526 lb.
Gross weight	6,040/6,750 lb.	5,667/5,747 lb.
Armament	eight 0.303 in. Browning.	four 7.9 mm. or two 7.9 mm. and two 20 mm MG/FF
Engine	Merlin 1,030 bhp. at takeoff. 965 hp. at full throttle height.	DB601 1,100 bhp. at takeoff. 950. hp at full throttle height.
Maximum speed at sea level	246 mph.	283 mph.
5,000 feet	264 mph.	302 mph.
15,000 feet	310 mph.	338mph.
20,000 feet	306 mph.	343 mph.
25,000 feet	293 mph.	328 mph.
Maximum speed at full throttle height	311 mph. at 17,500 feet	348 mph. at 17,500 feet.
Service ceiling	32,800 feet	35,200 feet.
Operational ceiling	31,400 feet	31,900 feet.

Figure 2. Comparison between Hurricane I and Bf109E.

164

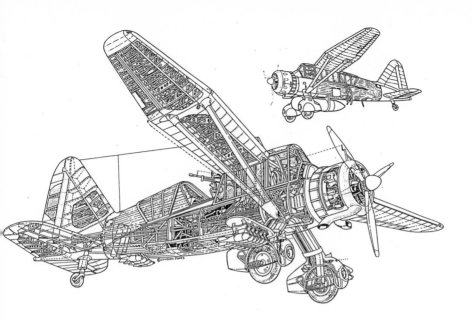

4. Westland Lysander

The Lysander was Westland's answer to the Air Staff's requirements for a replacement for the army co-operation Hawker Audax. Although the Handley Page Gugnunc may have demonstrated what eventually became known as STOL (short take-off and landing) in modern terminology, the Lysander was to demonstrate this in production and operational form prior to and during the war years. It became obvious to the RAF in the 1930s that standardising on the Hart series of aircraft namely the Hind, Osprey, Demon and Audax would not answer the situation. A jack of all trades range of aircraft, would not always be the answer to their problem. Westlands canvassed around the army co-operation squadrons for the pilot's opinions and these were the main points stipulated: For army co-operation aircraft there was needed good forward and downward visibility for the pilot, good low speed control, ability to land and take-off in a small space, hardly the known capabilities of the Audax! Petter and his staff spent many hours on these discussions, so as to ensure success, or at least give their design the features that would give it a chance in competition with other manufacturers' designs.

At Westland, under Arthur Davenport's instructions, the chief stressman, John Digby, drew up an outline general arrangement drawing of a high-wing aircraft, with the crew in an enclosed cockpit. The aircraft featured a retracting undercarriage and the pilot seated forward of the mainplane leading edge. Petter had fundamental changes made to this, which altered the mainplane outline and configuration considerably, the undercarriage also being made non-retractable. The mainplane was based on a D nose mainspar, with

Lysander N1200 at Abingdon in 1939 being viewed by NCO aircrew of No. 15 Squadron.

taper from mid-span outboard on the leading and trailing edges. It also tapered inboard to the centre-section to provide the pilot with a better view. The high-wing had its bending and torsion loads taken by large 'V' struts connected to the undercarriage arch to the midspan of the wings. The undercarriage arch comprised of a single heavy guage square-section extrusion formed in the shape of a wide inverted 'U'.

To improve the handling at low speeds, and thus provide a slow approach speed with short landing and take-off runs, leading-edge slats were linked to slotted trailing-edge flaps.

The P8 Lysander first prototype was K6127, and it made its first flight on 15th June, 1936, flown by Harald Penrose. It was still in its red doped fabric, the undercarriage was unfaired and the engine drove a fixed pitch wooden propeller. Early flight tests soon showed up problems, the two major ones being longitudinal instability and insufficient elevator control with power 'off', as at that time the tailplane was of the fixed type. When the aircraft went to A&AEE for trails, the pilots there also reported the instability and elevator problems. This resulted in Westlands having to increase the tailplane area as well as making the tailplane adjustable by manual control from the cockpit.

Further flight trials by Penrose showed a vast improvement, but raised a further problem, because on landing it was necessary to move the tailplane to a large negative angle. This was quite satisfactory under normal landing conditions, but if it became necessary to execute an overshoot procedure, the control column had to be held firmly forward as the tailplane trim was wound off. Should an engine fail under such circumstances, the possibility of the aircraft getting into a stalled position was real indeed. Petter refused to authorise any further alteration to the tailplane, and surprisingly enough the A&AEE test pilots accepted the aircraft, as the cockpit was placarded to this effect,

166

and the Pilot's Notes covered this handling problem. However, during the 'Lizzie's service this problem led to a number of fatal crashes.

On 11th December, 1936, the second prototype K6128 was flown and was sent to A&AEE for trials. It had a Mercury IX engine and a three blade two-pitch propeller. During the trials, while being flown by Squadron Leader Collings, the fabric tore off the wings during the diving tests which made it difficult to control; nevertheless, it was landed safely, even if a little fast!

In June, 1938, approximately two years after the prototype first flew, No. 16 Squadron received their first Lysander, the squadron commanding officer being Squadron Leader T. Humble. No. 4 Squadron received six Mk IIs by the end of the year, and Nos. 4, 13 and 26 Squadrons were fully equipped with Lysanders within the first few months of 1939. By 3rd September, 1939, there were 263 of the type delivered to the RAF and, to help in the conversion onto type, a number were converted to dual control, the first being L4740.

The Air Ministry had ordered 114 aircraft under the initial order, L4673 being the first production aircraft, and these were fitted with the Mercury XII engine. Following these came the Mk II aircraft, which although having the same dimensions as the Mk I, were powered by the Perseus XII. The first production Mk II being L4739, which was sent for testing in December 1938. In service the Perseus engine was found to be giving more trouble and also proving not so reliable as the Mercury engine, so the decision was made to taper off Lysander II production. Then with the introduction of the Mercury XVA the Lysander Mk III was introduced.

The Lysander pilot had two 0.303 inch Browning machineguns, one fixed in each spat and firing forward, the wireless-operator air-gunner having either a Vickers 'K' or Lewis 0.303 inch machinegun on a Fairey mounting. In order to allow the Lysander to carry bombs, small bomb wings, which were easily detachable, could be fitted to the spats, and on these bomb racks were fitted. The aircraft was very enjoyable and easy to fly. From the pilot's cockpit, visibility was good both for flying and taxiing. The biggest problem was the handling when overshooting or at maximum angle of climb off the ground as already mentioned. Wing Commander David Annand of No. 26 Squadron flew 480 hours on Lysanders, and described the Lysander as "... easy to fly and had good visibility", but says of the dual control version, "I did not enjoy sitting in the rear giving dual for landing. There was no forward visibility." Its visibility and manoeuvrability were probably the main reasons that more were not lost in France, and probably made it ideal for Air Sea Rescue and Special Operations Executive operations later.

Chapter Seven
Aircraft of the German Luftwaffe

A trick of fate, the action of one man, or the death of one man can sometimes have an effect on history out of all proportion to what actioned it. In the case of the German Luftwaffe, the death of General Wever in 1936 would spell the end of the long-range heavy bomber in Germany, and thus the inability of the Luftwaffe to operate in a strategic rôle. Without this ability the Luftwaffe were unable to strike at distant targets, such as the Russian factories in the Urals, and was thus relegated in general to the tactical rôle. For this rôle the Luftwaffe concentrated on single and twin engined bomber aircraft, single and twin engined fighters, as well as army co-operation aircraft. These were totally successful in Western Europe where distances were short, and against meagre fighter opposition, but the theory started to come apart when they met an organised and concentrated fighter opposition in the Battle of Britain. In fact, in the Battle of France where concentrations of fighters were met, especially Hurricanes, the Luftwaffe began to suffer heavy losses and the upgunning of its fighters and bombers began. The theory of the dive bomber, as demonstrated in peacetime in the USA, was to receive wholehearted support in Germany, and resulted in the Junkers Ju87, which in conjunction with armour and fighters cleared a path through France for the German Army. Yet this same theory and aircraft would prove as ineffective as the Fairey Battle once combat with fighters commenced, necessitating an even greater umbrella of Luftwaffe fighters, and the Battle of Britain soon saw the withdrawal of the Ju87 from the shores of England. The success of the Ju87 in Poland, Belgium and France, led many politicians as well as army 'experts' and others in Britain to scream for dive bombers for the RAF and army. However, history was to prove that the dive bomber was a 'dead turkey' as was the Battle, once the enemy held air superiority, and that the fighter-bomber would be the only effective answer. What should have been given priority in evaluation was the manner and effectiveness of the German Blitzkrieg, the training and efficiency of the German troops, and the Panzerwaffe tactics. What was outstanding in the Battle of France, and would be demonstrated effectively in the Battle of Britain, were the fighter tactics and formations. For whereas the RAF fighters appeared to be tied to paper attack formations and attacks worked out pre-war at Fighter Command, the Luftwaffe had digested the lessons learnt in the First World War as well as the Spanish Civil War. The

Luftwaffe attacked in loose formations. Flying in pairs, they attacked out of the sun, and flew top escorts to their bombers. The RAF flew in tight 'V' formations, where more time was spent watching the next man's wingtip than quartering the sky for the enemy.

The dive-bomber theme appeared to take over the bomber concepts and specifications that emanated from the RLM pre-1939, which resulted in the Junkers Ju88 and He177 with dive-bombing capabilities, though not to the same extent as the Ju87. Unfortunately for the Luftwaffe, as well as for the German aircraft industry, there was rivalry between Milch and Hermann Göring; Hugo Junker was not in favour with the regime; Udet was an expert flyer but not suited to the position of Technical Office of the Air Ministry (Technischen Amt); Messerschmitt was not in favour until the production of the Bf109; whilst Göring himself was not fitted technically or mentally to be head of the Luftwaffe.

It has been claimed that German Luftwaffe officers considered that the failure to produce a successful four-engined bomber was due to Udet's preference for twin-engined bombers. How much truth there was in this is hard to judge, for with the launch of the Luftwaffe and Hitler's aggressive intentions, there was a need to equip a large bomber force in the shortest possible time, and obviously twin-engined aircraft could be built in greater numbers more quickly than four-engined ones.

Germany's greatest bottleneck was the production of high powered engines to power their warplanes, and in a number of cases British or French engines were brought in to power prototype aircraft, with both Bristol and American engines being produced under license. Having said that, the airframe situation was very good, and the designed airframes were as good as, if not better than, those produced in other countries. This resulted in the employment of seven operational monoplane types during combat in the Battle of France. These were the Bf109, Bf110, Do17, He111, Hs126, Ju87 and Ju88.

1. Messerschmitt Bf109

This aircraft was a natural progression after the success of the Messerschmitt 108 tourist aricraft, which set a new standard in design and performance. The Bf109 was designed by Dipl-Ing. Willy Messerschmitt of Bayerische Flugzeugwerk (BFW) in 1934, and was intended to be powered by the 610 hp. Junkers Jumo 210A engine. Messerschmitt introduced a number of features in the design which reduced the weight yet maintained the structural strength, unfortunately, in respect of the undercarriage position and layout he introduced the Achilles heel of the design.

The German Reichsluftfahrtministerium (RLM) issued a specification for a new fighter in 1934, to which Messerschmitt tendered, though it has been said that he had been told by RLM officials that in no way would he get a production contract. Messerschmitt's design philosophy was to use up to date materials and methods, simple construction, aerodymanic devices on a small area wing and a retractable undercarriage. All these were incorporated in the Bf109, which featured a stressed skin all-metal wing with high wing loading of 24 lb./sq. inch, a thickness/chord ratio of 14.5%; this being offset by the use of Handley Page leading edge slots and slotted flaps and ailerons.

Although Messerschmitt was personally responsible for overall design, the chief of the design office at BFW was Walter Rethel, so the initial design of the Bf109 centred around these two men. It was decided that the focal point of the design should be the Jumo 210A engine (although at the same time making provision for the possible fitment of the Daimler Benz inverted V12 engine), and to design the most compact and functional airframe around it. The wing of the original Bf109 was of extremely light construction, based on a single spar with only five full ribs, reinforced by spanwise stringers. This wing was not designed to accept a heavy armament, one of Messerschmitt's few failings.

In September 1935 the Bf109V-1 made its first flight, but due to the unavailability of the Junkers engine it was necessary to carry out the test flying powered by a Rolls-Royce Kestrel, driving a two-blade Schwarz fixed pitch propeller. The undercarriage at this stage was hand-cranked up and down, and its narrow track combined with the aircraft's high nose angle was causing problems. As there was no time to rectify these problems before the aircraft was dispatched to the Rechlin test centre, it was dispatched in its original condition. Touching down there the starboard undercarriage attachment point broke, the airfield being renowned for its roughness. The damage was easily repairable, and the Bf109 was soon involved in the test programme, but the pilots were not impressed with the long nose which blanketed their view on taxiing, the difficulty in ground handling and the high wing loading.

The German authorities in the end insisted that the undercarriage track was widened, Messerschmitt's answer was to modify the aircraft on the spot by splaying the legs, which gave the Bf109 its characteristic look on the ground.

The only real competition to the Bf109 in performance was the He112, which, although having an inferior top speed and rate of climb, impressed the test pilots more with its good handling and better

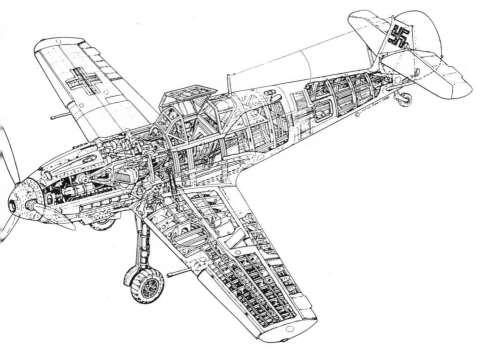

vision for approach and taxiing. It also had a lower wing loading, more comparable to a biplane. In the end development contracts were given to both types for ten further prototypes, and in January 1936 the V2 fitted with the Jumo 210A engine of 610 hp. joined the flight trials. On this model the undercarriage legs were already angled-out, and the legs and their attachments strengthened.

The specification had called for a single-seat fighter armed with two machineguns firing through the propeller, but as news of British multi-gun fighters filtered through, upgunning commenced. The third prototype was the first to have armament fitted, which was initially two MG17s, later to be increased to three MG17s, with the third one firing through the propeller boss.

A full year elapsed between the flight of the prototype and the arrival of the first pre-production aircraft, the first production BF109 was the B-1 series powered with the Jumo 210 engine with two-speed supercharger, a number of which were supplied to the Kondor Legion in Spain. By the Autumn of 1938 the C version with 20mm motor-cannon was being supplied to the Luftwaffe. But the cannon had problems, so the BF109C had two 7.9mm installed in the wings outboard of the wheelbays to supplement the two fuselage mounted MG17s.

Messerschmitt Bf109B prewar, fitted with Junkers Jumo 210 engine and two synchronized 7.9 mm machine guns.

The Bf109 had shown a tendency to swing swiftly to the left on take-off. Modifications eased this problem, but never eliminated it. Early flights also reported severe flutter in the ailerons and sometimes in the tailplane. In the dive the rudder became quite heavy as speed increased, becoming very heavy in a fast dive, then reversing trim.

At about the same time as the C version entered service, the D series also entered service. Whereas the C version had the Jumo 210G of 730 hp, the D version was powered with the Jumo 210D of 680 hp. The V10 prototype had been fitted with an early example of the DB600 engine and was the prototype of the Bf109D-0, which was fitted with the 960 hp DB600Aa engine.

The major production version of the Bf109 was the E type, the prototype of this version being the V14. In this model the wing was extensively redesigned and strengthened, with a spar having increased flanges, thirteen full ribs, with the root rib not only being extra strong but having a triangulated reinforcement as well. Even with this wing the limiting factor as regards armament was the position of the main spar at approximately mid-chord, and the thinness of the wing outboard of the wheel-wells.

With the introduction of the Bf109E the armament initially stayed at four 7.92 mm MG17 machineguns. Then on the E-3 model the MG/FF 20 mm cannon was introduced. This was a drum fed development of the Oerlikon cannon. Problems with this cannon were caused mainly by vibration, which could not easily be rectified, so the pre-production batch of E-0s were delivered with four MG17s. With the introduction of the E-1 the armament was two fuselage mounted MG17s and two MG/FFs in the wings. This was followed by the E-3 with an engine mounted MG/FF cannon, but again severe vibration made pilots wary of using it.

Bf109E-1 of 3/JG1 flown by Unteroffizier Hans Schubert.

The Bf109s powered by the Jumo 211 and DB601 engines had the engines mounted on forged magnesium alloy cantilever strut braced mountings in the inverted position, a position favoured by the RLM, as it gave an improved forward sighting line for the pilot. At the same time it allowed the installation of the fuselage mounted armament without raising the cowling line. With the introduction of the DB601 engine into the E airframe, the firm was forced to move away from the chin radiator of the earlier models, the extra power requiring greater cooling area. Ducted radiators were installed, one under each wing, requiring more wing strengthening to accommodate the weight and bulk.

The DB601A engine also introduced the Bosch direct fuel injection system and an oil system having a tank capacity of 6.48 gallons, with an oil cooler under the engine integral with the lower cowling. Messerschmitt had introduced on the Bf109B, C and D aircraft the variable pitch propeller. Now with the introduction of the 109E there was introduced the three-blade constant-speed, fully feathering VDM propeller. This was electrically operated and had the feature peculiar to some Continental engines, of having a hollow propeller hub through which a cannon or machinegun could fire

At the start of war in September 1939, the Luftwaffe fighter units had well over 1,000 Bf109s of various versions on their inventory, and by the beginning of May, 1940, there were over 1,000 Bf109s facing the Allies on the Western Front. These were dispersed amongst the following units, JG1, 2, 3, 26, 51, 53, 54, I/LG2 and JGr21.

If the Bf109 had any problems in handling, it mainly centred around its undercarriage when taxiing, although in the air while pulling tight turns the leading slats did tend to pop out unevenly, which caused a lateral wobble which could upset the pilot's aim in combat. This, combined with the rather tight cockpit and lack of rudder trim could impose a tiring load on the pilot, but even allowing for this, the Bf109 was a lethal weapon and in normal flight a delight to fly. Landing it could be a different proposition, for it could bite!

173

2. Messerschmitt Bf110

With the unveiling of the Luftwaffe, new specifications were issued for aircraft to replace those already in service. One of the RLM specifications issued in 1934 was for a Kampfzerstörer. This specification was later altered and split into two separate types, one of which resulted in the Bf110 design. When this emerged it was seen as a twin-engined low-wing monoplane with heavy armament, for which three prototypes had been ordered, all powered with the 900 hp. DB600A engine. The V1 model made its first flight on 12th May, 1936, but when evaluated at the Rechlin test centre it was considered that its manoeuvrability was not satisfactory and that it was also heavy to fly, in spite of having a maximum speed of 314 mph.

Four pre-production Bf110A-0s were then built, each armed with four MG17s in the nose and one MG15 in the rear cockpit, power being provided by two 680 hp. Jumo 210Da engines. These engines did not bestow on the aircraft sufficient performance, so ten Bf110B-0s were produced in early 1938 powered by 670 hp. Jumo 210Ga engines. With these aircraft development was carried out for the B-1 initial production type. In this model two 20mm MG-FF cannon were added in a more streamlined nose.

The idea of the Zerstörer is generally considered to have originated with Göring, being an aircraft with a fighter's speed and a bomber's range, heavily armed and powered by two engines. The idea appears to have been accepted with enthusiasm by the authorities, possibly because it suited them with Göring as chief of the Luftwaffe. Certainly, the Zerstörer was Göring's pride and joy, the long-range fighter escort for his bombers, but it would in the end require its own fighter escorts.

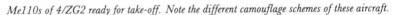

Me110s of 4/ZG2 ready for take-off. Note the different camouflage schemes of these aircraft.

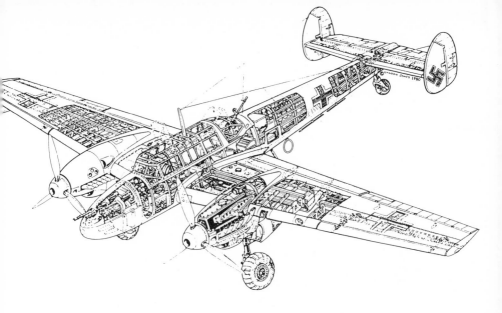

With the introduction of the Bf110B series the engine nacelles were improved and lengthened to eliminate turbulence, the nose was aerodynamically improved by lengthening, and the top portion of it could be slid forward to give access to the four MG17 machineguns. The B-1's two 20mm cannon were installed below the pilot and were loaded by the radio operator. With the installation of the DB601A engines in the V3 prototype the large radiator under the engine were replaced by shallow radiators under each wing outboard of the engine nacelles, with a small oil cooler integral with each engine under-cowling.

From the B-1 series onwards the wings were reduced in span by clipping the wingtips. With the DB601A engines installed giving a take-off power of 1,050 hp., the performance was improved to 336 mph. at 19,685 feet. The first series with these improvements was the Bf110C, the Bf110C-1 entering service in April, 1939, with I(Z)LG1. Further development introduced the Bf110C-3 and C-4, the latter introducing some armour plate for the crew. By May, 1940, the Luftwaffe inventory included 355 Bf110s, of which 248 were immediately available, 300 aircraft having been delivered by the end of 1939.

The C-4, when introduced, had an improved MG-FF cannon and a maximum speed of 349 mph. at 22,965 feet, and a maximum speed at sea level of 294 mph. The main type that served with Luftflotten 1 and 3 on 5th May, 1940, was the C-1.

Performance wise the Bf110 was good for a twin-engined two-seat fighter, and although the view forward and to the side was good for the pilot, and stability was good, it failed to be manoeuvrable enough to mix it with single-seat fighters like the Dewoitine D520, Hurricane

An Me110 has its DB601 engine canged in the field.

and Spitfire. In combat with the Hurricane or D520 its only hope was to 'pour on the coals' and get away, so as a day fighter with single engined aircraft around, it was a failure. There have been numerous accounts to prove the effectiveness of the Bf110, and though there is no denying its effectiveness as a night-fighter, it was disastrous as a day fighter.

Wingspan	53 ft. 3.25 in.
Wing area	413.33 sq. ft.
Length	39 ft. 6.25 in.
Empty weight	11,440 lb.
Maximum loaded weight	14,850 lb.
Total fuel capacity	279 imp. gals.
Armament	Two 20 mm cannon plus five 7.9 mm machineguns.
Maximum speed	335 mph. at 19,680 ft.
Maximum climb rate	10,000 ft. in 10.2 min.
Service ceiling	32,800 ft.

Figure 3. Basic data of Bf110.

176

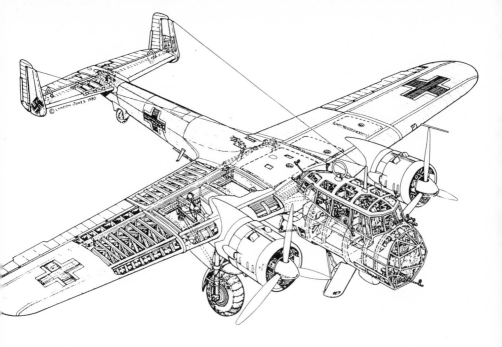

3. Dornier Do17

In 1933, with the upsurge of German aviation, Deutsche Lufthansa (DLH) issued a specification for a high speed mail-cum-passenger aircraft to provide a fast commercial service on DLH's European routes. Dorniers were interested in the requirements, and against them produced their Do17 design. This was completed during 1934, and the characteristic feature of the design was its exceptionally slim fuselage side profile, although in plan form the centre fuselage was broader than normal. As well as its high structural strength, the performance and handling were outstanding and it fully met Lufthansa's performance requirements. The Do17 prototype was a shoulder wing aircraft with a single fin and rudder, and powered by two BMW VI engines of 660 hp. The whole airframe was of metal construction and metal covered, except for the control surfaces. It had a two-seat flight cabin and two passenger cabins. The aircraft was passed to Lufthansa in 1935 for evaluation and two further prototypes produced for evaluation. The passenger accommodation was too restrictive and impracticable, and it was rejected by Lufthansa for those reasons.

The three Do17s were returned to Dornier and were apparently left well alone until a liaison officer from RLM flew one and suggested that they should be reworked or redesigned as bombers. Dornier undertook this work and in 1935 produced the V4 prototype as a bomber. This Do17 was now approaching the shape that we know. Twin fins and rudders had replaced the single fin and rudder, and the flight cabin now included a radio operator behind the pilots.

The first that Britain knew about this '*Schnellbomber*' was in October 1935, when one of the prototypes was demonstrated at Bückeberg. It participated in the 1937 Military Aircraft Competition at Zurich, its performance there being outstanding, and its slim fuselage soon got it dubbed 'The Flying Pencil'. What was not known was that the prototype had a number of features not incorporated in the production aircraft being delivered. Some of the theory behind the interest in the Do17 was that it would possess sufficient speed to outpace enemy fighters. The RLM wanted the minimum of modifications made to the new model before acceptance for military trials. The first military prototype had three crew, fuselage length reduced to 56ft. 3¼ in., and all the portholes had been eliminated.

Dorniers were continuing development of the type. One of these development aircraft was the V5, which was powered with Hispano-Suiza 12Ybrs liquid cooled engines of 775 bhp. This could attain a maximum speed of 243 mph. The V7 prototype was the first one to incorporate defensive armament, having one 7.9mm machinegun above and one below the cabin facing to the rear. It also introduced the glazed nose for the bombadier.

The first true production models were the Do17E-1 and F-1, for which the V9 prototype was the test vehicle. The E-1 was the bomber version and the F-1 was the reconnaissance version. This had the bombsight and bombgear replaced with cameras and provision for an increased fuel load. On the E-1 model the bomb bay could accommodate 1110 lb of bombs stowed horizontally, or with a reduced range the bomb load could be increased to 1650 lb. Manufacturing steps were taken with the production versions to make considerable 'breakdown' of the structure possible to speed production and sub-contracting. Fifteen of the Do17F-1s were despatched to Spain to the Kondor Legion in early 1937, in order to gain operational experience with the type. It had virtual immunity to interception by the fighter aircraft flown by the Government pilots, and this inclined the Luftwaffe to accept the theory of the fast, lightly armed bomber, though not all of the Luftwaffe leaders accepted this. In 1938 the Do17E and F models began to equip a number of Gruppen, the armament being three 7.9mm MG15 machineguns.

The Do17M model was the next to be introduced. This was based on the V8 prototype, which had been fitted with two DB600A engines rated at 1,000 hp. for take-off, which propelled it to a maximum speed of 264 mph. When it was decided to put it into production, it was found that this particular engine type was in short supply, which forced Dornier to investigate other engine suppliers. Eventually, the choice fell on the Bramo-Fafnir 323A-1 air-cooled radial engine which

*A Dornier Do17E with 750 hp BMW VI engines. Used by the Luftwaffe for reconnaissance.
(Dornierwerke)*

developed 900 hp. at take-off and 1,000 hp. at 10,200 ft. The
incorporation of this engine presented no problems and the production
line was quickly turning out Do17M bomber and P reconnaissance
aircraft, production commencing at the end of 1937. Fairly soon
afterwards there was again a shortage of the chosen engine, which
caused Dornier to re-engine the Do17P version with the BMW132N.
This developed 865 hp. at take-off and 665 hp. at 14,760 ft, which
increased the Do17P's operating range, without a military load, to
1,367 miles.

Do17s in formation.

Do17Z-2s of KG3.

Experience of the Do17s in Spain and investigations by Dornier resulted in a number of changes to the Do17's structure. These were mainly to improve its operational capabilities, and also changed its side profile from the 'Flying Pencil' outline of the early Do17. One of the bad features of the early variant was the lower MG15 machinegun, which had a very limited arc of fire and could not be fired directly to the rear. In the reconstruction of the front fuselage the roof of the cabin was raised, the nose portion housing the bombaimer was completely glazed, and the lower fuselage lowered to allow the incorporation of a rearward firing MG15, operated by a prone gunner.

These features were first incorporated on the Do17S, which was a high-speed reconnaissance model powered by DB600G engines and accommodation for four crew members; but only three of these were produced when the Do17Z was introduced. On this model a switch back to the Bramo-Fafnir 323A-1 was made, the DB600 engines being in doubtful supply, as there was considerable demand of these engines for the Luftwaffe fighter programme.

The Do17Z-1 model was similar in construction to the Do17S, and similar to the Do176M-1, with the exception of the front fuselage, but the model was now completely underpowered with the addition of a fourth crew member and the extra equipment. It was reported that its good handling characteristics had not been compromised, and was as good as its predecessors.

In retaining the improved features Dornier, in conjunction with the RLM, made the decision to restrict its bomb carrying capacity to a maximum of 1,100 lb. until the BMW323P engine was made available. This engine version had a two-speed supercharger and developed 1,000 hp. at take-off and 940 hp. at 13,120 feet. With the new engines installed the aircraft became the Do17Z-2, and the bomb-carrying capacity was restored to 2,200 lbs. With this bomb load the fuel capacity was reduced, which reduced the range to 205 miles with the maximum bomb load.

The operational Do17s commenced World War II with a defensive armament of three 7.9mm MG15 machineguns, but soon afterwards it was found necessary to add a further machinegun in the nose for the observer. Operational necessity also led to an increase in machineguns as the events of 1940 exposed this weakness in many Luftwaffe aircraft.

On 3rd September, 1940, there were 373 Do17s with the front line units of KG2, KG3, KG76 and KG77. These aircraft were of various models, Do17M-1, Do17E-1, Do17Z-1 and Do17Z-2. Production over 1939 was 600 aircraft, but in spite of its good handling charac-teristics, reliability and popularity with the aircrew, the production was tapered off, for it had neither the bomb carrying capability of the He111 nor the speed of the Ju88. Flying crews enjoyed the layout of the Do17 with its shoulder wing, for this allowed low-level flying with a good view to the side and forward. The aircraft was also used for shallow dive bombing, up to speeds of 370 mph. During the attack through the Low Countries and France, the Do17s mainly struck at communications, airfields and dumps. During the Dunkirk evacua-tion KG2 and KG3 bombed the troop concentrations there.

Berthold Kruger, lead observer of the IV/KG2 attack on Vraux, said of the Do17:

"We had many times before the war practised low flying and the Do17 proved herself outstanding for the task. She was a high-wing monoplane with excellent sighting for the pilot forward and below. As the propellers did not reach under the under-edge of the fuselage, the pilot could actually fly very low (below the crown of tree level) as the plane reacted excellently to each movement of the controls."

	Do17E-1	Do17M-1	Do17Z-2
Wingspan	59 ft.	59 ft.	59 ft.
Wing area	592.014 sq. ft.	592.014 sq. ft.	592. 014 sq. ft.
Length	53 ft. 3¾ in.	53 ft. 3¾ in.	51 ft. 9 in.
Empty weight equipped	9,920 lb.		11,484 lb.
Maximum loaded weight	15,520 lb.	17,640 lb.	18,931 lb.
Engines and bhp.	BMW VI	Bramo 323A	Bramo 323P
	750 hp.	900 hp.	1,000 hp.
Max speed at sea level	220 mph.	214 mph.	186 mph.
Max speed at 13,120 ft.	193 mph	225 mph.	224 mph.
Max speed at sea level	196 mph.	188 mph.	168 mph.
Max cruise at height	163 mph. at	218 mph. at	186 mph. at
	13,120 ft.	10,670 ft.	13,120 ft.
Max range with military load	310 miles	319 miles	205 miles with 2205 lb. bombs

Figure 4. Comparison between three Dornier Do17 types.

An He111 of KG40.

4. Heinkel He111

In early 1934 a specification was issued by the RLM in conjunction with Lufthansa (DLM), for a high-speed, twin-engined aircraft embodying all the up to date aerodynamic and structural improvements of the period under the guise of a transport aircraft. It has been claimed that the specification's requirements were so framed as to make the aircraft suitable as a ten seat passenger aircraft for DLH or as a medium bomber for the Luftwaffe. The structural integrity and construction was obviously too high for an economic airliner but necessary for a successful bomber. Nevertheless, Heinkels' design staff utilised all the technology available and experience gained from their past designs, such as the He70, to try and meet the conflicting points brought on by the requirements and rôles. It is noticeable, however, that very few He111s were produced as airliners. With the creation of the Luftwaffe during that period, as well as re-armament, it is difficult to reconcile the German's statement regarding the specification, and the operation of the He111 as an economically viable airliner is hard to accept.

The initial specification was issued to Heinkel and Junkers, with five prototypes being ordered from each manufacturer. Heinkel's approach was to utilise the ellipitical wing as used on the He70, as it offered the best lift to drag and efficiency, whilst the fuselage shape and structure was one of the most efficient. The He111's first appearance in civil form was made to the press at Berlin's Templehof airport on 10th January 1936, when it was revealed as an elegant, strong looking

182

monoplane. It was powered by two BMW VI engines of 660 bhp. at
take-off, with low-drag elliptical shaped wings. The design development had commenced at Heinkels in early 1934, and resulted in the
first flight of the He111A on 24th February, 1935. This was the
bomber version, which had a long glazed nose that terminated in a
single 7.9mm machinegun, whilst provision was made for similar
weapons in the mid-fuselage position. It was intended that it was to
carry a 2,200 lb. bomb load at a normal loaded weight of 16,755 lb.

It can be assumed that this first aircraft was not satisfactory, for
Heinkel had already commenced construction of a development. The
Official trials at Rechlin confirmed this, and were far from
encouraging. When the He111A was flown unladen it retained the
pleasant handling characteristics of the prototype V1, but when it was
test flown with the military load it was found to be both sluggish and
unresponsive, and its performance was unimpressive. In its maximum
loaded condition the test flights recorded 217 mph. in level flight with
a service ceiling of 17,720 feet. On the strength of the above the RLM
rejected the Heinkel He111A, but Heinkel had already commenced
flight testing of the V5. This was powered by the DB600 engine of
1,000 hp. and had its first flight early in 1936. Flight testing was
satisfactory and the V5 received RLM approval, going into
production as the He111B.

The He111B-2 was powered with the fully supercharged DB600CG
engine, which was rated at 950 hp. at take-off and 910 hp. at 13,120
feet, with a supplementary coolant radiator on each side of the engine
beneath the wing leading edge. The next aircraft were the C and G

183

models, which were transport variants, with six Cs and two Gs going to DLH. In these versions the bomb bay area was the 'smoking' compartment.

The He111D series was a result of the development and refining of the basic design, with a view to improving its performance. In this model the surface radiators had been deleted and a much deeper radiator had been introduced. The ejector exhausts led to a single ejector exhaust each side of the engine. The all-up-weight had now increased to 19,423 lb. but the maximum speed had risen to 255 mph. at 13,120 feet. Introduced in 1938 was the He111E-O bomber, which was powered with Jumo 211A-1 engines, had semi-retractable radiators, a maximum bomb load of 3,748 lb. at an all up weight of 22,720 lb. which was later increased to 23,370 lb.

In 1937 there started a further series of design studies at Heinkel. This was to improve the aerodynamic shape and improve visibility. The results completely changed the nose, which was shortened and broadened, the whole being glazed and the instrument panel attached to the cockpit roof. This shape would be incorporated in all future models, yet no attempt was made to upgun the armament, which remained at three 7.9mm MG15s. The engines were now DB601A-1s giving 1,100 hp. at take-off driving three blade VDM propellers.

The He111 H and P models were planned simultaneously, although production of the H did not begin until May, 1939, the prototype for the H being the V19, which first flew in January 1938. When World War II commenced the assembly lines were in the process of switching from the H-1 to the H-2, crew members now numbered five and the defensive armament had increased to six 7.9mm machineguns. Power was supplied by Jumo 211D-1 engines rated at 1,200 hp. The H-4 entered service early in 1940 and by May of that year there were He111s in KG1, KG4, KG26, KG27, KG53 and KG55.

In France in 1939-40 the He111 was no longer the potent weapon for day operations it had been in Spain 1937-38, and with its inadequate defensive armament it required a fighter escort. It must be remembered that its maximum bomb load of 4,410 lb. was comparable with that of the Wellington, with some of its performance figures in excess of that of the British aircraft. It was past its heyday by 1940, certainly as a day bomber, but, for that period of time, its handling characteristics were good and the aircraft stable around all axis. The fuel system comprised two tanks per engine, a main and a reserve, yet rather strangely for such a well engineered aircraft, no crossfeed was fitted. This meant that in the case of one engine failing, the fuel on that side could not be fed to the other engine in case of fuel shortage.

Heinkel He111 of 6/KG1 in flight with companion in distance . . . obviously no RAF fighters around. Note that it has been upgunned.

A further failing in the aircraft's design must surely have been the greenhouse effect of the huge amount of cockpit glazing and framing which must have posed problems in bad weather. Provision was made to raise the pilot's seat and controls and to allow the pilot to slide back the entry panel and for him to sit above the glazing. He was protected by a small retractable windscreen. This feature had only been introduced with the deletion of the stepped cockpit and the change to a completely glazed nose.

	He111B-2	He111P-4	He111H4-1
Wingspan	74 ft.	74 ft.	74 ft. 1¾ in.
Wing area	942.917 sq. ft.	942.917 sq. ft.	931.07 sq. ft.
Length	57 ft. 5 in.	53 ft. 9½ in.	53 ft. 9½ in.
Empty equipped weight	12,875 lb.	Not known	19,136 lb.
Maximum loaded weight	22,046 lb.	29,762 lb.	30,865 lb.
Engines and bhp.	DB600.CG	DB601A-1	Jumo 211F-1
	950 bhp.	1100 bhp.	1,400 bhp.
Max speed and height	230 mph. at	247 mph. at	255 mph at
	13,120 ft.	16,400 ft.	13,125 ft.
Max cruise at sea level	174 mph.	194 mph.	–
Max cruise and height	202 mph. at	232 mph. at	205 mph. –
	13,120 ft.	16,400 ft.	height not known
Service ceiling	22,966 ft.	26,250 ft.	27,885 ft.
Max range with			
Bomb load	565 miles	1,224 miles	1,212 miles

Figure 5. Comparison between three He111 versions.

Henschel Hs126 of Aufklarungsgruppe 10 'Tannenburg'.

5. Henschel Hs126

In 1935 there was produced by the Henschel company a short-range reconnaissance aircraft for the Luftwaffe, the Hs122, three prototypes being constructed and tested. The first prototype was powered by the Rolls-Royce Kestrel engine and the other two by 600 hp. Siemens 22B radial engines. These were followed by a small batch of pre-production aircraft of this all-metal parasol monoplane, but when tested its performance was found to be no better than aircraft already in service, such as the He46.

In early 1936 the Henschel design staff began a project based on the Hs122, which used basically a redesign of the Hs 122 in that it retained the parasol wing layout and the Hs126 V-1 prototype was converted from the Hs122A-04 airframe. The Hs126 incorporated a redesigned wing and the strutted undercarriage of the Hs122 was replaced by a cantilever one, with the cockpit being semi-enclosed. This first prototype was flown powered by the 610 hp. Jumo 210 engine, but the V-2 was powered by the 830 hp. Bramo-Fafnir 323A-1 radial engine, as was the third prototype. This latter aircraft differed in a number of ways, having the same vertical surfaces as the first prototype, which differed from the second prototype, and the angle of the undercarriage legs was set at right-angles to the fuselage datum.

In February, 1937, Göring announced that the Hs126 would be the new army reconnaissance aircraft. The Mobilisation Plan of April 1938 envisaged 85 Hs126 aircraft at first line units and 25 employed on training, but by June 1938 only 13 had been produced. RLM production plans envisaged that by the end of the financial year 1939-40 there would be 786 Hs126s available. With the issue of the Production Plan 11, it was decided that of the 689 Hs126s required, 218 would be produced by April 1939 and the remainder after. Another projection was for ten army reconnaissance squadrons of Hs126s and FW189s by Autumn 1942.

A pre-production batch of ten Hs126A-0s were produced by the end of 1937, which were basically similar to the V3, and were soon delivered to units for evaluation. The aircraft proved popular and a vast improvement on the existing range of reconnaissance aircraft, having excellent handling characteristics and performance for a close-support reconnaissance type.

Production settled on the definitive Hs126B-1 powered by the Bramo-Fafnir 323A-1, which developed 830 hp. at 13,120 feet. This aircraft had been preceded by the A-1 powered by the BMW 132 Dc engine, which entered service in 1938. But it was the B-1 model with enhanced performance which was the main model used. This started entering service in mid-1939. It had a fuselage of stressed-skin metal monocoque, which was built in two sections and joined on the centreline. The mainplane was built around two main girder spars and had slotted ailerons fitted inboard of the ailerons. The flaps were hydraulically operated. The tailplane was attached to the fin and braced by four struts, with all control surfaces balanced statically and aerodynamically.

By the start of the war the Hs126 equipped the majority of army co-operation reconnaissance units, with 257 on the Luftwaffe's inventory, and by the start of May 1940 there were 344 in reconnaissance Staffeln. The Hs126 was armed with a fixed forward firing MG17 machinegun with a free mounted 7.9mm MG15 in the rear cockpit. Five 22 lb. bombs or one 110 lb. bomb could be carried under the fuselage. On operations the aircraft was rarely flown above 6,000 feet, sometimes flying low to use the countryside contours or features as protection while providing tactical information direct to their assigned army corp.

From 1st April 1937 until 30th September, 1938, there were 101 Hs126 aircraft produced and the final production run finished with a total of 752 aircraft. The Hs126 units suffered heavy casualties during the German Army advance, and many returned to Germany for re-equipment in July 1940.

	Henschel 126	Lysander I
Wingspan	47 ft. 6¾ in.	50 ft. 6¾ in.
Wing area	340.14 sq. ft.	260 sq. ft.
Length	35 ft. 7 in.	30 ft. 6 in.
Empty weight	4,476 lb.	4,065 lb.
Loaded weight	6,813 lb.	5,920 lb.
Armament, guns	2 mgs.	3 mgs.
bombs	110 lb.	500 lb.
Max speed at sea level	193 mph.	206 mph.
Max speed	221 mph.	229 mph.
Climb	7.2 min. to 13,120 ft.	3.1 min. to 5,000 ft.
Service ceiling	27,232 ft.	26,000 ft.

Figure 6. Comparison between Hs126 and Lysander aircraft.

Ju87B-1 of II/StG2. (Immelmann)

6. Junkers Ju87

It would be fair comment to state that this aircraft stemmed from the interest shown by Ernst Udet in a dive-bombing demonstration in 1933, which was carried out in the USA by Curtiss 'Helldivers'. The small aircraft with only two crew appealed to him and fitted in with Hitler's idea of a large quickly assembled air force. The Ju87 brought the name 'Stuka' to the English language. A shortened version of Sturzkampfflugzeug (German for dive bomber) was applied in general to the Ju87. Even when Udet was appointed Inspector of Fighters in 1936 the dive bomber still retained his interest, so Junkers had his firm backing in any official discussions.

With the acceptance of the dive bombing theory, it was seen as the offensive tool for use in support of German ground forces. The Ju87 most probably had its origins in the Junkers K47, which was built in Sweden in 1928. In 1935 a competition was launched for a Sturz-kampfflugzeug for the Luftwaffe. The Junkers design team project was a monoplane having anhedral on the inner plane and dihedral on the outer wing. This produced an inverted gull-wing, which at its lowest point had an extended fairing to cover the undercarriage. The

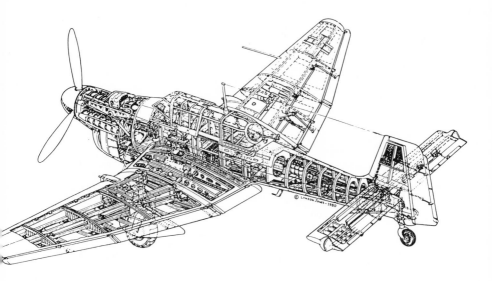

V1 was powered with the Rolls-Royce Kestrel engine and had square shaped twin fins and rudders.

The first prototype was soon lost during testing, when during a terminal velocity dive, tail flutter occurred. So the V2 was modified with a single vertical tail surface, and though it was still powered by a Kestrel engine, it now had a large deep radiator. The V3 was the first prototype to be fitted with the Junkers Jumo 210A 610 hp. engine, with a three-blade propeller. The V4 was the first on which was introduced the fork to swing the bomb clear of the propeller in a dive and also introduced the automatic pull-out control for dive bombing. Special dive brakes of slat-type were introduced. These were designed to restrict the dive speed to a maximum of 375 mph., which was the speed that the design team considered was safe before structural failure.

The initial programme called for 250 aircraft. The first, the Ju87A, first appeared in 1937 and three of these went to the Kondor Legion in Spain. This model had a fixed forward firing 7.9mm MG17 in the starboard wing and a free mounted 7.9mm MG15 in the rear cockpit. The Ju87A-0 was the first to be fitted with the Askania designed automatic pull-out device. The Ju87A-1 had a maximum speed of 199 mph. at 12,000 feet in an unladed condition, whereas the Ju87B-0 with the Jumo 211D engine had a maximum speed of 234 mph at 15,000 feet with a bomb load. The Ju87B was the result of the Junkers design team's new look at the design and their proposals. This resulted

A Ju87B-2 of 7/StG1 suffering from a little damage.

in re-engineering with the 1210 hp. Jumo 211 engine and replacement of the trouser type covering for the undercarriage with streamlined struts and spats. Armament was increased to two forward firing MG17 machineguns and an improved canopy for the gunner. The bomb load was now increased to 1,100 lb.

Ten pre-production Ju87B-0s were produced in 1938 after the V6 prototype was modified as the B-0 prototype. This introduced the features mentioned previously, as well as enlarged vertical tail surfaces. The Ju87B series was the model most produced during the early war years, with the B-1 being replaced in production in late 1939 by the B-2. The B-1 model was the type encountered over France in 1939-40.

On 15th August, 1939, an artillery shoot in conjunction with a Luftwaffe dive bombing demonstration was held at Neuhammer. It ended with a tragic accident that eliminated 26 Luftwaffe personnel from any further war preparations. Aircraft of 1/StG76 were detailed to carry out the exercise, commencing their dive from 12,000 feet, but due to changing weather conditions after briefing, when low clouds were forecast, a thick mist had moved over the training area. This resulted in the leader just managing to pull out in time, but thirteen of the Ju87s dived into the wood without any chance of survival.

At the start of 1940 there were ten Groups equipped with the Ju87, with 720 aircraft available in May 1940, 419 of which were in frontline units. By that date the Stuka myth had been born, for with almost overwhelming air superiority over Poland the Ju87 had wreaked havoc wherever it was sent to operate. Over France, in a number cases, the Ju87s when met by RAF and French fighters, were despatched quickly. The aircraft was too stable longitudinally, and therefore of limited manoeuvrability. Though described as easy and pleasant to fly, it was also too slow, and thus an anachronism in any area where the enemy held air superiority. Although this lesson was not learnt in France it was repeated over the British coast in the Battle of Britain. In a dive the aircraft was steady, the elevators being moderately light in the dive initially, but becoming heavier as the speed built up.

The German Luftwaffe planned the mass production of the Ju87, and the RLM production plans envisaged that by the end of 1939–40 financial year there would be 973 aircraft of this model produced. The Ju87 design was an anachronism by May 1940, but as long as the Luftwaffe held air superiority, and the enemy was short of anti-aircraft weapons (or too petrified to use them) the 'Stuka' could accurately place its load. The material damage in France against troops was only severe when the Ju87s attacked badly disciplined troops, or troops without ack-ack weapons, but the morale effect was greater. What was outstanding was the speed of answering any call from the advancing German troops who treated the Ju87 as quick call artillery. Some crews flew up to nine sorties a day in France.

These were the pre-requisites of a successful Ju87 operation, but this was totally ignored by the dive-bomber protagonists as well as the 'experts' of the British Army. For that service, as well as politicians, were to demand that dive-bombers be produced. Fortunately, the Air Ministry and the Ministry of Aircraft Production refused to sanction the interruption of the British aircraft programme, for at that stage in the war the RAF needed fighters. As was to be proved in North Africa and Italy, it was the fighter-bomber that was to be feared not the Ju87, which required a fighter escort.

The Ju87 would be used in every area that the German tentacles reached out for, and was successful as long as the Luftwaffe maintained a measure of air superiority. It created its own legend as well as a host of myths, and the myths live on as long as there are ex-members of the Stukagruppen or Dunkirk warriors around.

	Battle	Junkers 87B
Wingspan	54 ft.	45 ft. 3½ in.
Wing area	422 sq. ft.	343.3 sq. ft.
Length	52 ft. 1¾ in.	36 ft. 1 in.
Weight, empty	6,647 lb.	5,980 lb.
take-off	10,900 lb.	9,560 lb.
Engine type	RR. Merlin	Junkers Jumo 211
Engine bhp. at take-off	1,030 bhp.	1,200 bhp.
Armament, guns	*two 0.303 in. mg.	three 7.9 mm mg.
bombs	1,000 lb.	**1,200 lb.
Max speed at sea level	210 mph.	211 mph.
Max speed at height	252 mph. at 15,000 ft.	238 mph. at 13,410 ft.
Rate of climb, initial	895 ft/min.	
maximum	980 ft/min.	
Service ceiling	23,500 ft.	26,248 ft.

*during 1940 increased to three.   **later increased with increased bhp.

Figure 7. Comparison between Battle and Ju87.

191

7. Junkers Ju88

The Technical Office of the RLM, in early 1935, issued their requirements for a Kampfzerstörer (bomber-destroyer) aircraft, but after due consideration the RLM changed the specification and introduced the Zerstörer (destroyer) requirements. There was also a requirement for a high speed bomber, the Schnellbomber. Amongst these requirements were:

- Lightly armed fast aircraft
- a crew of three
- one machinegun
- normal bomb load of 1,100 lb.
- maximum bomb load of 1,765 lb.
- top speed of 310 mph,
- radius of action of 750 miles
- capable of operating from short, rough runways.

Two design studies were projected by the Junkers design team, the second of which was the Ju88. Project work commenced in January 1936 and the RLM, after deliberation, settled on the Ju88 design. Construction was authorised and began in May 1936.

The first prototype, the Ju88V-1, was registered D-AQEN and first flew on 21st December 1936, being powered by two 1,000 hp. DB600A engines. It was a three-seat, low-wing, all-metal monoplane having an extensively glazed crew compartment with the lower part of the nose glazed. It was noticeable for its annular engine cowlings housing radiators in the front. The original undercarriage, as opposed to later models, had twin oleo legs for each main unit. These were electrically operated and retracted to the rear, with the tailwheel unit being retracted into the fuselage. Unfortunately, the V1 was lost fairly early on in its testing and was replaced by the V2. This was similar and carried the registration D-AREN.

The V3 prototype had its first flight on 13th September, 1937, and was the result of some redesign at Junkers and the re-engineering with the 1,000 hp. Jumo 211A engine. This engine was also fitted with the annular engine cowling and radiator, and would be the type of engine that powered all Ju88A series aircraft. The V3 was noticeable for having the redesigned cockpit canopy and nose similar to production aircraft. This aircraft was sent to Rechlin in late 1937, where it was extensively tested. The results satisfied the RLM to the point that the Ju88 was selected for further development and production.

The V4 was completed in February, 1938, and had an increased maximum weight, a change in the glazed nose and the fitting of a ventral gondola or 'bola'. With this and a fourth crew member with a

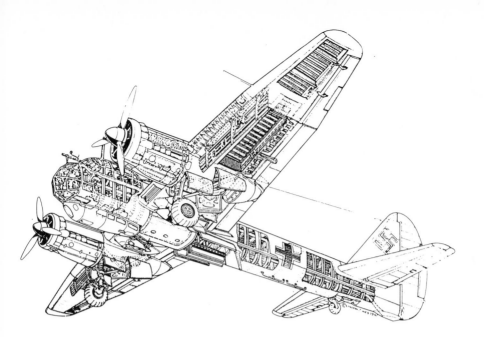

7.9mm MG15 machine gun in the rear of the gondola, which was offset to starboard, the weight was increased.

By this time the RLM had added a dive-bombing capability to the specification and so the V6 aircraft, when produced, was fitted with dive brakes hinged beneath the front main spar. This prototype also had the single oleo type main wheel units which were hydraulically operated. It also had four blade propellers, and was the prototype for the pre-production Ju88A-0 model. The V7, V8 and V9 differed very little from the V6, although the V7 was later fitted with 20mm MG/FF cannon as a prototype for the Ju88C Zerstörer. Fitment with the dive-brakes beneath the front main spar did not help an airframe that was highly stressed and already suffering 'teething' problems. This necessitated limitations being imposed on high speed manoeuvres on the early aircraft, whilst diving attacks were limited to 60 degree angles. By the time of the Battle of France, most of the airframe's shortcomings had been rectified, all except its inadequate armament.

Upon the insistence of Göring, Udet and Jeschonnek, the Ju88 was put into mass production even before all the testing of the prototypes had been completed. General der Kampflieger, Werner Baumbach, has since made the point that the aircraft had not been thoroughly tested and a large number of troubles showed themselves in service. The aircraft arrived at the units without effective night flying aids and 2,500 changes were required to fulfill the dive-bombing requirements. The modifications had still not been completed when, on 30th September, 1938, Hermann Göring gave instructions to Dr Kappenburger,

A Ju88A-1 of KG30 after a mishap (Büttner)

General Manager of Junkers, to create an armada of Ju88 bombers. Kappenburger was also given the necessary power to achieve this.

In production form there was a wide range of the Ju88A series, but the most common was the A-4, which was powered by the Jumo 211J-1 engine, although the A-1 was the type mainly seen over France. The Ju88A-1 which entered service in 1939 had a crew of four, a range of 550 miles with a 2,000 lb. bomb load, or a range of 250 miles with a maximum bomb load of 3,800 lb. and flying at 190 mph.

It was originally intended to introduce the Ju88 in late 1938 but due to the long gestation period in eliminating its shortcomings, there were only eighteen Ju88s on the Luftwaffe inventory in September 1939. These were with I/KG30. By the end of 1939, production had only reached 102, so there was little seen of the Ju88s until during the Dunkirk period of the battle.

In its bomber production form it was characterised by the multi-panel nose, as first installed on the V4. In this form, even making allowances for grouping the aircrew together for morale purposes, the impression was of a cramped interior for four crewmen. The centre of gravity, just behind the mainwheels, meant that opening up the engines on take-off had to be done steadily and slowly, or a swing developed. While the cruising speed was high (230 mph. at 17,390 feet) the initial rate of climb when fully loaded at 26,680 lbs. was not impressive, being 770 ft/min. up to 17,000 feet. Its maximum speed was high, at 293 mph., being faster by 26 mph. than the Blenheim IV, and so it formed an elusive target for the Hurricane to catch, unless intercepted early.

In the Battle of France the Ju88 was used mainly as a fast bomber, with reconnaissance potential, and gained the reputation of being a 'hot' aircraft for landing. This was probably true after the leisurely and ladylike handling of the He111, but this must not be allowed to cloud any assessment of this aircraft. In France, in 1939, its speed gave the Hurricane I with its fixed pitch propeller very little chance of catching it.

Epilogue

The Battle of France clearly signalled to the Air Staff of the Royal Air Force the failure of some of their tactics; the vulnerability of unescorted bombers, the inadequacy of the Battle and Blenheim armament and the capability of the German light flak. Despite the clear warnings against daylight operations, with the introduction of the new four-engined heavy bombers, they would again try daylight raids without fighters!

Some of the best and bravest of the RAF aircrews were consumed in the fire that was the Battle of France. Executing orders in the face of overwhelming air superiority and murderous flak, pressing in attacks in the face of hopeless odds; this was their "Charge of the Light Brigade". The battle resulted in the RAF suffering shattering losses, both in men and machines, yet the RAF were to inflict on the Luftwaffe its first heavy casualties. The Germans were to *officially* admit losses of 1,284 aircraft of all types.

At Dunkirk the aircraft of 11 Group were called upon to provide an air umbrella that they did not have the resources for, yet the BEF expected. The BEF themselves had not learnt the lesson of using rifle and machine-gun fire against low-flying aircraft and dive-bombers. All the same, and in spite of army jibes, the aircraft of 2 and 11 Groups, as well as the BAFF, were fighting the army's battle, often over enemy troops and away from the escape route to Dunkirk. For many aircrew there would be no Dunkirk, as they were killed or cremated in their crashing and burning aircraft.

Not only the RAF but also the Armée de l'Air were to suffer appalling losses in their fight against the new Hun invaders. Fortunately, some of them were to continue their fight in the RAF after the occupation of their homeland. At this crucial point in France's history there came to the fore an unknown General, who was one of France's greatest patriots, who threw in his lot with Great Britain when the future for this country was extremely bleak. This man was General de Gaulle, who would lead France once again back into the battle and a senior place at the peace table.

While the Royal Air Force can be blamed for using the wrong tactics during the battle, its morale could never be faulted, nor its determination to win. Yet the BEF were shown up time and again to be a generation behind the Germans in their military efficiency, operations and morale.

For some unexplainable reason British history and historians

195

A No. 142 Squadron Battle L5231 still in its shotdown location in winter 1940 . . . the Battle of Britain had since been won. (J. De Vos)

appear to treat Dunkirk as a British victory, yet it was the defeat of two armies, the British and French. The countries failed to provide modern weapons and organisation, their top Generals failed to understand modern warfare, not to mention the disarmament attitude practiced by the socialist dominated Governments in the early 1930s. For these failures thousands of Allied servicemen died, were injured or captured. For these failures the aircrews of the BAFF, 2 Group and the Armée de l'Air were sacrificed.

The Battle of France was to bring to the English language the word 'Blitzkrieg'. This dashing cut-and-thrust tactic supported by artillery, tanks and aircraft, was to bring to the British Army a new experience. While expecting air support, they failed to understand air support or anti-aircraft defence, and like the Royal Navy they completely underrated air power or the defence against air power.

Even in regard to logistics, transportation and communications the British Army in many cases failed. Witness the greasing-up of guns and tanks for the short journey across the Channel, mortars without ammunition, Lewis 0.303 inch machineguns instead of Bofors anti-aircraft guns, troops in one ship and their equipment in another. During evacuation there was artillery and equipment left on the quayside for the Germans, even when there was time left to load it. No wonder the BEF used the RAF and French Army as scapegoats! Remember also, it was a French perimeter rearguard that many British troops withdrew through at Dunkirk, it was a French Army

Vroenhoven Bridge over the Albert Canal in 1989; the bridge at Veldwezelt was replaced post-war. As can be seen, the destruction of the bridges would have left the Albert Canal as a formidable anti-tank ditch. (J. de Vos)

rearguard that fought on at Dunkirk until surrender on June 4th . . . when perfidious Albion had departed.

Not all French Army units fought so well. Whilst some panicked and were routed, some others fought to the last man. Some British Army units were outstanding, some actions best forgotten, some British troops were reported roaming the countryside undisciplined and without arms. By 16th June the Battle of France was all over. The BEF had been in many cases outmanoeuvred and defeated; the Battle and Blenheim squadrons had been bled and depleted to the point of exhaustion; large quantities of stores of the Army and RAF had been left in France; while Fighter Command had been reduced in numbers of aircraft to a point originally considered below safety. But at last we knew where we stood, the German enemy was across the Channel and had won the first round, from now on it was up to the Royal Air Force.

On May 10th F/O D. A. Cameron baled out of his No. 226 Squadron Battle near Diekirch, Luxembourg, where he landed in a tree. He was taken to the nearby city hospital where he later died from his wounds. Cameron now lies in a lone plot in the Suen cemetery. His grave has been tended by Mme de Winter for 50 years.

Appendix
Belgian Battles over Maastricht

On 11th May, 1940, the ten remaining Battles of 9/II/3 and 5/III/3 units, having escaped the bombing of their airfields at Brussels-Evere and Belsele, were at their emergency airfield at Aalter, (midway between Ghent and Bruges). From there they were preparing to strike at the bridges across the Albert Canal. At 03.15 hours the engines were warming up ready for an early morning reconnaissance, but just as the crews were ready to go, this was cancelled. Finally, between 05.45–06.00 hours the sun was well up nine Battles took off, flying in three sections of three aircraft. The crews and targets thus:

Battle T73	Capitaine Pierre and Leutenant Cloquette	} Veldwezelt bridge.
T60	Adjudant Verbraeck and Adjudant Dome	
T58	Adjudant Timmermans and 1st Sergeant Rolin	
T70	Capitaine Glorie and Sous Leut Vanden Bosch	} Vroenhoven bridge.
T64	Adjudant Binon and Caporal Legand	
T61	Adjudant Delvigne and Sergeant Moens	
T62	Adjudant Jordens and Sergeant de Ribaucourt	} Briegden bridge.
T68	1st Sergeant Wieseler and Adjudant de Coninck	
T71	Adjudant Vandevelde and Caporal Bergmans	

Although fighter cover was to have been provided by six Gladiators, these were attacked in the target area by Bf109s and only two returned to base.

Near Ghent the first section was attacked by two German fighters, the first victim being T60. Verbraeck was hit in the back by four bullets but continued until some minutes later, when Dome warned the pilot that he could not fire his machineguns anymore as his hands were shattered by bullets. Verbraeck crash landed near to Dendermonde and both were taken to hospital. T58 was shot down near Hasselt and both crew killed. T73 arrived at Veldwezelt, made one pass and then turned again into the murderous flak and dropped his bombs, scoring a near miss, then escaping back to Aalter.

The second section received the attention of 'friendly' heavy tracer from near Louvain, then near Tirlemont 'friendly' ack-ack opened up on them. Over Tongres vicious and intense flak opened up on the section with hits on the aircraft. Into the attack on Vroenhoven bridge, T64's bombs fell into the canal, whilst T70 and T61 had their bombs hang-up. Making a second pass both T70 and T61 were hit by flak and shot down, only Vanden Bosch managing to bale out, but too low. He suffered a broken back and foot.

The third section was fired at by 'friendly' troops near Lier and T71 forced to land, with Bergmans seriously wounded. T62 was also hit and set on fire, and although Jordens flew on for a while the fire became too intense and both crew members had to bale out, only to be shot at by Belgian infantry. Only T68 arrived at Briegden, dropping its bombs on the bridges, but missing and being immediately hit by flak. Upon force landing in friendly territory, Wieseler found his bombs hung-up and de Cominck with a broken leg.

In the aftermath of battle it has been reported that of all the Battle pilots, only Capitaine Pierre had ever dropped real bombs on the ranges from a Battle, there were no delay action fuses for the bombs, several of the crews did not know how to drop the bombs, there were no bomb-sights fitted to the Battles and, even worse, some of the microphones of the intercom had gone away for servicing. The only way that the observer-gunners could attract their pilot's attention was by shaking the control surface push-pull rods that passed through their cockpit area.

Amongst a number of Belgian air and groundcrews that escaped to Britain to continue the fight, was Adjudant Verbraeck. While serving with No. 11 Squadron in the Middle East, fate crossed his path once too often. When the Luftwaffe bombed LG 104 on 22nd November, 1941, he was among those killed.

Appendix 2

Luftwaffe Facing The Allies. 10th May 1940

Luftflotte 2 (Kesselring) .. IV Fliegerkorp (Keller)

Lehrgeschwader I	Junkers 88
Kampfgeschwader 3	Heinkel 111
Stukageschwader 3	Junkers 87

VIII Fliegerkorp (von Richthofen)

Stukageschwader 1	Junkers 87
Stukageschwader 2	Junkers 87
Stukageschwader 77	Junkers 87
Jagdgeschwader 27	Bf109
I/Jagdgruppe 21	Bf109
II/Lehrgeschwader 2	

Jagdfliegerführer 2 (Doring)

Jagdgeschwader 3	Bf.109
Jagdgeschwader 26	Bf.109
Jagdgeschwader 51	Bf.109
Zerstörergeschwader 26	Bf.110

Luftflotte 3 (Sperrle) .. 1 Fliegerkorp (Grauert)

Kampfgeschwader 1	Heinkel 111
Kampfgeschwader 76	Do17/Ju88
Kampfgeschwader 77	He111/Ju88

II Fliegerkorp (Loerzer)

Kampfgeschwader 2	Dornier 17
Kampfgeschwader 3	Dornier 17
Kampfgeschwader 53	Heinkel 111
II Stukageschwader 1	Junkers 87
IV Lehrgeschwader 1	Junkers 87

V Fliegerkorp (von Greim)

Kampfgeschwader 51	Junkers 88
Kampfgeschwader 55	Heinkel 111

Jagdfliegerführer 3 (Massow)

Jagdgeschwader 52	Bf.109
Jagdgeschwader 53	Bf.109
Zerstörergeschwader 76	Bf.110

Appendix 3

Comparison between bombers. 10th May 1940

	Blenheim 4	Dornier D17Z-2	Heinkel 111H4	Leo 451
Wingspan	56 ft. 4 in.	59 ft. 0½ in.	74 ft. 1½ in.	74 ft. 0 in.
Wing area	469 sq. ft.	592.014 sq. ft.	931.07 sq. ft.	710.4 sq. ft.
Length	42 ft. 9 in.	51 ft. 9½ in.	53 ft. 10 in.	56 ft. 6 in.
Engine type	Bristol Mercury 15	Bramo-Fafnir 323 P	Junkers Jumo 211	Gnome-Rhone 14N39
Engine power (each engine)	920 hp.	1,000 hp.	1,350 hp.	1,069 hp.
Empty weight	9,790 lbs.	11,488 lbs.	19,136 lbs.	16,600 lbs.
Loaded weight	13,500 lbs.	18,940 lbs.	30,864 lbs.	25,132 lbs.
Crew	3	4	5	4
Armament	two 0.303 in. mgs.	four 7.9 mm mgs.	three 7.9 mm mgs.	one 20 mm + three 7.5 mm mgs.
Bomb Load	2,000 lbs.	2,205 lbs.	4,410 lbs.	2,800 lbs.
Maximum speed at height	266 mph. @ 11,800 ft.	224 mph. @ 13,100 ft.	258 mph. @ 15,400 ft.	285 mph. @ 13,100 ft.
Cruising speed at height	180 mph. @ 15,000 ft.	186 mph @ 13,120 ft.	224 mph.	
Service ceiling	22,500 ft.	22,950 ft.	21,982 ft.	29,530 ft.
Operational ceiling.	27,000 ft.	26,904 ft.	26,500 ft.	26,500 ft.
Range, normal	1,950 miles	721 miles	1,212 miles	750 miles

Notes: (a) Armament on Blenheim, Dornier Do17Z and He111H4 were all increased after encounters with the enemy.

(b) Range is obviously dependent on load carried, maximum load carried will decrease the range.

Appendix 4

The 'Y' Service

This organisation was a branch of the Royal Air Force, and came under the AI4 Department, which was responsible for Air Intelligence. The 'Y' Service monitored all enemy radio and radar signals, and so produced the raw material for Ultra. In their ceaseless monitoring of enemy radio transmissions, decoding low-grade messages and plain language transmissions, they presented the tactical information, warning of raids, identifying of enemy control systems and much more.

During the Battle of France the 'Y' Service were not only understaffed but also underequipped, and with the continual retreat were never able to carry out their full function. Only during the Battle of Britain and after was the 'Y' Service to expand and have an important part to play in the war. The information supplied also enabled decisions to be made that would affect immediate combats before radar came into the act.

Many of the first 'Y' Service operators were pre-war amateur radio enthusiasts, both civilian and service, some were Post Office trained wireless operators, all were used to searching and listening to radio traffic. Their equipment was the Hallicrafters S27 VHF receiver, that covered the frequencies 2 – 10 metres, an oscilloscope and aerial array. With this the initial listening watch was on the short range VHF traffic.

The operator's service training commenced with technical training at Cranwell, mainly to cover wireless procedures, the flying often being carried out on the old Vickers Valencias. From there most of the operators were posted to various secret signals establishments, which, even at that early date, were recording and decoding Luftwaffe signal transmissions.

Appendix 5

Aircraft / Aircrew Losses

In an air battle, claims and losses are always difficult to assess, due mainly to over claiming (in good faith) on the part of both combatants. This is partly due to the speed of the engagement and combat, as well as the numbers of aircraft engaged in the combat. In the Battle of France and the Low Countries this assessment was made even more difficult by the loss of many squadron operational record books. The following have been collated by John Foreman, who very generously made the information available to the author.

ROYAL AIR FORCE OPERATIONAL LOSSES,
French Campaign
May – June 1940

Legend:

KIA	killed in action	
MIA	missing in action	
FTR	aircraft failed to return	
ret	crew returned without aircraft	
PoW	prisoner of war	
b/o	baled out	
*	Not directly involved in the Battle of France	

Note: For bomber losses only the captain is named.

Sqn. No.	A/C serial	A/C type	Pilot	Fate

10th May 1940

Sqn. No.	A/C serial	A/C type	Pilot	Fate
1		Hurricane	P/O Mould	Shot down: b/o
1		Hurricane	F/O Lorimer	Shot down: b/o
1		Hurricane	F/Lt Walker	Shot down: crashed
3	L1925	Hurricane	F/O Lines – Roberts	Shot down: force landed
12	L5190	Battle	P/O Matthews	MIA
12	L4949	Battle	F/Lt Simpson	FTR: ret
12	P2243	Battle	F/Lt Hunt	Force landed: ret
18		Blenheim	P/O Dixon	MIA
18	L1405	Blenheim	P/O Harding	MIA
40	L8776	Blenheim	P/O Burns	MIA
40	L8828	Blenheim	F/O Rowan	MIA
40	L8831	Blenheim	Sgt Thomas	MIA
57	L9245	Blenheim	P/O Thomas	MIA
57	L9246	Blenheim	F/Lt Wyatt	Force landed
73		Hurricane	F/Lt Lovett	Shot down
85		Hurricane	P/O Mawhood	Shot down
87		Hurricane	Sgt Nowell	Shot down: force landed Senon
103	K9372	Battle	F/Lt Wells	FTR: PoWs
103	K9270	Battle	Sgt Lowne	FTR: Belgium 1 PoW, 2 KIA
103	K9264	Battle	P/O Drabble	KIA
105	P2200	Battle	P/O O'Brien	MIA
105		Battle	F/O Rowan	MIA

105		Battle	Sgt Thomas	MIA
105		Battle	Sgt Robertson	MIA
142	L5231	Battle	F/O Roth	MIA
142	L5578	Battle	P/O Laws	KIA
142	L5238	Battle	Sgt Spear	FTR: ret
150	K9390	Battle	F/Lt Parker	KIA: Luxembourg
150	L5540	Battle	F/O Roberts	Shot down: PoWs
150	L5539	Battle	Sgt White	MIA
226	K9183	Battle	F/Lt Kerridge	Luxembourg, 1 KIA, 2 PoWs
226	L5247	Battle	F/O Cameron	FTR: pilot dead, 2 PoWs
600	L6616	Blenheim	S/Ldr Wells	MIA: Pernis NL.
600	L1335	Blenheim	F/O Moore	MIA: Waalhaven
600		Blenheim	P/O Rowe	MIA
600	L1515	Blenheim	P/O Anderson	MIA: Spijknisse
600		Blenheim	P/O Haine	FTR: ret
604	L1517	Blenheim	F/O Joll	FTR: ret

11th May 1940

1		Hurricane	P/O Richey	Shot down: b/o
17		Hurricane	F/Lt Donne	MIA
17		Hurricane	F/O Slee	MIA
17		Hurricane	P/O Hulton – Harrop	FTR: PoW
17		Hurricane	S/Ldr Tomlinson	FTR: ret
17		Hurricane	Sgt Lock	MIA
18	L9255	Blenheim	Sgt Le Voi	FTR: PoWs
18	L8861	Blenheim	F/O Bellis	Belgium KIA
18		Blenheim	P/O Holmes	Crash landed Chaons, flak
53	L9459	Blenheim	F/O Pantom	FTR: ret
54		Spitfire	P/O McKenzie	* MIA
73		Hurricane	P/O McFadden	Shot down: safe
79		Hurricane	F/Lt Edwards	Shot down: force landed on fire. ret
79		Hurricane	P/O Appleton	Shot down: force landed Le Touquet
85		Hurricane	F/Lt Lee	FTR: ret
87		Hurricane	F/O Campbell	Shot down
87		Hurricane	P/O Edwards	Shot down: KIA
87		Hurricane	P/O Mackworth	Shot down: KIA
87		Hurricane	Sgt Nowell	Shot down: b/o
87		Hurricane	P/O Saunders	KIA
87		Hurricane	F/O Joyce	Shot down
87		Hurricane	F/O Strickland	Shot down: b/o
88	P2251	Battle	F/Lt Madge	FTR: 1 dead, 2 PoWs
88	P2261	Battle	P/O Skidmore	KIA
88	P2202	Battle	P/O Mungovan	2 KIA, 1 PoW Belgium
103		Battle		Crash landed
110	L9175	Blenheim	F/O Gratton	MIA
110	N6208	Blenheim	Sgt Bennett	Shot down: PoWs
218	P2326	Battle	F/Lt Crews	FTR: west St. Vith
218	K9325	Battle	F/O Hudson	FTR: PoWs
218	P2249	Battle	P/O Murray	FTR: PoWs
218	P2203	Battle	Sgt Dockrill	KIA
235		Blenheim	P/O Smith	* MIA
235		Blenheim	P/O Savile	* MIA
501		Ensign		* Crashed Cat. E

11th/12th May 1940

77	N1366 Whitley	F/O Parrott	* MIA

12th May 1940

1	Hurricane	F/Lt Lewis	Shot down: b/o
1	Hurricane	F/O Drake	Shot down: b/o
1	Hurricane	S/Ldr Halahan	Shot down: belly landed
12	P2204 Battle	F/O Garland	Shot down: KIA
12	P2322 Battle	F/O Thomas	Shot down: PoWs
12	L5439 Battle	P/O McIntosh	Shot down: PoWs
12	L5527 Battle	Sgt Marland	Shot down: KIA
12	L5241 Battle	P/O Davey	Crash landed: air gunner PoW
15	L8847 Blenheim	F/O Bassett	KIA: Maastricht
15	P6911 Blenheim	F/O Oakley	KIA: Maastricht
15	L8849 Blenheim	F/O Douglas	KIA: Maastricht
15	P6912 Blenheim	P/O Frankish	KIA: Maastricht
15	P6914 Blenheim	Sgt Hall	KIA: Maastricht
15	N6151 Blenheim	Sgt Pepper	FTR: Maastricht. PoWs
21	L8739 Blenheim	F/Lt Watspm	KIA: Maastricht
79	Hurricane	P/O Parker	Shot down: b/o. ret
79	Hurricane	F/Lt Edwards	Shot down: b/o
85	Hurricane		Shot down: b/o. ret
103	P2693 Battle	P/O Morton	Belgium: KIA
103	K5512 Battle	F/O Morgan – Dean	MIA
105	K9485 Battle	P/O Hurst	Bouillon: KIA
107	P4905 Blenheim	F/O Edwards	2 PoW, 1 KIA
107	L8748 Blenheim	F/O Rotheram	Shot down: crash landed Belgium
107	L8733 Blenheim	P/O Thornton	KIA: Belgium
107	P4914 Blenheim	P/O Keedwell	KIA: Belgium
139	N6216 Blenheim	S/Ldr Scott	KIA: Maastricht
139	P4826 Blenheim	F/Lt Lee	MIA: Maastricht
139	N6219 Blenheim	F/O Gray – Smith	MIA: Maastricht
139	N6215 Blenheim	F/O McPherson	KIA: Maastricht
139	N6229 Blenheim	Sgt Harrison	MIA: Maastricht
139	P4923 Blenheim	S/Ldr Tideman	Crash landed 1 KIA, 2 ret
139	L9416 Blenheim	F/Lt Pepper	FTR: crash landed. ret
150	P2336 Battle	P/O Campbell – Irons	KIA: Belgium
206	N7353 Hudson	P/O Gray	* MIA
218	K9353 Battle	Sgt Horner	KIA
218	P2183 Battle	P/O Bazalgette	Shot down: pilot dead. 2 ret
501	Hurricane	F/O Rayner	Shot down
501	Hurricane	F/O Smith	Shot down
615	Hurricane	P/O Fredman	KIA: Belgium

13th May 1940

1	Hurricane	P/O Lorimer	Shot down: crash landed
3	L1901 Hurricane	P/O Ball	FTR: PoW
3	N2653 Hurricane	F/O Lines – Roberts	Killed in collision
3	N2654 Hurricane	F/O Adam	Killed in collision
4	P9063 Lysander	P/O Vaughan	KIA: Belgium
57	P6930 Blenheim	P/O Drimmie	Observer KIA Belgium

59		Blenheim	P/O Chamberlain	MIA
66		Spitfire	F/O Brown	* MIA: ret
73		Hurricane	P/O Marchand	Shot down: wounded
85		Hurricane	S/Ldr Oliver	Shot down: b/o. ret
103		Battle	F/O Cunningham	MIA
226	K2353	Battle	F/O Waddington	Force landed Brussels
264		Defiant	F/Lt Skelton	* MIA: PoW (a/g ret)
264		Defiant	P/O Chandler	* MIA
264		Defiant	P/O Greenhone	* MIA
264		Defiant	P/O Thomas	* MIA: pilot ret
264		Defiant	P/O McLeod	* MIA: pilot ret
607		Hurricane	F/O Thompson	KIA: Belgium

14th May 1940

1		Hurricane	F/Lt Hanks	Shot down: Force landed
1		Hurricane	F/O Clisby	KIA
1		Hurricane	F/O Lorimer	KIA
3	L1932	Hurricane	P/O Carey	Shot down: wounded
3	L1591	Hurricane	Sgt Allen	FTR: ret
3	L1908	Hurricane	P/O Jeffries	Shot down: b/o. ret
3		Hurricane	F/Lt Stephens	Shot down: force landed Mauberg
4	L4745	Lysander	F/O Clarke	KIA: Blegium
12	L4950	Battle	F/O Vaughan	MIA
12	L5188	Battle	Sgt Winkler	MIA
12	L5186	Battle	Sgt Johnson	MIA
12	L4952	Battle	F/Lt Clancy	FTR: PoWs
21	L8738	Blenheim	Sgt Outhwaite	MIA
21	L8742	Blenheim	P/O Gilmore	MIA
21	P6890	Blenheim	F/O Sarll	Shot up: belly landed base
26		Lysander	P/O Walker	Shot down: wounded
57		Blenheim	P/O Spencer	Shot down: Belgium 1 KIA
59	P6926	Blenheim	F/O Hawke	KIA
73		Hurricane	Sgt Pyne	MIA
73		Hurricane	Sgt Dibden	MIA
73		Hurricane	P/O Roe	MIA
79		Hurricane	P/O Wood	FTR: ret
79		Hurricane	P/O Appleton	MIA
88	L5190	Battle	Sgt Ross	MIA
103	K5516	Battle	P/O Cunningham	KIA
103		Battle	F/O Fitzgerald	FTR: force landed. ret
103		Battle	Sgt Beardsley	FTR: force landed. ret
105	L5523	Battle	F/Lt Samuels	MIA
105	L5585	Battle	F/O Wall	MIA
105	K9181	Battle	F/O Gibson	MIA
105	K9342	Battle	P/O Lascelles	FTR: ret
105	L5238	Battle	P/O Ridley	MIA
105	L5230	Battle	P/O White	MIA
105	L5250	Battle	P/O Murray	MIA
110	N6210	Blenheim	P/O Rose	KIA
110	P6889	Blenheim	Sgt Cater	Shot up: crash landed Attigny. wounded
110	L9241	Blenheim	Sgt Storrow	FTR: crash landed near Orchies. ret
110	L9214	Blenheim	F/O Wright	FTR: PoWs

110	L9217	Blenheim	P/O Mullins	FTR: air gunner dead. 2 PoWs
114	L9464	Blenheim	P/O Jordan	KIA
139	N6230	Blenheim	F/O Newberry	* MIA} No. 114 Sqn. Crews
139		Blenheim	P/O Power	* MIA} with No. 139 Sqn.
139	P4827	Blenheim	Sgt Brady	MIA} aircraft.
139	L9197	Blenheim	F/O de Montmorency	MIA}
142	P2246	Battle	S/Ldr Hobler	FTR: force landed. ret
142	P2333	Battle	Sgt Spear	KIA: pilot ret
142	L5517	Battle	F/Lt Rogers	MIA
142	K9333	Battle	P/O Oakley	Force landed Eely
105	L4946	Battle	F/O Ing	MIA
150	K9483	Battle	P/O Posselt	MIA
150	P2182	Battle	P/O Boon	MIA
150	P5232	Battle	Sgt Barker	MIA
218	L5232	Battle	P/O Harris	MIA
218	L5235	Battle	P/O Imrie	MIA
218	L5422	Battle	F/O Crane	MIA
218	P2324	Battle	F/O Foster	MIA
218	6 x	Battle		MIA
226	P2267	Battle	S/Ldr Lockett	MIA
226	L5438	Battle	F/Sgt Dunn	MIA
226	K9343	Battle	Sgt Moseley	MIA
504		Hurricane	S/Ldr Parnall	MIA
504		Hurricane	Sgt Hamblett	MIA
504		Hurricane	P/O Sibley	MIA
504		Hurricane	P/O Hay	Shot down: force landed
504		Hurricane	F/O Royce	Shot down: b/o
607		Hurricane	F/O Cuthbert	MIA
607		Hurricane	F/Lt Sullivan	KIA: Belgium
615		Hurricane	F/O Murton – Neale	KIA: Belgium
803	L2925	Skua	Lt/Cdr Lucy	* Shot down

15th May 1940

1		Hurricane	P/O Ritchey	Shot down: b/o
1		Hurricane	F/Lt Walker	Shot down: force landed
1		Hurricane	F/Lt Hanks	Shot down: b/o
1		Hurricane	F/O Clisby	* MIA
1		Hurricane	F/O Lorrimer	* MIA
3	L1643	Hurricane	Sgt Williams	MIA
3	N2534	Hurricane	F/Lt Carter	MIA
3	N2422	Hurricane	P/O Hallifax	MIA
4		Lysander	P/O Barbour	MIA
13		Lysander	P/O Ollerenshaw	KIA: Belgium
15	L8856	Blenheim	P/O Harriman	Force landed, ret
40	N6217	Blenheim	W/Cdr Barlow	KIA
40	P4913	Blenheim	F/Lt Edwards	KIA
53	L9399	Blenheim	P/O Bone	Shot down by Hurricane near Tournai: KIA
59	L4859	Blenheim	P/O Murdoch	FTR: observer buried at Louvain
59	N6168	Blenheim	F/Lt Smithers	Crashed on return
73		Hurricane	F/O Orton	Shot down: b/o
73		Hurricane	Sgt Humphries	MIA
73		Hurricane		Shot down
85		Hurricane	F/O Allen	FTR: b/o. ret

85		Hurricane	P/O Ashton	FTR: ret
85		Hurricane	P/O Pace	FTR: crash landed on fire. ret
139	L9411	Blenheim	P/O De Souza	MIA
504		Hurricane	S/Ldr Parnall	KIA: Belgium
607		Hurricane	F/O Russell	MIA
615		Hurricane	P/O Fowler	MIA

15th/16th May 1940

9	N3015	Wellington		* MIA: in sea
44	P4386	Hampden	P/O Ashfield	* MIA

16th May 1940

1		Hurricane	P/O Ritchey	Shot down: b/o
3		Hurricane	S/Ldr Gifford	MIA
4		Lysander	F/O Wood	MIA
18	L8863	Blenheim	Sgt Thomas	Shot up: landed Vitry. Pilot died
53	L4860	Blenheim	P/O Lovell	Shot down: Blegium
53	L4843	Blenheim	P/O McPherson	FTR: PoWs
53	L4852	Blenheim	F/Lt Daly	Shot down by Hurricane at Glisy
59	N6168	Blenheim	F/Lt Smithers	Shot down by Hurricane. Crash landed Vitry
79		Hurricane	Sgt Cartwright	Shot down: force landed
85		Hurricane	P/O Angus	Shot down: KIA
85		Hurricane	P/O Rawlinson	KIA: Belgium
85		Hurricane	Sgt Crozier	FTR: ret
139	L9411	Blenheim		MIA
615		Hurricane	F/Lt Thornley	MIA
615		Hurricane	P/O Jackson	MIA
615		Hurricane	F/O Young	MIA
803		Skua	Lt Harris	* MIA: Rombaksfjord: rescued

17th May 1940

1		Hurricane	F/O Palmer	Shot down: b/o ret
2		Lysander	P/O Rearden	Shot down
3	L1609	Hurricane	P/O Jones	Shot down: b/o
3		Hurricane	Sgt Hillwood	Shot down: force landed
3	N2141	Hurricane	F/Lt Hope	Shot down: force landed
16		Lysander	P/O White	MIA
17		Hurricane	S/Ldr Tomlinson	FTR: ret
17		Hurricane	F/O Lines	MIA
18		Blenheim	F/O Stuart	KIA
18		Blenheim	P/O Whelan	Crash landed
53	L4861	Blenheim	P/O Royle	MIA
53	L4841	Blenheim	P/O Huggett	KIA
57		Blenheim	P/O Ritchie	Force landed: ret
79		Hurricane	P/O Herrick	MIA
79		Hurricane	Sgt Valentine	Shot down: force landed. ret
82	P8830	Blenheim	F/O McConnell	MIA
82	P9210	Blenheim	Sgt Grierson	MIA
82	P4852	Blenheim	S/Ldr Delop	FTR: ret. wounded
82	P4903	Blenheim	Sgt Wrightson	MIA

82	P4838	Blenheim	F/O Crofton	MIA
82	P4898	Blenheim	P/O Christenson	MIA
82	P4854	Blenheim	P/O Toft	MIA
82	P9213	Blenheim	F/L Watson	MIA
82	P4851	Blenheim	F/O Fordham	MIA
82	P4893	Blenheim	Sgt Newbatt	MIA
82	P4904	Blenheim	Sgt Watkins	MIA
82	P8858	Blenheim	Sgt Morrison	Severely damaged
213	"O"	Hurricane	Sgt Valentine	FTR: ret. wounded
615		Hurricane	F/Lt Sanders	Shot down: force landed

18th May 1940

3	N2364	Hurricane	P/O Gardner	Shot down: force landed
4		Lysander	F/O Ford	KIA: Belgium
15	P6917	Blenheim	F/Lt Chapman	KIA
15	L9030	Blenheim	P/O Robinson	Landed at Poix. Scrapped
15	L8853	Blenheim	S/Ldr Lawrence	KIA: air gunner PoW
15	L8852	Blenheim	F/O Dawson – Jones	KIA
16		Lysander	F/O Walker	MIA
53		Blenheim	P/O Royle	MIA
53		Blenheim	P/O Huggett	MIA
56	N2439	Hurricane	F/O Rose	Shot down
56	N2437	Hurricane	F/Lt Soden	KIA
59	R3702	Blenheim	P/O Durie	FTR: Air gunner ret. 2 KIA Belgium
85		Hurricane	F/O Wilms	MIA
85		Hurricane	P/O Chambers	MIA
85		Hurricane	F/O Allen	MIA
111		Hurricane	P/O Morewood	Shot down: force landed
111		Hurricane	Sgt Craig	Shot down: force landed
111		Hurricane	F/Lt Darwood	KIA
145	P2600	Hurricane	P/O Newling	FTR: b/o. ret
151		Hurricane	Sgt Atkinson	FTR: ret
206	N7329	Hudson	F/Sgt Turner	* MIA
206	N7400	Hudson	F/O Hutcheson	* MIA
253	L1600	Hurricane	P/O Ford	FTR: ret
253	L1660	Hurricane	P/O Strang	FTR: ret
253	L1655	Hurricane	P/O Bell – Salter	FTR: ret
253	L1667	Hurricane	Sgt Brackley	FTR: ret
504		Hurricane	P/O Rennison	MIA
504		Hurricane	F/Lt Owen	MIA:b/o
601		Hurricane	F/Lt Hope	Shot down: force landed
	P5647	Walrus	Lt Benson Dare	* Shot down Tromso from *HMS Devonshire*

18th/19th May 1940

77		Whitley	F/Lt Raphael	* MIA: in sea

19th May 1940

1		Hurricane	P/O Stewart	Force landed: France
1		Hurricane	F/O Richey	Shot down: b/o wounded
1		Hurricane	Sgt Soper	Shot down: crash landed
3	N2535	Hurricane	P/O Rose	Shot down: b/o

4		Lysander	P/O Plumb	Shot down: KIA Lille
4		Lysander	P/O Oldairs	Shot down: KIA Lille
12	L5538	Battle	P/O McElligott	Shot down: pilot died
12	N2178	Battle	F/O Barr	MIA
15		Battle	F/Lt Chapman	* MIA
15		Battle	Sgt Laurence	* MIA
15		Battle	F/O Dawson	* MIA
16		Lysander	F/O Reed	Shot down: KIA
16		Lysander	P/O Dromgoole	Shot down: KIA
16		Lysander	P/O Hughes	Shot down: force landed
17		Hurricane	P/O Harris	MIA
17		Hurricane	Sgt Pavey	FTR: ret
26	N1290	Lysander	P/O Halliday	MIA
32		Hurricane	F/O Milner	FTR: PoW
59	L4856	Blenheim	P/O Wylie	Force landed
73		Hurricane	P/O Hobart	Shot down: force landed
73		Hurricane	P/O Thompson	Shot down: force landed
85		Hurricane	P/O Woods – Scawen	Shot down: b/o
85		Hurricane	Sgt Little	Shot down
111		Hurricane	P/O Bury	MIA
111		Hurricane	P/O Moorwood	MIA
111		Hurricane	S/Ldr Thompson	FTR: ret
142	K7696	Battle	P/O Taylor	Shot down: PoWs
142	L5226	Battle	Sgt Godsall	Shot down: 2 PoWs
142	P5238	Battle	Sgt Ebert	Shot down: crash landed
145	N2598	Hurricane	P/O Lucas	MIA
150	P5235	Blenheim	P/O Osment	MIA
206		Hudson	Sgt Judge	* MIA
213		Hurricane		Shot down: b/o
213		Hurricane	P/O Stone	Shot down: force landed
229	L2142	Hurricane	F/Lt Rosier	Shot down: badly burnt
229	L1803	Hurricane	P/O Bussey	MIA
229	L1770	Hurricane	P/O Dillon	KIA: Belgium
233		Hudson		* MIA
253		Hurricane	P/O Ratford	MIA
253	N2590	Hurricane	F/Lt Harris	FTR: ret wounded
253		Hurricane	F/Lt Anderson	MIA
253		Hurricane	Sgt McKenzie	MIA
504		Hurricane	Sgt Mapletoft	MIA
504		Hurricane	S/Ldr Hill	FTR: b/o, wounded E. Lille
504		Hurricane	P/O Hardacre	Shot down: b/o
601		Hurricane	F/O Riddle	FTR: ret
601		Hurricane	F/O Hubbard	FTR: ret
601		Hurricane	F/Lt Hope	Shot down: force landed. ret
604		Blenheim	F/O Gillies	* MIA (night?)
605		Hurricane	P/O Paxton	FTR: b/o. ret wounded
615		Hurricane	P/O Pexton	FTR: ret
PDU		Spitfire	P/O Coleman	* MIA

19/20th May 1940

77	N1417	Whitley	W/Cdr Cognan	* MIA
77	N1376	Whitley	F/S Hall	* MIA

20th May 1940

32		Hurricane	Sgt North	MIA
48	"G"	Anson	F/Lt Dodds	* MIA: in sea
79		Hurricane	P/O Parker	MIA
79		Hurricane	P/O Dorrien – Smith	MIA
85		Hurricane	S/Ldr Peacock	KIA: shot down nr. Arras
85		Hurricane	P/O Barton	MIA
85		Hurricane	P/O Shrewsbury	KIA: shot down nr. Arras
85		Hurricane	Sgt Howes	Shot down: force landed
226	K9176	Battle	Sgt Annan	MIA
229		Hurricane	P/O Ravenhill	Shot down: crashed, ret

20th/21st May 1940

77	N1384	Whitley	F/O Pryde	* MIA
102	N1528	Whitley	F/Lt Owen	* MIA
115	P9298	Wellington	F/Sgt Moore	* MIA
115	R3152	Wellington	P/O Morris	* MIA

21st May 1940

1		Hurricane	Sgt Albonico	Shot down
4		Lysander	F/Lt Graham	Shot down: KIA Clairmarais
4		Lysander	P/O Davey	Shot down: Clairmarais
4		Lysander	P/O Peace	KIA: Belgium
15	R3706	Blenheim	F/Lt Webster	Shot up: force landed, ret
18	L9325	Blenheim	P/O Light	MIA
18	L9185	Blenheim	P/O Rees	Shot down by Spitfires
74	N3243	Spitfire	P/O Aubert	FTR: ret
74		Spitfire	F/O Byrne	* MIA: PoW
253		Hurricane	P/O Gower	* MIA
253		Hurricane	S/Ldr Elliott	MIA
263	N5693	Gladiator	F/Lt Mills	* Crashed after combat
263	N5693	Gladiator	P/O Richards	* Crashed Harstad: combat
601		Hurricane	F/O Riddle	FTR: ret

21st/22nd May 1940

51	P4980	Whitley	Sgt Bowles	* MIA
75	R3157	Wellington	F/O Collins	* MIA
99	L7803	Wellington	P/O Dyer	* MIA
102	N1528	Whitley	P/O Womersley	* MIA: force landed France
115	P9297	Wellington	F/O Laslett	* MIA

22nd May 1940

2		Lysander	F/O Doidge	MIA
18	R3598	Blenheim	P/O Dickens	MIA
32		Hurricane	Sgt Turner	FTR: ret
56	N2431	Hurricane	P/O Wicks	FTR: ret
57	L9184	Blenheim	P/O Saunders	MIA
59	L9266	Blenheim	F/O Bird	MIA
59		Blenheim	P/O Durie	MIA
82	P4838	Blenheim	Sgt Hartfield	MIA
103		Battle	Sgt Crich	Shot down: crash landed

107	P4925	Blenheim	P/O Millar	FTR: ditched. rescued
110	L8761	Blenheim	S/Ldr Hall	MIA
206	N5698	Hudson	P/O Craig Adams	* Shot down
206	N7402	Hudson	P/O Giles	* MIA
206		Hudson	P/O Clark	* MIA
229		Hurricane	P/O Gower	* MIA
263	N7409	Gladiator	P/O Clark	* MIA
601		Hurricane	F/O Cuthbert	MIA
605		Hurricane	F/O Austin	FTR: ret
605		Hurricane	F/O Leeson	FTR: PoW
605		Hurricane	Sgt Moffat	MIA
605		Hurricane	F/O Wright	MIA
605		Hurricane	P/O Currant	Shot down: crash landed. wounded

23rd May 1940

15	L9403	Blenheim	P/O Masters	MIA
24		S73		* Shot down: Murville
24	OOAUI	DC3		* Shot down: Arques
32		Hurricane	P/O Flinders	FTR: ret
32		Hurricane	Sgt Nowell	FTR: ret
40	P4909	Blenheim	W/Cdr Llewellyn	MIA
40	L8832	Blenheim	F/O Jacoby	MIA
53	R3691	Blenheim	F/O Pepys	MIA
74	K9875	Spitfire	S/Ldr White	FTR: ret
74		Spitfire	F/O Byrne	MIA
92		Spitfire	P/O Learmond	MIA
92		Spitfire	S/Ldr Bushell	FTR: PoW
92		Spitfire	F/O Gillies	FTR: PoW
92		Spitfire	Sgt Klipsch	MIA
92		Spitfire	F/Lt Green	Shot down: wounded
242	N2809	Hurricane	F/O Graafstra	MIA
242	N2730	Hurricane	F/O Madore	MIA
242	P3392	Hurricane	P/O Smiley	MIA
242	P2550	Hurricane	P/O Benzie	FTR: ret
253		Hurricane	P/O Ford	MIA
263	N5719	Gladiator	Sgt Whall	* Crashed: b/o

22nd/23rd May 1940

88	P2356	Battle	P/O Wickham	MIA

23rd/24th May 1940

44	L4171	Hampden	S/Ldr Johnson	* MIA
58	N1361	Whitley	P/O McLaren	* MIA
78		Whitley		* MIA

24th May 1940

15	R3614	Blenheim	P/O Henderson	* KIA: crashed on approach Wyton.
54	P9455	Spitfire	F/O Linley	MIA
54	P9388	Spitfire	Sgt Phillips	MIA

59		Blenheim	P/O Carruthers	FTR: Force landed Trapagny. ret
73		Hurricane	F/O Bell – Sayers	Baled out
73		Hurricane	P/O Carter	MIA
74	K9321	Spitfire	F/O Hoare	FTR: PoW
74	K9992	Spitfire	F/Lt Treacey	FTR: ret
74	K9952	Spitfire	Sgt Mould	FTR: ret
74	N3243	Spitfire	P/O Aubert	FTR: ret
92		Spitfire	P/O Cazenove	* MIA: ret
235		Blenheim	F/O Ryan	* MIA: off Ameland
242	P3272	Hurricane	P/O Mitchell	MIA
242	P3266	Hurricane	P/O Hill	MIA

25th May 1940

1		Hurricane	F/O Thorn	MIA
15	P6913	Blenheim	P/O Harriman	MIA
40	L4920	Blenheim	Sgt Tonks	MIA
54	N3096	Spitfire	Sgt Buckland	MIA
54	N3188	Spitfire	P/O Allen	FTR: b/o. rescued
54	N3103	Spitfire	P/O Gribble	FTR: ret
103		Battle	Sgt Beardesley	FTR: ret
262	L5467	Battle	P/O Anderson	KIA
501		Hurricane	P/O Sylvester	FTR: ret

25th/26th May 1940

21	L8734	Blenheim	Sgt Rawson	Pilot PoW, 2 KIA Belgium
37	L7793	Wellington		* MIA: Ostend: ret
49	P1316	Hampden	P/O Butler	* MIA
88		Battle	P/O Anderson	MIA
103	L5514	Battle	F/O Leyden	Pilot PoW, 2 KIA

26th May 1940

17		Hurricane	F/Sgt Jones	MIA
17		Hurricane	F/Lt Adye	Shot down: b/o
19		Spitfire	S/Ldr Stephenson	FTR: PoW
19		Spitfire	Sgt Irwin	MIA
19		Spitfire	P/O Watson	MIA
19		Spitfire	F/O Ball	Wounded
53	L8853	Blenheim	P/O Bailey	MIA
59		Blenheim	P/O Shaw	MIA
65		Spitfire	F/O Wellford	Shot down
65		Spitfire	P/O Hart	FTR: ret
73		Hurricane	P/O Sydenham	MIA
79		Hurricane	F/Sgt Jones	MIA
79		Hurricane		
150	L5459	Battle	F/O Vernon	FTR: pilot ret
605	N2346	Hurricane	P/O Muirhead	MIA

27th May 1940

26		Lysander	P/O Deas	MIA
26		Lysander	P/O Howard	MIA
26		Lysander	P/O Dixon	MIA

53	L8735	Blenheim	P/O Villiers – Tothill	MIA
53	R3703	Blenheim	P/O Aldridge	b/o by St. Margarets.
54		Spitfire	P/O Deere	FTR: ret
54		Spitfire	F/Lt Pearson	MIA
56	P3478	Hurricane	P/O Maxwell	Shot down: b/o
56	P3311	Hurricane	F/Lt Lee	FTR: ditched. rescued
56	P3355	Hurricane	P/O Fisher	Shot down: wounded
65		Spitfire	F/O Proudman	Shot down: b/o. wounded
74	L1084	Spitfire	P/O Stevenson	FTR: ret
74	K9875	Spitfire	F/Lt Treacey	FTR: ret
107	L9391	Blenheim	W/Cdr Embry	FTR: pilot ret
107	N6192	Blenheim	Sgt Warman	MIA
145	P2743	Hurricane	P/O Elson	MIA
145	P2523	Hurricane	P/O Rayner	MIA
145	P2711	Hurricane	Sgt Bailey	MIA
145	P2710	Hurricane	P/O Forde	FTR: ret
145	P3314	Hurricane	P/O Wakeham	FTR: ret
145	P2713	Hurricane	P/O Ashton	MIA
263		Gladiator	F/Lt Hull	* Shot down: wounded
263		Gladiator	Lt Lydekker	* Shot down: wounded
601	P2568	Hurricane	F/Lt Hope	FTR: ret
601	P3486	Hurricane	F/O Lee – Steere	KIA
605	L2119	Hurricane	F/O Forbes	MIA
605	P3423	Hurricane	S/Ldr Perry	MIA
605	P3581	Hurricane	F/O Danielson	MIA
610		Spitfire	F/O Metcalfe	MIA
610		Spitfire	Sgt Medway	KIA
613		Lysander	P/O Jenkyns	* MIA

28th May 1940

16		Lysander	F/O Clapham	MIA
21	L8744	Blenheim	Sgt Bailes	FTR: observer KIA
54		Spitfire	F/O Deere	FTR: ret
59	R3664	Blenheim	P/O Peters	FTR: b/o. air gunner died. ret
65		Spitfire	P/O Smart	FTR: ret
213	"E"	Hurricane	F/O Winning	KIA
213	"B"	Hurricane	Sgt Boyd	Shot down: ditched, rescued
213	"C"	Hurricane	P/O Stone	Shot down: KIA
213	"R"	Hurricane	Sgt Lishman	Shot down: b/o. rescued wounded
213	P2721	Hurricane	Sgt Butterfield	Shot down: b/o. rescued
242	N2651	Hurricane	P/O Deacon	MIA
242	L1746	Hurricane	P/O Jones	KIA
264	L6959	Defiant	F/Lt Whitehouse	Shot down: Dunkirk
264	L7007	Defiant	P/O McLeod	Shot down: Dunkirk
264	L6953	Defiant	Sgt Daisley	Shot down: Dunkirk

28th/29th May 1940

77	N1432	Whitley	P/O Geach	* MIA

29th May 1940

46		Hurricane	P/O Drummond	* Shot down: b/o
46		Hurricane	P/O Banks	* Shot down: Narvik

48	"X"	Anson	P/O Allington	* MIA: rescued
56	N2659	Hurricane	P/O Dryden	FTR: ret
56	L1972	Hurricane	Sgt Elliott	MIA
64		Spitfire	F/Sgt Flynn	FTR: b/o rescued
64	L1052	Spitfire	S/Ldr Rogers	MIA
64	K9832	Spitfire	F/O George	MIA
64	K9906	Spitfire	P/O Hackney	MIA
88	P2313	Battle	F/O Evitt	MIA
151	P3303	Hurricane	P/O Newton	MIA
151	P3321	Hurricane	P/O Courtney	Shot down: b/o. wounded
235		Blenheim	P/O Booth	* MIA
235		Blenheim	F/Lt Manwaring	* MIA
222	P9376	Spitfire	P/O Broadhurst	Force landed, write off
500	"L"	Anson	Sgt Hoskins	* MIA: rescued
500	"Z"	Anson	P/O Chaffey	* MIA: rescued
610		Spitfire	F/O Kerr	MIA
610		Spitfire	F/O Kerr – Wilson	MIA
610		Spitfire	S/Ldr Franks	MIA
610		Spitfire	Sgt Jenkins	MIA

30th May 1940

26		Lysander	F/Lt Bryant	* MIA
48	"J"	Anson	P/O Tilson	* MIA
269	N7335	Hudson	Sgt Townsend	* MIA
500	"N"	Anson	P/O Wheelwright	* MIA

30th/31st May 1940

38	R3162	Wellington	F/O Rosewarne	* MIA

31st May 1940

2		Lysander	P/O Dearden	KIA
16		Lysander	P/O Shepley	MIA
16		Lysander	P/O Biden	MIA
24	W6457	DH89	F/O Ogilvie	Shot down near Beauvais
64	K9813	Spitfire	Sgt Hatch	MIA
213	"W"	Hurricane	S/Ldr McGregor	Shot down, ditched, rescued
213	"G"	Hurricane	F/O Robinson	Shot down: b/o. ret
213	"P"	Hurricane	P/O Sizer	Shot down: crash landed. ret
213	"D"	Hurricane	F/O Gray	MIA
213	"A"	Hurricane	Sgt Boyd	KIA
222	N3295	Spitfire	P/O Davies	Force landed near Dunkirk. ret
242		Hurricane	P/O Stewart	MIA
245	P2658	Hurricane	P/O McGlasham	FTR: ret
264	L6968	Defiant	P/O Hickman	KIA
264	L6961	Defiant	P/O Whitley	Collision: safe
264	L6980	Defiant	P/O Young	Collision: safe
264	L6975	Defiant	F/Lt Cooke	MIA
264		Defiant	P/O Barrett	MIA
609		Spitfire	F/Lt Persse – Joynt	MIA
609		Spitfire	F/O Gilbert	MIA
609		Spitfire	Sgt Bennett	FTR: ret

610		Spitfire	P/O Keighly		FTR: b/o. rescued
610		Spitfire	F/O Chambers		MIA
	2 x	Skuas		*	MIA: Nieuport

31st May/1st June 1940

37	P9288	Wellington	*	MIA

1st June 1940

2		Lysander	F/O Doidge		MIA
17		Hurricane	P/O Manger		FTR: crash landed. ret
19		Spitfire	Sgt Potter		FTR: ditched
26		Lysander	P/O Patterson		MIA
26		Lysander	P/O Wilson		KIA
41		Spitfire	P/O Stapleton		MIA
41		Spitfire	F/O Legard		MIA
43	N2584	Hurricane	P/O Carswell		FTR: rescued wounded
43	L1758	Hurricane	Sgt Gough		MIA
73		Hurricane	P/O Potts		MIA
73		Hurricane	Sgt Milner		MIA
73		Hurricane	P/O Scott		FTR: force landed near Paris. ret
145	P3400	Hurricane	P/O Duncan		MIA
222	P9339	Spitfire	P/O Massey – Sharpe		MIA
222	P9317	Spitfire	P/O Falkus		MIA
222	N3232	Spitfire	Sgt White		KIA
222	P9377	Spitfire	P/O Morant		FTR: ret 2.6.40
245	N2709	Hurricane	P/O West		MIA
245	P2597	Hurricane	P/O Marsland		MIA
254		Blenheim	P/O Alexander	*	MIA
254		Blenheim		*	MIA
609		Spitfire	F/O Russell		MIA
609		Spitfire	F/O Dawson		MIA
616		Spitfire	F/O Bell		MIA
	7 x	Swordfish		*	MIA

2nd June 1940

32		Hurricane		MIA
66		Spitfire	F/Sgt Hayman	MIA
66		Spitfire	Sgt Hunt	FTR: b/o. rescued
66		Spitfire	Sgt Robertson	FTR: b/o. rescued
111		Hurricane	P/O Wilson	FTR: b/o. off Manston. rescued
266	N3197	Spitfire	P/O Stevenson	MIA
266	N3092	Spitfire	Sgt Kidman	MIA
611		Spitfire	F/O Crampton	MIA
611		Spitfire	F/O Little	MIA

3rd June 1940

12	P2269	Battle	P/O McIntyre	MIA
17		Hurricane	F/O Meredith	MIA
73	2 x	Hurricanes		MIA
501		Hurricane		MIA
501		Hurricane		FTR: b/o. rescued

3rd/4th June 1940

83	P1178 Hampden	P/O Haydon	* MIA

4th June 1940

1	Hurricane	F/O Hillcoat	Shot down: crash landed. safe
1	Hurricane	P/O Hancock	Crashed Boos after combat

4th/5th June 1940

9	P9232 Wellington	S/Ldr Peacock	* MIA
77	N1522 Whitley	P/O Meigh	* MIA

5th June 1940

233	"S" Hudson	F/O Dunn	* MIA: Norway

5th/6th June 1940

9	N2993 Wellington	F/O Nicholson	* MIA
83	P1348 Hampden	S/Ldr Field	* MIA

6th June 1940

17	Hurricane	Sgt Holman	MIA
26	Lysander	P/O Fevez	MIA
40	L8827 Blenheim	S/Ldr Patton	MIA
40	L9410 Blenheim	P/O James	MIA
40	P4927 Blenheim	Sgt Rice	MIA
40	P4917 Blenheim	P/O Wakeford	FTR: force landed. ret
40	R3692 Blenheim	P/O Engstrom	FTR: pilot ret, 2 PoW
73	Hurricane	F/O Kain	Killed, flying accident Echimmines
111	Hurricane	Sgt Brown	FTR: ret wounded

7th June 1940

12	P2162 Battle	Sgt Field	KIA
17	Hurricane	S/Ldr Emms	MIA
17	Hurricane	P/O Whittaker	MIA
43	N2585 Hurricane	Sgt Hallowes	FTR: ret
43	L1931 Hurricane	F/O Edmonds	MIA
43	L1847 Hurricane	F/O Wlikinson	MIA
43	L2116 Hurricane	F/Lt Rowland	Shot down: wounded
43	L1737 Hurricane	Sgt Ayling	Shot down: crash landed Boos
43	L1608 Hurricane	Sgt Ottewill	Shot down: severe burns
43	L1726 Hurricane	P/O Woods – Scawen	Shot down: b/o. ret
103	Battle	Sgt Brown	Shot down: ret
107	R3686 Blenheim	F/O Pleasance	Shot down: ret
150	L5288 Battle	F/O Vernon	KIA
151	P3529 Hurricane	P/O Pettigrew	MIA
601	P3484 Hurricane	F/O Hubbard	FTR: ret
601	P3490 Hurricane	F/O Robinson	Shot down: ret wounded

8th June 1940

12	L5546 Battle	F/O Brereton	FTR: PoW
15	R3746 Blenheim	S/Ldr Burke	KIA
15	N6177 Blenheim	P/O Myland	* Crash landed Tangmere. written off
21	L9023 Blenheim	F/O Durnford	KIA
32	Hurricane	P/O Grice	FTR: ret
32	Hurricane	P/O Cherrington	MIA
32	Hurricane	P/O Kirlcoldie	MIA
82	R3618 Blenheim	P/O Mackenzie	FTR: 1 dead, 2 PoWs
103	P2315 Battle	P/O Thorogood	FTR: force landed Paris. ret
103	N2259 Battle	Sgt Beardesley	FTR: PoWs
110	R3670 Blenheim	P/O Arderne	FTR: ret
150	Battle	F/Lt Weeks	MIA
151	Hurricane	P/O Blomeley	MIA
501	4 x Hurricanes		MIA

8th/9th June 1940

3 x Blenheims		* MIA

9th June 1940

17	Hurricane	P/O Leary	FTR: ret
107	R3739 Blenheim	F/O Buckley	FTR: pilot dead, 2 PoWs
107	L9323 Blenheim	F/O Bamford	MIA
107	R3685 Blenheim	P/O Bennett	FTR: ret
501	Hurricane	Sgt Lacey	Force landed, written off

9th/10th June 1940

61	P4336 Hampden	S/Ldr Lawrence	* MIA

10th June 1940

82	Blenheim	P/O Percival	MIA
103	P2328 Battle	P/O Thomas	KIA

11th June 1940

15	R3588 Blenheim	P/O Myland	FTR: force landed near Cherbourg
15	L9024 Blenheim	F/O Clarke	Collision, pilot killed
15	L8851 Blenheim	P/O Werner	Collision, all dead
21	L8743 Blenheim	P/O Rogers	MIA
21	L8746 Blenheim	P/O MacDonald	MIA
21	R3674 Blenheim	Sgt Outhwaite	MIA
40	Blenheim	Sgt Bartlam	MIA
59	P3631 Blenheim	P/O Hopkins	FTR: forced down by Ms406s. ret
88	Battle	F/Lt Ditfield	MIA
88	Battle	P/O Talman	FTR: force landed Vitry
107	Blenheim	P/O Reid	* MIA
142	L5200 Battle	P/O Perriman	MIA
226	Battle	Sgt McLoughlin	KIA

269	"G"	Hudson	Sgt Lascelles	* MIA: Norway
269	"P"	Hudson	Sgt Robsob	* MIA: Norway

11th/12th June 1940

10	P4954	Whitley	S/Ldr Keast	* MIA
44	P1325	Hampden	Sgt Jeffrey	* MIA
77	N1340	Whitley	Sgt Songest	* MIA

12th June 1940

15	R3747	Blenheim	P/O Takedeli	KIA
40	R3893	Blenheim	Sgt Barton	FTR: PoWs
88	L5334	Battle	F/Lt Pitfield	KIA
88		Battle	P/O Talmon	Shot down: force landed. ret
107	R3810	Blenheim	P/O Reid	KIA
142		Battle	F/Lt Martin	MIA
254	"N"	Blenheim	Sgt Brown	* MIA: Norway

12th/13th June 1940

144		Hampden	W/Cdr Watts	* MIA

13th June 1940

12	L5451	Battle	P/O Shorthouse	MIA
12	L5580	Battle	P/O Parkhouse	MIA
12	L5531	Battle	P/O McPhie	MIA
21	R3676	Blenheim	P/O Blanckensee	KIA
21	L9269	Blenheim	F/Lt Petley	FTR: force landed. ret
82	R6910	Blenheim	F/Lt Breese	MIA
82	P6925	Blenheim	P/O Williams	FTR: PoWs
82	L8829	Blenheim	Sgt Merritt	FTR: PoWs
88		Battle	Sgt Haywood	FTR: ret wounded
107	R3616	Blenheim	P/O Stidtson	KIA
142		Battle	F/Lt Hewson	FTR: ret
142		Battle	P/O Sutton	FTR: ret
142		Battle	Sgt Holliday	FTR: PoWs
150	L5437	Battle	Sgt Beale	KIA
150	L5524	Battle	P/O Gulley	FTR: pilot dead, 2 PoWs
150	L5591	Battle	S/Ldr Bradley	Shot down: force landed, ret
500	"M"	Anson	Sgt Sparks	* MIA

13th/14th June 1940

9	L7787	Wellington	Sgt Hewitt	* MIA

14th June 1940

1		Hurricane	F/Lt Brown	FTR: ret
1		Hurricane	Sgt Warcup	MIA
12	L5396	Battle	P/O Blowfield	MIA
12	L5383	Battle	Sgt Wilcox	FTR: observer ret
21	R3742	Blenheim	P/O Saunders	MIA
40	R3693	Blenheim	P/O Lewis	MIA
40	N3592	Blenheim	S/Ldr Gleed	MIA

103		Battle	F/O Hawkins	FTR: PoWs
103		Battle	Sgt Brumby	FTR: PoWs
111		Hurricane	Sgt Roscoe	FTR: ret
224	"Q"	Hudson	P/O Wood	* MIA: Norway
245		Hurricane	P/O Southwell	MIA

15th June 1940

12		Battle	F/Lt Hunt	MIA
73		Hurricane	Sgt McNey	MIA
103	2 x	Battles		MIA
150	L5541	Battle	Sgt Benjamin	Crash landed, ret
233	"U"	Hudson	P/O Asquith	* MIA: Norway
233	"V"	Hudson	P/O Greenaway	* MIA: Norway
233	"W"	Hudson	P/O Ewart	* MIA: Norway
254	"F"	Blenheim	P/O Gylard	* MIA :Norway

16th June 1940

59	R3818	Blenheim	P/O Everton – Jones	FTR: PoWs

17th June 1940

17th/18th June 1940

58	N1463	Whitley	F/Sgt Ford	* MIA

18th June 1940

151	P3313	Hurricane	P/O Wright	* FTR: b/o. rescued
151	P3324	Hurricane	Sgt Aslin	* KIA
24CF Pool		Hurricane	P/O Maycock	* MIA: force landed nr. Loudon
24CF Pool		Blenheim		* MIA

18th/19th June 1940

9	N2897	Wellington	P/O Butler	* MIA: in sea
19		Spitfire	F/O Petre	* Shot down: b/o
23		Blenheim	S/Ldr O'Brien	* Crashed after combat
23		Blenheim	S/Ldr Close	* Shot down by E/A
23		Blenheim	P/O Barnwell	* MIA
58	N1460	Whitley	P/O McInnes	* MIA
77	N1499	Whitley	Sgt Masham	* MIA

19th June 1940

PDU	P9392	Spitfire	P/O Nicholson	* MIA

19th/20th June 1940

99	R3200	Wellington	F/L Pickard	* MIA: in sea

20th/21st June 1940

9	L7807 Wellington		* MIA: in sea
58	N1442 Whitley	F/O Walker	* MIA
61	P4355 Hampden	P/O Smith	* MIA

21st June 1940

224	"P" Hudson	F/Lt Williamson	* MIA: Norway
233	"X" Hudson	S/Ldr Feeny	* MIA: Norway

21st/22nd June 1940

44	P4346 Hampden	F/Lt Barrett	* MIA

22nd June 1940

615	Hurricane	P/O lloyd	* MIA

23rd June 1940

107	R3688 Blenheim	P/O Essan	* MIA: Steenwijkerwold

23rd/24th June 1940

144	Hampden	P/O Taylor	* MIA

Luftwaffe Casualties May – June 1940

10th May 1940

I/JG1	Bf109E	Missing. Lt Ditel wounded	100%
I/JG1	Bf109E	Missing. Ogfr Scheibe lost	100%
I/JG2	Bf109E	Shot down by Hawk 75 over Ardennes	100%
5/JG26	Bf109E	Shot down by Fokker DXXI near Kesteren	100%
9/JG26	Bf109E	Shot down by Fokker DXXI at Meordijk	100%
3/JG27	Bf109E	Shot down by Gladiator (Fw Hoppe)	100%
2/JG53	Bf109E	Shot down by Flak at Thionville	100%
III/JG53	Bf109E	Shot down by Bloch 152 N France	100%
I/LG2	Bf109E4	Crashed German Bight. Pilot killed	100%
1/TrGr.186	Bf109E	Shot down by Fokker DXXI. Oblt Robitsch captured	100%
4/ZG1	Bf110	Shot down by Fokker DXXI Holland	100%
I/KG1	He111	Shot down by RAF fighter Amiens/Cambrai	100%
II/KG1	He111	Shot down by RAF fighter Amiens/Cambrai	100%
III/KG1	6 x He111	Shot down by RAF fighter Amiens/Cambrai	100%
I/KG2	Do17Z	Shot down by Hurricane Rheims	100%
I/KG2	Do17	Bdly damaged by Hurricane Rheims	80%
II/KG2	Do17Z	Shot down by Hurricane France	100%
II/KG2	2 x Do17Z	Shot down by Hawk 75 Suippes	100%
II/KG2	2 x Do17Z	Shot down by MS406 Suippes	100%
III/KG2	Do17Z	Shot down by Hurricane Rheims	100%
Stab/KG3	Do17Z	Shot down by Hurricane at Thionville	100%
II/KG3	5 x Do17Z	Shot down by Hawk 75 at Metz	100%
III/KG3	Do17Z	Shot down by Hurricane Suippes	100%
III/KG3	Do17Z	Shot down by Flak at Metz	100%
III/KG3	3 x Do17Z	Shot down by Hawk 75 at Metz	100%
I/KG4	He111	Shot down near Waalhaven by Fokker G – 1	100%
Stab/KG4	He111	Shot down by Flak over Holland	100%
II/KG4	4 x He111	Shot down by Flak over Holland	100%
III/KG4	2 x He111	Shot down by Fokker DXXI Holland	100%
9/KG4	3 x Ju88A	Shot down by Fokker G – 1 Holland	100%
2/KG27	2 x He111	Shot down by MS406 at Norrent – Fontes	100%
3/KG27	He111	Shot down by MS406 at Norrent – Fontes	100%
Stab II/KG27	He111	Shot down by MS406 at Norrent – Fontes	100%
II/KG27	He111	Shot down by Flak over Dunkirk	100%
Stab III/KG27	He111	Shot down by Hurricane over Seclin A/f	100%
Stab I/KG30	Ju88	Shot down by Dutch fighter over S Holland	100%
I/KG30	2 x Ju88	Shot down by Dutch fighter over S Holland	100%
I/KG30	Ju88	Shot down by Flak over S Holland	100%
III/KG30	2 x Ju88	Shot down by Flak at Charleroi	100%
Stab III/KG54	He111	Shot down by Fokker DXXI De Kooy/ Den Helder	100%
8/KG54	6 x He111	Shot down by Fokker DXXI De Kooy/ Den Helder	100%
1/KG55	3 x He111	Shot down by Flak at Touel	100%
II/KG55	2 x He111	Shot down by MS406 at Nancy	100%
III/KG55	He111	Shot down by Flak at Nancy	100%
III/KG55	3 x He111	Shot down by Hawk 75 at Xaffeuillers	100%
Stab/KG76	Do17Z	Missing over France	100%
II/KG76	Do17Z	Missing over France	100%
III/KG76	Do17Z	Missing over France	100%

5/KG77		Do17	Shot down by Belgian fighter at Schaffen/Diest	100%
I/LG1		He111	Shot down over Brussels/Evere by Belgian fighter	100%
1/LG1	2 x He111		Shot down by RAF Hurricane near Oudenarde	100%
II/LG1		He111	Shot down over Brussels/Evere by Belgian fighter	100%
9/LG1		Ju88	Shot down by Flak at Wevelghem	100%
I/StG.76	7 x Ju87		Shot down by Flak over Belgium	100%
II/StG.2		Ju87	Shot down by Flak	100%
I/TrGr.186	2 x Ju87		Shot down by Flak	100%
3(F)/121		He111H	Shot down by Flak at Metz	100%
2(F)/ObdL		Do215B	Missing	100%
1(H)/14		Hs126	Shot down by Flak	100%
3(H)/14		Hs126	Shot down by French fighter	100%
1/406		Do18	Shot down into sea by Hudson 120m SW Jutland	100%
F.d.Luft	4 x He115		Destroyed; cause not known	100%
Staffel Schwilden	1830 He59		Shot down by Dutch Artillery R.Maas	100%
Staffel Schwilden	1995 He59		Shot down by Dutch Artillery R.Maas	100%
Staffel Schwilden	2593 He59		Shot down by Dutch Artillery R.Maas	100%
Staffel Schwilden	2599 He59		Shot down by Dutch Artillery R.Maas	100%
Z/KG30		Ju88C2	Crashed near Narvik	100%
I/KGzbV.1	5 x Ju52		Shot down by Flak near The Hague	100%
I/KGzbV.1	14 x Ju52		Crash – landed near The Hague	100%
Stab/ KGzbV.2	2 x Ju52		Crashlanded Delft/The Hague	100%
Stab/ KGzbV.2		Ju52	Destroyed by Dutch forces Katwijk A/f	100%
3/KGzbV.9		Ju52	Shot down nr Ijmuiden by Po631	100%
KGzbV.9		Ju52	Shot down by Flak Waalhaven A/f	100%
KGzbV.9	4 x Ju52		Destroyed on ground by Dutch Forces The Hague	100%
KGzbV.9	3 x Ju52		Shot down by Flak at Ockenburg	100%
KGzbV.9	11 x Ju52		Crashlanded Ockenburg/Ypenburg	100%
KGzbV.9	10 x Ju52		Crashlanded Delft/The Hague	100%
KGzbV.11	34 x Ju52		Destroyed by Dutch forces Katwijk A/f	100%
KGzbV.12	11 x Ju52		Shot down by Flak Ypenburg airfield	100%
KGzbV.12	6 x Ju52		Shot down by Flak at Ockenburg	100%
KGzbV.12	20 x Ju52		Destroyed by Dutch forces Ockenburg	100%
KGzbV.172	2 x Ju52		Shot down by Flak Waalhaven A/f	100%

11th May 1940

1/JG21		Bf109E	Shot down by Hurricane Rotterdam	100%
JG26		Bf109E	Shot down by MS406 at Antwerp	100%
1/JG27		Bf109E	Shot down by by Fokker DXXI Ziel. Uffz Scheffler PoW	100%
I/JG53		Bf109	Crashed on take – off from Metz	100%
V/LG1	2 x Bf110		Shot down by RAF Hurricanes at Charleville	100%
I/ZG2	2 x Bf110		Shot down by by Fokker DXXI Holland	100%
I/ZG26		Bf110	Shot down by MS406 at Schellebelle	100%
II/ZG76	2 x Bf110		Shot down by Hawk 75 at Hirson	100%

223

???	Bf109	Missing	100%
KG1	He111	Shot down by Hurricane at Hirson	100%
KG1	He111	Shot down by Hawk 75 at Hirson	100%
8/KG2	Do17Z	Shot down by RAF Hurricanes at Charleville	100%
1/KG27	He111	Shot down by RAF Hurricane at Gembloux	100%
1/KG27	He111	Shot down by RAF Hurricane at Gembloux	100%
II/KG27	2 x He111	Shot down by RAF Hurricane at Gembloux	100%
II/KG27	2 x He111	Shot down by Po631 at Calais	100%
III/KG28	He111	Shot down by MS406 at Aulnoye	100%
III/KG53	He111	Shot down by Hurricane at Vassincourt	100%
KG54	3 x He111	Shot down by Hawk 75 at Antwerp	100%
II/KG54	4 x He111	Shot down by Hawk 75 at Antwerp	100%
1/KG55	He111	Shot down by French fighter at Orleans	100%
1/KG55	He111	Shot down by Flak at Vassincourt	100%
III/KG55	He111	Shot down by French fighter at Orleans	100%
III/KG77	Do17Z	Shot down by Flak Luttich – Geyer	100%
I/LG1	He111	Shot down by Flak at Lockeren	100%
I/LG1	3 x He111	Shot down by Bloch 152 at Antwerp	100%
Stab/StG.2	Ju87	Shot down by by Hawk 75 at Bouillon	100%
I/StG.2	5 x Ju87	Shot down by RAF Hurricanes at Tirlemont	100%
III/StG.2	4 x Ju87	Shot down by by Hawk 75 at Bouillon	100%
???	He111	Missing	100%
Aufk.St			
zbV/7	Do17M	Damaged in combat with Fokker DXXI	
		Den Helder	35%
3(F)/122	Ju88A1	Shot down by Spitfires Dutch coast	100%
3(F)/123	Do17P	Shot down by Hurricane at Rheims	100%
3(H)/14	Hs126	Shot down by MS406 at Dinant	100%
2/806	He111	Shot down by naval Flak North Sea	100%
3/906	3 x He115	Crashlanded at Vlissingen	100%

12th May 1940

I/JG1	2 x Bf109	Shot down by Blenheim at Maastricht	100%
JG2	2 x Bf109	Shot down by MS406 at Bouillon	100%
I/JG27	3 x Bf109	Shot down by RAF Hurricane at Maastricht	100%
JG51	3 x Bf109E	Shot down by Fokker DXXI at Noordijk	100%
I/JG54	Bf109E	Shot down by Flak at Luxeuil	100%
2/JG54	Bf109E	Shot down by Flak at Herbevilliers	100%
I/ZG76	Bf110	Badly damaged by Blenheim Bergen	80%
II/ZG76	Bf110	Shot down by MS406 at Cambrai	100%
Z/KG30	Ju88C2	Crashed at Vaernes	100%
V/LG1	2 x Bf110	Shot down by RAF Hurricane at Rheims	100%
KG2	3 x Do17Z	Shot down by Flak N France	100%
II/KG3	Do17Z	Shot down by Flak N France	100%
KG27	He111	Shot down by Hurricane at Courtrai	100%
KG27	2 x He111	Shot down by French fighters at Antwerp	100%
II/KG30	Ju88	Shot down by Defiant Ijmuiden	100%
III/KG30	Ju88	Shot down by naval Flak Dutch coast	100%
III/KG51	He111	Missing France	100%
I/KG53	He111	Shot down by French fighter at Mourmelon	100%
I/KG53	He111	Crashlanded after combat Mourmelon	80%
II/KG53	He111	Missing France	100%
III/KG53	He111	Missing France	100%
KG54	He111	Shot down by Flak near Breda	100%
II/KG55	He111	Missing France	100%

II/KG55	He111	Shot down by Bloch 152 at Chateaudun	110%
KG77	Do17Z	Shot down by Hurricane at Brussels	100%
3/KGr.126	He111H	Shot down by Flak Ijsselmeer	100%
I/LG1	He111	Shot down by Blenheim Hook of Holland	100%
II/LG1	He111	Shot down by Defiant at Ijmuiden	100%
II/LG1	He111	Shot down by Spitfire at Ijmuiden	100%
III/LG1	He111	Shot down by Hurricane at Antwerp	100%
2/StG.1	Ju87	Crashed at Vaernes	100%
I/StG.2	Ju87	Shot down by Hurricane at St Trond	100%
II/StG.2	Ju87	Shot down by by French fighter at Bouillon	100%
7/StG.2	Ju87	Shot down by Hurricane at St Trond	100%
I/StG.76	Ju87	Shot down by Hurricane at St Trond	100%
1(F)/10	Do17P	Shot down by French fighter Ardennes	100%
1(F)/121	Ju88	Shot down by Hurricane over Dutch coast	100%
1(F)/121	Do17P	Shot down by Fokker DXXI near Amsterdam	100%
1(F)/122	He111	Missing from Narvik	100%
3(F)/123	Do17P	Shot down by RAF Hurricane Belgium	100%
2(H)/12	Hs126	Shot down by Hurricane at Diest	100%
2(H)/13	Hs126	Shot down by RAF Hurricane at Bouillon	100%
4(H)/13	Hs126	Shot down by RAF Hurricane Wavre	100%
1(H)/23	Hs126	Shot down by RAF Hurricane Luttich	100%
1(H)/41	Hs126	Shot down by Hurricane at St Trond	100%
KGzbV.106	Ju52	Crashed at Vaernes	100%

13th May 1940

III/JG3	Bf109E7	Shot down by RAF Hurricane Antwerp/Brussels	100%
1/JG20	Bf109E	Shot down by Spitfire Rotterdam	100%
I/JG21	Bf109E	Shot down by Hawk 75 N France	100%
1/JG26	Bf109	Shot down by MS406 Breda.	
		Uffz Hermann Stock KIA	100%
5/JG26	Bf109E	Shot down in combat Numansdorp. Pilot PoW	100%
6/JG77	Bf109E	Crashed on take – off from Stavanger.	80%
II/ZG1	Bf110	Shot down by Blenheim Dutch coast	100%
I/ZG26	2 x Bf110	Shot down by RAF Hurricane Antwerp/Brussels	100%
II/ZG76	Bf110	Shot down by MS406 Philippeville	100%
II/ZG76	Bf110	Shot down by MS406 Charleroi	100%
V/LG1	3 x Bf110	Shot down by MS406 Sedan	100%
I/KG1	He111	Shot down by MS406 Charleroi	100%
KG2	Do17Z	Missing Sedan	100%
1/KG4	He111	Shot down by Flak at Middelburg	100%
II/KG4	He111	Shot down by Flak Hook of Holland	100%
KG27	He111	Shot down by RAF Hurricane Antwerp/Brussels	100%
III/KG28	He111	Shot down by MS406 Philippeville	100%
II/KG30	Ju88	Shot down by Defiant at Rotterdam	100%
II/KG53	He111	Shot down by Flak Montmedy	100%
KG54	He111	Shot down by Flak at Middelburg	100%
Stab/KG55	He111	Shot down by Flak Charleroi	100%
III/KG55	He111	Shot down by Flak Charleroi	100%
StG.2	Ju87	Missing Sedan	100%
I/StG.76	Ju87B	Shot down by Flak	100%
StG.77	Ju87	Missing Sedan	100%
II/StG.77	2 x Ju87	Shot down by Flak Tirlemont	100%
LG1	He111	Shot down by RAF Hurricane Antwerp/Brussels	100%
3(F)/11	Do17P	Shot down by fighter NW Belgium	100%
4(F)/11	Do17P	Missing N Rheims	100%

3(F)/22	Do17P	Shot down by RAF Hurricane N Rheims	100%
I(F)/121	Ju88	Shot down by RAF Hurricane Antwerp/Brussels	100%
3(F)/122	Ju88A1	Missing NW Belgium	100%
9(H)/LG2	Hs126N	Shot down by D520 NW Belgium	100%

14th May 1940

1/JG2	4 x Bf109	Shot down in combat Sedan	100%
III/JG2	3 x Bf109	Shot down by RAF Hurricanes S Sedan	100%
1/JG26	2 x Bf109	Shot down in combat S Brussels	100%
I/JG51	Bf110	Shot down by fighter	100%
1/JG53	Bf109	Destroyed by exoploding Blenheim Ziele	100%
1/JG53	2 x Bf109	Shot down by RAF Hurricanes S Sedan	100%
III/JG53	Bf109	Shot down by French fighter. Hptm Molders baled out	100%
II/ZG26	Bf110	Shot down(?) NW Germany	100%
II/ZG76	Bf110	Shot down by French fighter Namur	100%
I/ZG52	2 x Bf110	Shot down by D520 St Menehould	100%
V/LG1	2 x Bf110	Shot down by RAF Hurricane Chalons	100%
II/KG2	Do17Z	Shot down by D520 St Menehould	100%
II/KG4	He111	Shot down by Fokker DXXI Rotterdam	100%
4/KG26	He111	Shot down by Skua Narvik	100%
I/KG27	He111	Crashlanded at base after combat S Brussels	80%
III/KG27	He111	Crashlanded at base after combat S Brussels	100%
9/KG27	He111	Crashlanded at base after combat S Brussels	100%
3/KG51	Ju88	Shot down by RAF Hurricane Chalons	100%
8/KG51	2 x He111	Shot down by RAF Hurricane Chalons	100%
2/KG53	2 x He111	Collided over Verdun	100%
3/KG53	He111	Shot down by Flak Verdun	100%
3/KG53	He111	Crashlanded at base – Flak Verdun	80%
I/LG1	He111	Crashlanded at base after combat S Brussels	100%
II/LG1	He111	Shot down in combat S Brussels	100%
IV/LG1	2 x Ju87	Shot down in combat S Brussels	100%
II/LG2	Hs123	Damaged by Flak Tirlemont. Lt G.Dorffel safe	80%
Stab/StG.1	Do17M1	Crashlanded at base – Flak	100%
II/StG.2	Ju87	Missing S Sedan	100%
III/StG.2	Ju87	Shot down by Flak Gembloux	100%
III/StG.51	Ju87	Shot down by Flak Forgnies	100%
Stab/ StG.77	Ju87	Shot down by Flak S Sedan Obst Schwartzkopf lost	100%
I/StG.77	3 x Ju87	Shot down by RAF Hurricanes S Sedan	100%
I/StG.77	Ju87	Missing S Sedan	100%
I/TrGr.186	Ju87	Missing S Sedan	100%
3(F)/12	Do17P	Shot down by French fighter Luxembourg	100%
3(F)/122	Ju88	Shot down by RAF Hurricane Courtrai	100%
3(H)/21	Hs126	Shot down by French fighter Sedan	100%
2/506	He115	Destroyed at List RU	100%
KGzbV.108	He59	Crashlanded in sea off Trondheim	100%

15th May 1940

II/JG2	2 x Bf109	Shot down by Hawk 75 Rheims	100%
JG51	2 x Bf109	Shot down by RAF Hurricane Belgium	100%
JG51	Bf109	Shot down by Belgian CR42	100%
I/JG53	2 x Bf109	Shot down by D520 Sedan	100%

2/JG77		Bf109E	Shot down by French fighters Dinant.
			Uffz Klopper b/o	100%
I/ZG26	2 x	Bf110	Shot down by RAF Hurricane Belgium	100%
III/ZG26	2 x	Bf110	Shot down by RAF Hurricane Belgium	100%
II/ZG76		Bf110	Missing N France	100%
V/LG1	2 x	Bf110	Shot down by RAF Hurricane Rheims	100%
1/ZG52	3 x	Bf110	Shot down by RAF Hurricane Rheims	100%
1/ZG52	2 x	Bf110	Damaged by RAF Hurricane Rheims	50%
KG2		Do17Z	Shot down by Hawk 75 Rheims	100%
III/KG2	2 x	Do17Z	Shot down by RAF Hurricane Mourmelon	100%
III/KG4		Ju88A	Shot down by Flak Holland	100%
KG26		He111H4	Damaged by Skua Narvik	20%
9/KG26		He111H4	Engine damage Alston Is	60%
1/KG30		Ju87	Shot down by Flak from RN destroyer
			Dutch coast	100%
III/KG51	2 x	He111	Missing Valenciennes	100%
I/KG53	2 x	He111	Shot down by MS406 Suippes	100%
I/KG53		He111	Crashlanded at Valmy	100%
II/KG76		Do17Z	Shot down by French fighters Flavion	100%
KGr.126		He111H	Shot down Channel	100%
I/StG.2		Ju87	Shot down by Flak Luttich	100%
II/StG.2		Ju87	Shot down by Falk Montherne	100%
9/StG.2		Ju87	Missing Gembloux	100%
StG.77	2 x	Ju87	Missing Gembloux	100%
1(F)/10		Do17P	Shot down by MS406 Mezieres	100%
4(F)/14		Do17P1	Damaged by Flak Channel coast – crashlanded	50%
1(H)/14		Hs126	Shot down by Hawk 75 Signy l'Abbaye	100%
3(H)/21	2 x	Hs126	Shot down by D520 SW Sedan	100%
1(H)/23		Hs126	Shot down by French fighter Namur	100%
1(H)/41		Hs126	Shot down by RAF Hurricane E Brussels	100%
SNFKdo		He59	Crashlanded Norway	100%

16th May 1940

II/JG21		Bf109E	Shot down by Hurricane Alost	100%
5/JG26		Bf109E	Shot down by French fighter.
			Fw Stoltz killed	100%
I/JG51		Bf109E	Crashlanded at Neufchateau	100%
I/JG54		Bf109E	Shot down by Flak Luxeil A/f. Pilot PoW	100%
III/ZG26		Bf110	Shot down by Lysander Lille	100%
III/JG26		Bf109E	Shot down by Hawk 75 Mons. Pilot PoW	100%
II/JG27		Bf109E	Damaged by Hurricanes Ghent	80%
V/LG1	3 x	Bf110	Shot down by MS406 Vitry	100%
I/KG4		He111	Shot down by Flak Walcheren. 5J+IK Lt Zeiss	100%
9/KG27		He111	Shot down by Flak Wavre	100%
6/KG30		Ju88	Shot down by Skua Narvik	100%
6/KG30		Ju88	Crashlanded Narvik	100%
III/KG55		He111	Shot down by D520 Verdun	100%
II/KG76	2 x	Do17Z	Shot down by MS406 Maubeuge	100%
I/KG77		Do17Z	Missing from Rheims	100%
II/KG77		Do17Z	Missing from Laon	100%
I/StG.2		Ju87B	Shot down by Flak Luttich	100%
II/StG.2		Ju87B	Missing Cambrai	100%
I/StG.77		Ju87B	Missing from Rheims	100%
7(F)/LG2		Do17P	Shot down by Hurricane Nivelles	100%
4(F)/11		Do17P	Shot down by MS406 Chimay	100%

3(F)/31	Do17P	Shot down by French fighter Strasbourg	100%
3(F)/123	He111	Forced down by Swiss Air Force.	
		Crew interned	100%
1(H)/11	Hs126	Missing Stenay	100%
3(H)/12	Hs126	Shot down by Flak Walcheren	100%
3(H)/21	Hs126	Missing Attigny	100%
1(H)/23	Hs126	Shot down by Flak Namur	100%
2(H)/23	Hs126	Missing La Chesne	100%
4(H)/31	Hs126	Shot down by fighter Beauvais	100%
KGzbV.108	2 x BV138	Destroyed	100%

17th May 1940

1/JG3	Bf109E	Shot down by Hurricane Valenciennes.	
		Lt Sprenger b/o	100%
3/JG3	Bf109E	Shot down by Hurricane Valenciennes.	
		Lt Haberland safe	100%
3/JG3	Bf109E	Shot down by Hurricane Le Cateau.	
		Lt Reumschussel safe	100%
I/JG20	2 x Bf109E	Shot down by Hawk 75 Walcheren	100%
4/JG26	2 x Bf109E	Shot down by MS406 Franco/Belgian border	100%
I/JG53	Bf109E	Crashed N Germany. Pilot injured	100%
I/JG77	Bf109E	Shot down in combat. Lt Envers missing	100%
V/LG1	3 x Bf110	Shot down by Hurricane Rheims	100%
I/LG2	2 x Bf109E	Shot down by MS406 Franco/Belgian border	100%
I/ZG1	Bf110	Shot down by MS406 Franco/Belgian border	100%
II/ZG26	Bf110	Shot down by Blenheim Le Cateau	100%
III/ZG76	Bf110	Missing Philippeville	100%
Stab/KG4	He111	Shot down by AC-2 Walcheren	100%
Stab/KG4	He111	Shot down by Hawk 75 Walcheren.	100%
III/KG30	Ju88	Shot down by Spitfires Haamstede	100%
I/KG54	3 x He111	Shot down by Hurricane Valenciennes	100%
II/KG76	2 x Do17Z	Shot down by French fighters Naubeuge	100%
II/KG76	2 x Do17Z	Shot down by RAF Hurricane Cambrai	100%
III/KG76	Do17Z	Shot down by RAF Hurricane Cambrai	100%
9/LG1	Ju88	Shot down by RAF Hurricane Douai	100%
IV/LG1	3 x Ju87	Shot down by RAF Hurricane near Brussels	100%
III/StG.51	7 x Ju87B	Shot down by Hurricane Valenciennes	100%
1(H)/14	Hs126	Missing St Quentin	100%
2(H)/14	Hs126	Missing Flander	100%
4(H)/31	Hs126	Missing N France	100%
2(H)/41	Hs126	Shot down by RAF Hurricane Nivelles	100%
3(H)/41	Hs126	Shot down by fighter Guise	100%
5/196	Ar196A2	Crashed Baltic	100%
5/196	Ar196A2	Destroyed.	100%

18th May 1940

6/JG2	Bf109E	Shot down by Hurricane near Brussels	100%
I/JG3	3 x Bf109E	Shot down by Hurericane Maubeuge	100%
II/JG26	Bf109E	Shot down by French fighter Tournai	100%
8/JG52	Bf109	Crashlanded at Thionville after combat.	100%
I/JG76	Bf109E	Shot down by MS406 La Fere	100%
I/ZG26	Bf110	Shot down by Hurricane Amiens	100%
I/ZG26	Bf110	Crashland after combat with Hurricanes	80%
II/ZG26	5 x Bf110	Shot down by Hurricanes Le Cateau	100%

II/ZG26	Bf110	Damaged by Hurricanes Le Cateau	100%
II/ZG26	Bf110	Damaged by Hurricanes Le Cateau	75%
II/ZG76	Bf110	Shot down by Hurricanes Vitry en Artois	60%
II/ZG76	2 x Bf110	Shot down by Hurricanes Vitry en Artois	100%
II/KG1	3 x He111	Missing Cambrai	100%
II/KG2	Do17Z	Shot down by Hurricane Amiens	100%
II/KG4	2 x He111	Shot down by Hurricanes Lowen	100%
II/KG27	He111	Shot down by Hurricanes Cambrai	100%
II/KG27	He111	Shot down by Hurricane Tournai	100%
III/KG30	Ju88	Shot down by Bloch 152 Ostend	100%
II/KG54	2 x He111	Shot down by Hurricanes Lens	100%
I/KG55	2 x He111	Shot down by Po631 Soissons	100%
II/KG55	2 x He111	Shot down by Po631 Soissons	100%
II/KG55	He111	Crashlanded near Sedan after combat	70%
I/KG76	Do17Z	Missing Cambrai	100%
I/KG76	Do17Z	Crashlanded at Köln after combat.	100%
II/KG76	2 x Do17Z	Missing Cambrai	100%
III/LG1	Ju88	Shot down by Hurricanes Vitry en Artois	100%
3(H)41	2 x Hs126	Shot down by Hurricane N France	100%
3(H)/123	Hs126	Shot down by Hurricane N France	100%
3(F)/10	Do17P	Shot down by Hurricane Avesnes	100%
4(F)/11	Do17P	Shot down by Hurricane Valenciennes	100%
4(F)/14	Do17P	Shot down by Hurricane Douai	100%
4(F)/14	Do17P	Shot down by Hurricane Vitry en Artois	100%
3(F)/31	Do17P	Shot down by Hurricane Vraux	100%
3(F)/121	He111	Missing N France	100%
??	Ju88	Destroyed on operations	100%

19th May 1940

I/JG2	Bf109E3	Missing. Pilot killed	100%
5/JG2	Bf109E	Combat Courtrai. Pilot wounded	?%
6/JG2	Bf109E	Tournai. Oblt Cratein wounded	?%
I/JG3	Bf109E	Shot down Philippeville	100%
I/JG3	Bf109E	Shot down in combat Engel Fontaine. Lt Schnabel wounded	100%
9/JG3	Bf109E1	Combat Lille – Tornai. Pilot wounded	100%
6/JG20	Bf109E	Motor damaged Eindhoven. Pilot wounded	100%
I/JG26	Bf109E	Shot down Lille	100%
II/JG26	Bf109E	Shot down near Lille	100%
4/JG26	Bf109E	Forcelanded near Brussels after combat	30%
4/JG26	Bf109E	Forcelanded near Lille after combat. Hptm Ebbighausen wounded	80%
I/JG52	Bf109E	Hoppenstadt	25%
1/JG76	Bf109E3	Missing. Pilot killed	100%
1/JG76	Bf109E1	Missing. Pilot wounded	100%
II/JG77	Bf109E	Combat Lille. Lt Stiebel killed	100%
II/JG77	Bf109E	Combat Lille. Oblt Schiffer killed	100%
I/LG2	3 x Bf109E	Missing	100%
Stab/ZG76	Bf110	Shot down by Flak Dover. Maj Grabmann wdd	100%
1/ZG76	Bf110	Hit by Flak, forcelanded at Koln	85%
1/ZG76	Bf110	Shot down at Valenciennes	100%
1/ZG76	Bf110	Crashed Duren, technical failure	60%
1/ZG76	Bf110	Crashlanded at Vogeleang	80%
4/ZG76	Bf110	Missing Denain	100%
5/ZG76	Bf110	Missing Douai	100%

III/KG2	Do17Z	Combat Senlis	100%
II/KG3	Do17Z	Forcelanded after combat	?%
II/KG3	Do17Z	Combat near Compeigne	20%
II/KG3	Do17Z	Shot down by Flak near Compeigne	100%
6/KG4	He111	Shot down by Flak Lokeren	100%
7/KG4	He111	Shot down by Flak Ostend – Boulogne	100%
7/KG27	He111	Missing	100%
8/KG27	4 x He111	Missing	100%
9/KG27	He111	Missing	100%
I/KG51	Ju88	Missing	100%
9/KG28	He111	Combat with fighters Douai. One man killed.	?%
9/KG28	He111	Combat with fighters Douai	50%
I/KG51	Ju88	Force – landed in bad weather	?%
II/KG51	Ju88	Missing	100%
II/KG51	He111	Cause not known	?%
III/KG51	Ju88	Missing	100%
III/KG51	He111	Shot down near Rethel	100%
III/KG51	He111	Shot down in combat	100%
III/KG53	He111	Crash – landed near Compeigne	100%
III/KG53	He111	Shot down by fighter Amiens	100%
Stab/ KG54	3 x He111	Combat Arras	100%
3/KG54	2 x He111	Missing Arras	100%
I/KG54	He111	Missing Arras	100%
4/KG54	4 x He111	Missing Lille	100%
6/KG54	He111	Missing Lille	100%
7/KG54	He111	Combat Arras	100%
9/KG54	He111	Shot down by Flak Le Havre	100%
9/KG54	He111	Combat Lille	100%
III/KG76	Do17Z	Missing	100%
7/KG76	Do17Z	Combat. Two men wounded	?%
LG1	Ju88	Missing Dunkirk	100%
II/StG.2	Ju87	Combat with fighters Maubeuge	15%
III/StG.51	Ju87R	Damaged by Flak	80%
4(F)/14	Do17P	Missing	100%
1(H)/11	Hs126	Missing Flanders	100%
1(H)/14	Hs126	Missing Flanders	100%
2(H)/41	Hs126	Missing Flanders	100%

20th May 1940

I/JG1	Bf109	Crashlanded Beaulieu	40%
I/JG1	Bf109	Crashlanded Namur	35%
I/JG1	Bf109	Crashlanded Namur	45%
I/JG1	Bf109	Crashlanded Namur	40%
II/JG2	Bf109D	Tyre damage Jever	100%
1/JG3	Bf109E	Combat Arras. Lt Wisser missing	100%
II/JG3	Bf109E	Combat Arras	100%
I/JG51	2 x Bf109E	Missing	100%
III/ZG26	Bf110	Missing near Sedan	100%
III/ZG76	Bf110	Missing	100%
Stab/KG4	He111	One man wounded by Flak Ghent	?%
4/KG4	He111	One man killed; enemy gunfire Oudenarde	?%
7/KG4	He111	Missing Channel coast	100%
Stab/KG27	Do17Z	Damaged in combat	15%
I/KG30	Ju88	One man killed by Flak Ostend	?%

9/KG76		Do17Z	Three men wounded	?%
2/LG1		He111	Missing Abbeville	100%
6/LG1		Ju88	Combat Amiens	100%
III/StG.1		Ju87	Missing	100%
III/StG.51		Ju87	Force – landed Jemelle	100%
3(F)/10		Do17P	Missing N France	100%
1(F)/22		Do17P	Missing	100%
4(F)/22		Do17P	Missing N France	100%
3(F)/122		Do17	Three men wounded in combat	?%
2(F)/122		Ju88	Force – landed at Dulman	100%
2(F)/123		Do17P	Combat	100%
2(H)/12		Hs126	Combat Stonne	100%
4(H)/22		?	Two men wounded	?%
3(H)/41	2 x	Hs126	Combat N France	100%
Auf.St.Flak		Do17M	Missing	100%

21st May 1940

III/JG2		Bf109E	Shot down in combat Roye.	
			Hptm Dr Erich Mix missing	100%
III/JG2		Bf109E	Damaged in combat Signy Les Petit.	
			Lt Missfeld wounded	90%
II/JG3		Bf109E	Forcelanded at Anschen. Lt Pollach killed.	100%
I/JG26		Bf109E	Crashlanded at Anrwero	60%
2/JG26		Bf109E	Crashed on take – off	50%
II/JG51		Bf109E	Hit by Flak Kehl	10%
II/JG53		Bf109E	Damaged in combat	25%
I/JG54		Bf109E	Crashed on take – off from Freiburg	8%
II/ZG1		Bf110	Shot down Soissons	100%
III/ZG26		Bf110	Combat Beauvais	100%
III/KG1		He111	Missing Boulogne	100%
III/KG2		Do17Z	Damaged Merou	5%
Stab/KG3		Do17Z	Damaged in combat Trier	60%
I/KG27		He111	Hit by Flak Calais	40%
I/KG27		He111	Damaged in combat Calais	50%
Stab/KG28		He111	Two men wounded Niedermenig	?%
4/KG54	2 x	He111	Missing Calais	100%
5/KG54		He111	Missing Calais	100%
II/KG76		Do17Z	Missing	100%
1/LG1		He111	Shot down Dunkirk	100%
II/LG1	?		Bombed at Guise	100%
6/LG1	?		Two men wounded in combat Boulogne	?%
9/LG1		Ju88	Combat Boulogne	100%
1/KGr.126		He111	Missing	100%
1(F)/121		He111	Missing	100%
4(F)/121		Ju88	Crashed Saar	100%
1(H)/12		Hs126	Shot down N France	100%
5(H)/13		Hs126	Shot down in combat Malmedy	100%
2(H)/31		Hs126	Combat Flanders	100%
2(H)/23		Hs126	Bombed	100%

22nd May 1940

I/JG1		Bf109	Missing	100%
I/JG1		Bf109	Combat Arras	100%
I/JG21		Bf109	Missing	100%

3/JG26	Bf109E	Crashed on take – off from Woensdrecht	50%
I/JG27	Bf109	Missing	100%
I/ZG1	Bf110	Combat Douai	100%
III/KG27	2 x He111	Missing	100%
8/KG27	He111	Missing	100%
I/KG30	Ju88A	Missing Channel coast	100%
II/KG53	He111	Combat Rouen	50%
8/LG1	2 x Ju88	Combat Boulogne	100%
9/LG1	Ju88	Crash – landed at Düsseldorf after combat	100%
III/StG.2	Ju87	Missing	100%
III/StG.2	Ju87	Collided at Guise	7%
I/StG.77	Ju87	Damaged	85%
II/StG.77	Ju87B	Combat	100%
II/StG.77	Ju87B	Combat Rocroi	100%
II/StG.77	2 x Ju87B	Missing	100%
I(St)/ TrGr.196	2 x Ju87B	Crashed after combat	100%
3(F)/31	Do17P	Missing	100%
2(H)/23	Hs126	Missing Allonville. Oblt Schumann killed	100%
4(H)/31	Hs126	Missing Allonville	100%

23rd May 1940

I/JG1	Bf109E4	Missing. Pilot wounded	100%
I/JG27	Bf109E	Missing. Lt Wedigruber lost	100%
I/JG27	2 x Bf109E	Missing	100%
I/JG27	Bf109E	Combat Ypern	100%
9/KG4	He111	Unknown	?%
I/KG30	Ju88A	Flak Amsterdam.	100%
Stab/KG55	He111	Damaged over Paris. Two men wounded	?%
II/KG55	He111	Combat Trier	5%
III/KG55	He111	Missing	100%
I(St)/Tr Gr.186	Ju87	Forcelanded Cambrai	60%
I/KGr.126	He111	Missing	100%
1(F)/22	Do17P	Combat.	30%
3(F)/122	Do17P	Flak Arras	100%
2(H)/12	Hs126	Combat	100%
1(H)/14	Hs126	Enemy fire north France	100%
?	Ju88	Damaged by Flak, landed Schipol	?%

24th May 1940

I/JG1	Bf109E3	Missing	100%
Stab/JG27	Bf109E3	Damaged in combat	20%
Stab/JG27	Bf109E3	Damaged in combat	50%
I/JG27	Bf109E3	Damaged in combat	30%
I/JG27	Bf109E1	Missing from Le Cateau	100%
I/JG27	Bf109E	Combat Courtrai	60%
II/JG52	Bf109e	Combat Longwy. Lt Mund killed	100%
II/JG52	Bf109E	Combat Arlon.	45%
II/JG52	Bf109E	Collided Luxembourg A/f	30%
II/JG52	Bf109E	Collided Luxembourg A/f	30%
I/ZG26	Bf110	Damaged Sincey	60%
III/ZG76	Bf110	Combat	100%
II/KG2	Do17Z	Damaged Clairmont	30%

II/KG2	Do17Z	Destroyed Montdidier	100%
Stab/KG26	He111	Missing from Narvik	100%
II/KG26	He111	Crashlanded at Drontheim	45%
III/KG51	2 x He111	Missing	100%
I/KG54	He111	Missing Dunkirk	100%
I/KG54	He111	Two men wounded Dunkirk	?%
I/KG54	He111	One man wounded Dunkirk	?%
2/KG54	He111	Two men wounded Dunkirk	?%
I/KG77	Do17	Three men wounded in combat	?%
I/KG77	Do17	One man wounded in combat	?%
I/KG77	Do17	Two men wounded in combat	?%
I/KG77	Do17	Two men wounded in combat	?%
2/KGr.126	He111	Crashed Bremen	100%
II/LG1	Bf110	Damaged Trier A/f	70%
Stab/ StG.77	Do17M	Crashlanded Rocroi	80%
I/StG.77	Ju87B	Crashlanding Guise	30%
FAG ObdL	Bf110	Missing Dover	100%
4(F)/11	Do17P	Missing N France	100%
2(F)/22	Do17P	Missing Rocroi	100%
2(F)/123	Do17P	Two men wounded in combat	?%
2(F)/123	Do17P	Combat St Omer	100%
1(H)/14	Hs126	Missing	100%
2(H)/14	Hs126	Damaged in combat Laon	60%
4(H)/22	Hs126	Hit by Flak Urrall	3%
4(H)/23	Hs126	Damaged in combat Tassey	10%
4(H)/31	Hs126	Missing Moteaux	100%

25th May 1940

I/JG27	Bf109E1	Forcelanded near Le Cateau, fuel	45%
II/JG52	Bf109E	Crashlanded Luxembourg	35%
I/JG53	Bf109E2	Missing	100%
I/ZG26	Bf110C	Motor damage	80%
I/ZG52	Bf110	Crashlanded Couvia	80%
II/ZG76	Bf110C	Missing, Lt Peters killed	100%
Stab/KG3	Do17Z	Missing	100%
I/KG3	Do17Z	Missing	100%
I/KG3	Do17Z	Combat	?%
I/KG3	Do17Z	Combat	?%
I/KG3	Do17Z	Crashlanded at Wiesbaden	80%
I/KG3	Do17Z	Combat, 3 wounded	?%
II/KG51	Ju88A	Crashed Munich	100%
Stab/KG53	He111	Crashlanded Langendiebach	40%
I/KG53	He111	Combat Arras	10%
II/KG76	Do17Z	Missing	100%
Stab/StG.2	Do17	Missing, combat	100%
I/StG.2	2 x Ju87	Missing, combat	100%
II/StG.2	Ju87B	Missing	100%
Stab/ StG.77	Ju87B	Combat, 2 wounded	?%
II/StG.77	Ju87B	Combat, 1 wounded	?%
II/StG.77	Ju87B	Missing	100%
3(F)/11	Do17P	Crashed near Chimay, 2 killed, 1 wounded	100%
2(F)/122	Do17P	Combat Paris	60%

3(F)/122	2 x He111	Taxy accident Drontheim	100%
FAG			
St zbV	Do17Z	Lost Het Zoute	100%
4(H)/13	Hs126	Combat Armentieres, 1 wounded	?%
4(H)/22	Hs126	Combat. 2 wounded	?%

26th May 1940

I/JG1	Bf109E1	Combat Calais. Oblt Winschig killed	100%
III/JG2	Bf109E3	Missing, pilot wounded	100%
I/JG21	Bf109E1	Combat	70%
I/JG21	Bf109E1	Crashed on takeoff	95%
I/JG21	Bf109E3	Missing	100%
III/JG52	Bf109E1	Missing. Lt Planer killed	100%
II/JG53	Bf109	Crashlanded Luxembourg	100%
Stab/ZG1	2 x Bf110	Combat Calais	100%
I/ZG1	Bf110	Combat Ostend	100%
I/ZG1	Bf110	Combat	100%
I/ZG2	Bf110	Crashed on take – off Neufchateau	100%
I/ZG26	Bf110	Combat	25%
I/ZG2	2 x Bf110	Crashlanded at Neufchateau	100%
7/KG4	Ju88	Combat Dunkirk	100%
9/KG4	Ju88	Combat Dunkirk	100%
2/KG26	He111	Combat Harstadt, 1 wounded	?%
III/KG30	Ju88	Schipol	100%
III/KG54	He111	Celle	50%
Stab/KG55	He111	Combat Trier	60%
I/KG53	He111	Missing	100%
I/KG55	2 x He111	Missing	100%
I/KG77	Do17Z	Missing	100%
9/LG1	Ju88	Combat Calais	100%
I/StG.2	Ju87	Missing	100%
II/StG.51	Ju87	Missing St Aubin	100%
I/StG.76	Ju87	Combat	5%
I/StG.76	Ju87	Combat	100%
I/StG.77	2 x Ju87	Missing	100%
I/TrGr.186	Ju87B	Motor damage	10%
I/TrGr.186	Ju87	Enemy fire	80%
I/TrGr.186	Ju87	Flak	60%
I/TrGr.186	Ju87	Forcelanded	100%
3(F)/10	Do17P	Missing N France	100%
4(F)/121	Do17P	Missing	100%
3(H)/10	Do17P	Missing N France	100%
3(H)/13	Hs126	Unknown	60%
4(H)/21	Hs126	Combat near Albert, 2 wounded	?%

27th May 1940

I/JG1	Bf109E3	Combat	100%
I/JG1	Bf109E3	Combat, Lt Wassermaier killed	100%
3/JG26	Bf109E	Forcelanded at Bouchaute	40%
Stab/JG27	Bf109E3	Combat	40%
6/JG77	Bf109E1	Damaged by Blenheim Stavanger. Hptm Langer wounded	10%
II/ZG1	Bf110	Missing	100%
I/ZG26	Bf110	Combat Furnes	80%

I/ZG52	3 x Bf110	Missing	100%
I/ZG52	Bf110	Combat Calais	100%
Stab/KG2	Do17Z	Combat, 2 killed, 2 wounded	100%
1/KG2	Do17Z	Combat, 2 wounded	?%
II/KG2	Do17Z	Crashlanded Geisen	15%
III/KG2	2 x Do17Z	Missing	100%
III/KG2	Do17Z	Combat Ostend	100%
III/KG2	Do17Z	Forcelanded St Marie, weather	30%
I/KG3	3 x Do17Z	Missing	100%
I/KG3	Do17Z	Combat	40%
I/KG3	Do17Z	Flak, 1 wounded	?%
I/KG3	Do17Z	Combat	20%
3/KG3	Do17Z	Combat Hondeschoot, 5 wounded	?%
II/KG3	3 x Do17Z	Missing	100%
III/KG3	3 x Do17Z	Missing	100%
III/KG3	Do17Z	Flak, 1 wounded	?%
III/KG3	Do17Z	Flak, 2 wounded	?%
III/KG3	Do17Z	Crashlanded Rombies, combat	60%
III/KG3	Do17Z	Forcelanded at Koln, flak	50%
Stab/KG27	He111	Forcelanded at Sittard	20%
5/KG27	He111	Damaged by Flak Dixmunde	60%
III/KG27	He111	Shot down by Flak at Roulers	100%
Stab/KG51	Ju88	Crashlanded at Mannheim	80%
I/KG51	Ju88A	Crashlanded Abbeville, combat	60%
I/KG51	Ju88A	Crashlanded Brussels, Flak	60%
I/KG51	Ju88A	Crashlanded Brussels, Flak	60%
I/KG51	Ju88A	Crashlanded Mannheim, Flak	80%
II/KG51	Ju88A	Crashed at Köln, combat	50%
III/KG51	He111	Missing	100%
III/KG51	Ju88	One man wounded in combat	?%
I/KG53	3 x He111	Missing	100%
I/KG53	He111	Combat Forges	60%
1/KG54	He111	Combat Nieuport	60%
2/KG54	2 x He111	Missing Nieuport	100%
5/KG54	He111	Missing	100%
3(F)/11	Do17P	Missing	100%
4(F)/122	Ju88	Destroyed forcelanding N France	100%
3(F)/123	Do17P	Missing	100%
3(F)/123	Ju88A	Combat Koblenz	50%
4(H)/22	?	2 killed	?%

28th May 1940

8/JG3	Bf109E	Shot down Ostend	100%
2/JG26	Bf109	Shot down over Calais, pilot missing	100%
II/JG53	Bf109	Crashlanded at Cambrai	30%
Stab/KG26	2 x He111	Missing Rombaksfjord	100%
2/KG26	2 x He111	Missing Rombaksfjord	100%
III/KG30	Ju88	Shot down in combat Channel. Crew missing	100%
III/KG77	Do17Z	Shot down by Flak	100%
III/KG77	Do17Z	Damaged in combat	40%
III/KG77	Do17Z	Combat Guise	30%
2/KGr.100	He111	Shot down by Flak Narvik	100%
5/LG1	Ju88	Crashlanded at Düsseldorf, crew killed	100%
6/LG1	2 x Ju88	Shot down Dunkirk, crew missing	100%
II/LG2	?	One man wounded – no details	?%

II/LG2	Hs123	Crashlanded at St Pol	30%
7/LG2	Do17P	Combat Dixmunde	80%
I/StG.76	Ju87B	Shot down by Flak	100%
1(F)/122	He111	Three men wounded in combat Dijon	?%
3(F)/122	Hs126	Two men wounded Nancy	?%
2(H)/21	Hs126	Shot down Chateau Procienne, Two killed	100%
KGzbV.1	Ju52	Shot down by Flak at St Pol	100%

29th May 1940

I/JG3	Bf109	Missing Dunkirk, pilot killed	100%
I/JG3	Bf109	Missing Dunkirk, pilot missing	100%
I/JG21	Bf109E	Crashed forcelanding Monchy – Breton	100%
III/JG26	Bf109	Forcelanded at Beerst	60%
1/JG27	Bf109E1	Shot down by fighter Dunkirk	100%
II/JG27	Bf109E3	Crashlanded at Desvres after combat	70%
I/JG53	Bf109	Damaged in combat Dunkirk	60%
II/JG53	Bf109E	Crashlanded at Ham	40%
I/JG54	Bf109	Crashlanded after combat	60%
I/ZG52	Bf110	Two crew wounded – no details	?%
II/ZG76	Bf110	Combat St Omer	70%
II/ZG76	Bf110	Combat St Omer	10%
I/KG1	3 x He111	Missing	100%
I/KG1	He111	Crashlanded at Norrent after combat	70%
I/KG1	He111	Crashlanded at Ghent after combat	70%
Stab/KG2	Do17Z	Combat	60%
II/KG77	Do17	Crased at Bras	100%
II/LG1	Ju88	Missing Dinkirk	100%
I/StG.2	Ju87	Missing	100%
II/StG.2	Ju87	Bomb exploded at Cambrai	95%
3(F)/22	Do17M	Shot down Dunkirk, crew missing	100%
5(F)/122	Do17P	Shot down by fighter Dunkirk	100%
2(H)/21	Hs126	Combat Rethel, one wounded	?%

30th May 1940

2/JG26	Bf109	Shot down in combat Dunkirk, pilot missing	100%
I/KG3	Do17Z	Missing, crew missing	100%
7/KG4	2 x Ju88	Shot down in combat Dunkirk	100%
Stab/KG27	He111	Shot down in combat Dunkirk	100%
5/KG27	He111	Shot down in combat Dunkirk	100%
I/KG30	Ju88	Shot down in combat Schouwen Island	100%
II/KG30	Ju88	Shot down in combat Dunkirk	100%
5(F)/122	Do17P	Missing	100%
1(H)/41	Hs126	Flak St Lucienne, two wounded	?%
KGzbV.1	3 x Ju52	Destroyed at St Pol	100%
KGzbV.107	Ju52	Combat Ringebu	100%

31st May 1940

I/JG2	Bf109	Shot down by Flak	100%
III/JG3	Bf109	Missing	100%
I/JG20	Bf109	Missing Holland. Oblt Borries killed	100%
I/JG20	Bf109	Missing. Pilot killed	100%
I/JG21	Bf109	Forcelanded at Monchy – Breton	100%
8/JG26	Bf109	Combat Dunkirk	100%

9/JG26	Bf109	Combat Dunkirk	100%
I/JG53	Bf109	Forcelanded Compeigne	100%
1/KG27	He111	Combat Dunkirk, two wounded	?%
5/KG27	He111	Crashlanded after combat Dunkirk	30%
KG30	Ju88	Missing from Dunkirk	100%

1st June 1940

I/JG20	Bf109E	Crashed Martietal, pilot killed	100%
I/JG26	Bf109E	Combat. Pilot missing	100%
I/JG26	Bf109E	Combat. Lt Cruel missing	100%
I/JG26	Bf109E	Combat. Oblt Guerath wounded	100%
II/JG26	Bf109E	Combat Langmarck. Pilot missing	100%
6/JG26	Bf109E	Destroyed.	100%
6/JG26	Bf109E	Combat Dunkirk. Pilot wounded	100%
8/JG26	Bf109E	Combat and Flak Vreu. Lt Sprick wounded	100%
9/JG26	Bf109E	Combat. Pilot missing	100%
I/KG4	He111	Missing, crew lost	100%
I/KG53	He111	Combat Belfort, crew lost	100%
II/KG53	He111	Combat Beilersee, crew lost	100%
III/KG53	4 x He111	Combat Amberieu, crew lost	100%
I/KG55	He111	Missing, crew lost	100%
II/KG51	Ju88	Missing, crew lost	100%
II/KG51	He111	Missing, crew lost	100%
4.KG76	Do17Z	Combat Dunkirk. Crew lost	100%
2/KGr.806	He111	Motor damage PQ 6855. Crew lost	100%
2/KGr.806	He111	Motor damage Dogger Bank. Crew lost	100%
I/TrGr.186	2 x Ju87	Missing. Crew lost	100%
3(F)/22	Do17P	Missing, crew lost	100%
4(F)/121	Ju88	Missing, crew lost	100%
2(F)/122	Ju88	Missing, crew lost	100%

2nd June 1940

II/JG2	Bf109D	Crashed at Lindenses	100%
I/JG27	Bf109E	Destroyed	100%
I/JG27	Bf109E	Combat	100%
4/ZG76	Bf110C	Combat Heinekoog. Oblt Christiansen wdd	100%
I/KG51	Ju88	Combat	100%
4/KG54	2 x He111	Combat Dunkirk. Crew missing	100%
9/KG54	2 x He111	Combat Dunkirk. Crew missing	100%
I/StG.1	3 x Ju87	Missing Narvik. Crew lost	100%
II/StG.2	Ju87R	Combat Fort Philippe	100%
II/StG.2	Ju87R	Combat St Quentin	100%
II/StG.2	Ju87R	Combat near Dunkirk. Lt Busch killed	100%
II/StG.2	Ju87R	Forcelanded Wortheim	100%
III/StG.51	Ju87R	Forcelanded Wortheim	100%

3rd June 1940

Jafu 3	Bf109E3	Lost. Oberst von Massow missing	100%
III/JG2	Bf109E1	Shot down. Lt Schade believed killed	100%
4/JG26	Bf109E3	Shot down, pilot wounded	100%
II/JG52	Bf109E3	Missing. Oblt Gutbrod killed	100%
II/JG53	Bf109E4	Shot down	100%
III/JG53	Bf109E3	Missing	100%

8/KG4	Ju88	Crashlanded at Schipol	100%
I/KG26	He111H4	Shot down in combat Narvik	100%
Stab/KG51	Ju88	Shot down by Flak, crew lost	100%
6/KG76	Do17Z	Missing	100%
III/KG76	Do17Z	Missing.	100%

4th June 1940

III/JG53	Bf109E3	Shot down. Lt Flietz killed	100%
II/ZG1	Bf110C	Shot down	100%
I/ZG52	Bf110C	Shot down., Oblt Zieberth killed	100%
I/KG76	Do17Z	Forcelanded at Cambrai	100%

5th June 1940

I/JG1	2 x Bf109E1	Missing	100%
I/JG2	Bf109E3	Missing. Lt von Redan killed	100%
III/JG3	2 x Bf109E3	Shot down in combat	100%
I/JG27	Bf109E1	Missing	100%
I/JG27	Bf109E1	Missing. Oblt Kroos killed	100%
II/JG27	Bf109E1	Missing. Lt Falkensamme lost	100%
I/JG51	Bf109E1	Missing	100%
III/JG53	Bf109E4	Missing. Hptm Molders captured	100%
1/ZG1	Bf110	Collided, crew killed	100%
3/ZG1	Bf110	Collided, crew killed	100%
1/KG27	3 x He111	Shot down in combat Rouen	100%
3/KG27	2 x He111	Shot down in combat Rouen	100%
I/KG51	Ju88	Missing	100%
II/KG51	3 x Ju88	Missing	100%
II/KG53	He111	Motor fire near Mainz	100%
II/KG55	2 x He111	Missing	100%
III/LG1	Ju88	Missing	100%
7/LG1	2 x Ju88	Missing from Rouen	100%
II/LG2	Hs123	Destroyed taxiing at Pusieux	100%
II/LG2	Hs123	Shot down in combat	100%
II/LG2	Hs123	Motor fire	100%
III/StG.2	Ju87	Shot down by fighter near La Neuf crew missing	100%
I/TrGr.186	Ju87	Missing	100%
FAG ObdL	Do215	Missing North France	100%
3(F)/22	Do17	Shot down in combat Rheims	100%
3(H)/13	Hs126	Missing North France	100%
1(H)/23	Hs126	Shot down in combat Caceles	100%
3/KFl Gr.906	He115	Missing from Suffolk coast	100%

6th June 1940

I/JG2	Bf109E4	Missing. Lt Hoffmann killed	100%
Stab/JG3	Bf109E1	Shot down at Condes. Maj Quandt killed	100%
I/JG3	Bf109E1	Combat Vignacourt. Pilot killed	100%
II/JG3	Bf109E3	Combat Cavillon. Lt Haymann killed	100%
II/JG3	Bf109E3	Missing	100%
4/JG26	Bf109E3	Destroyed. Pilot killed	100%
I/JG27	Bf109E1	Missing. Lt Ungerberger lost	100%

II/JG27		Bf109E3	Taxi accident at Guise	100%
I/JG53		Bf109E1	Destroyed	100%
III/JG53		Bf109E1	Missing	100%
III/JG53		Bf109E4	Missing	100%
III/ZG2		Bf110C	Missing	100%
III/KG76	2 x	Do17Z	Missing	100%
I/LG2		Bf109E	Missing	100%
3/KFl Gr.506		He115	Destroyed at Drontheim	100%
4(H)/12		Hs126	Missing after combat Samoucy	100%
3(H)/14		Hs126	Shot down at Amiens. Oblt Bertram killed	100%
4(H)/22		Hs126	Shot down, crew killed	100%

7th June 1940

III/JG3		Bf109E3	Combat Abbeville, pilot missing	100%
III/JG3	2 x	Bf109E1	Combat Abbeville, pilot wounded	100%
4/JG26		Bf109E3	Combat Dieppe, Uffz Iberle killed	100%
4/JG26		Bf109E3	Combat Dieppe, pilot wounded	100%
5/JG26		Bf109E3	Combat near Ecuire, pilot missing	100%
III/KG2		Do17Z	Crashed	100%
6/KG26		He111	Missing from Narvik	100%
Z/KG30		Ju88C	Shot down by Flak Norway	100%
III/KG55		He111	Missing	100%
I/LG2		Bf109E	Shot down by Flak, pilot missing	100%
I/LG2		Bf109E	Missing	100%
3(F)/123		Do17P	Missing	100%
2(H)/12		Hs126	Missing north France	100%
KGzbV.105		Ju52	Crashed near Koblenz	100%
KGzbV.105		Ju52	Crashed near Charleville	100%

8th June 1940

7/JG3		Bf109E	Combat near Beauvais	100%
1/JG26		Bf109E3	Combat Beauvais. Pilot killed	100%
1/JG26		Bf109E3	Combat Beauvais. Pilot missing	100%
7/JG26		Bf109E1	Combat Neufchatelle, Lt Mietusch safe	100%
7/JG26		Bf109E1	Combat Neufchatelle, pilot wounded	100%
II/ZG1	2 x	Bf110	Missing	100%
II/ZG1		Bf110	Crashlanded after combat	100%
II/ZG1		Bf110	Crashlanded at Freiburg after combat	100%
1/KG1		He111H3	Missing north France	100%
2/KG1		He111H3	Missing north France	100%
II/KG76		Do17Z	Missing Aumale	100%
IV/LG1		Ju87R1	Crashed at Soissons	100%
I/StG.2	3 x	Ju87	Combat, crew missing	100%
II/StG.2		Ju87R1	Combat Rouen	100%
III/StG.2		Ju87	Combat, crew missing	100%
1(H)/11		Hs126	Crashed at Hennicourt, crew killed	100%

9th June 1940

II/JG3		Bf109E4	Combat Rheims. Lt Obehner killed	100%
II/JG27	4 x	Bf109E1	Lost.	100%
II/JG27		Bf109E3	Shot down Montdidier	100%
II/JG27		Bf109E3	Lost	100%

II/JG52		Bf109E1	Crashed near Epernay, pilot killed	100%
III/KG2		Do17Z	Crashlanded near Merch	100%
5/KG26		He111	Shot down PQ 1764	100%
I/KG51	2 x	Ju88	Collided at Lechfeld.	100%
III/KG55		He111P	Crashlanded at Eutingen	100%
Stab/StG.1		Ju87B	Lost	100%
Stab/StG.1		Do17M	Lost	100%
1/KFlGr.506		He115B	Combat, crew missing	100%
1/KGzbV.1		Ju52	Crashed at Mannheim	100%

10th June 1940

5/ZG76	Bf110	Missing near Vernueil	100%
1/StG.76	Ju87B	Zuss, one killed, one injured	100%
1/StG.76	Ju87B	Zuss, one killed	100%
2(F)/11	Do17P	Crashed at Rambouillet	100%
4(F)/11	Do17P	Combat near Soissons, crew missing	100%
4(F)/121	Do17P	Collided with Ju52	100%
1(F)/123	Do17Z	Missing	100%
1(H)/13	Do17P	Missing north France	100%
5(H)/13	Hs126	Combat Rethel, crew missing	100%
1(H)/14	Hs126	Crashlanded at Varvins	100%
3(H)/21	Hs126	Missing Channel	100%
1(H)/31	Hs126	Combat Gancourt, crew missing	100%

11th June 1940

2/JG3		Bf109E1	Combat Le Havre, pilot missing	100%
6/JG26		Kl35	Lost, Lt Karma believed safe	100%
II/ZG1		Bf110C	Crashed at Naalach	100%
Stab/KG28		Do17M	Missing Le Havre	100%
III/KG55		He111P	Destroyed	100%
4/LG1		Ju88	Crashed at Langenhagen.	100%
9/StG.51		Ju87B	Missing Pix	100%
3/KFl Gr.106		He115	Destroyed	100%
2/KFl Gr.906		Do18	Crashed at Haugesund	100%
1(H)/14		Hs126	Combat Rethel	100%

12th June 1940

I/JG27		Bf109E4	Missing, Lt Bosch captured	100%
I/KG51		Ju88A	Crashed at Lechfeld	100%
Stab/KG54	3 x	He111	Combat Le Havre, crew missing	100%
8/KG76		Do17Z	Crashed at Breux	100%
Wekusta 51		He111	Missing, Oblt Niessen & crew lost	100%
2(F)/123		Do17P	Shot down by Flak, crew missing	100%

13th June 1940

I/ZG26	2 x	Bf110C	Shot down by ground fire at Chartres. Crew missing	100%
9/KG4		Ju88	Destroyed	100%

2/KGr.126	He111	Destroyed	100%
II/StG.77	Ju87	Destroyed	100%
1/KFl			
Gr.906	He115	Crashlanded at Amsterdam	100%

14th June 1940

3/JG54	Bf109E4	Combat Evreux, Lt Angski killed	100%
I/KG1	2 x He111	Collided at Orleans, crew missing	100%
II/KG2	Do17Z	Combat, crew missing	100%
II/KG51	Ju88A	Crashlanded Heidelburg	100%
Stab/KG53	He111	Bombs exloded on Heidelburg AD	100%
I/KG53	3 x He111	Missing	100%
Stab/KG55	He111P	Shot down by Flak, crew missing	100%
Stab/KG77	Do17Z	Combat Joinville, crew missing	100%
Stab/KG77	Do17Z	Missing	100%
I/KG77	Do17ZM	Missing	100%
II/KG77	Do17Z	Missing	100%
IV/LG2	Ju87B	Shot down by Flak Vallette, crew missing	100%
I/StG.76	Ju87B	Missing	100%
4(F)/11	Do17P	Missing south France	100%
2(H)/10	Hs126	Combat near Brie, crew missing	100%
Wekusta 51	Do17P	Missing Honau	100%

15th June 1940

8/KG4	Ju88A1	Missing from Orleans	100%
9/KG4	Ju88A1	Missing north France	100%
III/StG.2	2 x Ju87B	Missing	100%
2(H)/10	Hs126	Missing Orleans	100%
3(H)/13	Hs126	Crash north France, crew killed	100%
1(H)/21	Do17	Missing Nancy	100%
1(H)/21	Hs126	Missing near Mersingen	100%
4(H)/21	Hs126	Missing near Troyes	100%

16th June 1940

II/JG51	Bf109E1	Crashed near Chartres	100%
5/KG30	Ju88A1	Flak Tours, one wounded	100%
5/KG30	Ju88A1	Shot down by Flak at Tours, crew killed	100%
1/KGr.126	He111	Missing near Winerburg	100%
2/KGr.126	He111	Missing	100%
I/TrGr.186	2 x Ju87B	Missing	100%
1(H)/12	Hs126	Missing Domveric; Flak	100%
3(H)/12	Hs126	Missing Joinville	100%
4(H)/21	Hs126	Missing	100%
KGzbV.101	Ju52	Forcelanded at Rouen	100%

17th June 1940

– nil –

18th June 1940

I/JG1	Bf109E4	Collided Chartreaux, pilot killed	100%
I/JG1	Bf109E1	Collided Chartreaux, pilot killed	100%
II/JG53	Bf109E1	Crashed at Freux, pilot killed	100%
II/JG53	Bf109E1	Forcelanded	100%
5/KG1	He111H2	Shot down by fighter Cherbourg, crew missing	100%
Stab/KG27	He111	Missing	100%
I/KG51	Ju88A	Missing	100%
9/LG1	Ju88	Crashed at Brest	100%
II/StG.1	2 x Ju87	Collided near Nivelles	100%
3/KFl Gr.106	He115	Missing Channel	100%

19th June 1940

I/JG2	Bf109E3	Crashed. Lt Grubel killed	100%
II/JG26	Bf109E3	Crashed Chateauroux, Lt Blohm killed	100%
II/JG26	Bf109E3	Crashed Chateauroux, Lt Ganster killed	100%
II/JG52	Bf109E2	Crashed at Karlsruhe, Lt Hofer killed	100%
Stab/KG4	He111	Missing England. Oblt Corpus & crew lost	100%
I/KG4	He111	Missing London	100%
II/KG4	He111	Missing England. Maj Fr von Massenbach & crew lost	100%
4/KG4	He111	Missing England. Hptm Prochnow & crew lost	100%
4/KG4	He111	Missing England. Oblt von Arnin & crew lost	100%
6/KG4	He111	Missing England. Lt Baschaus & crew lost	100%
I/KG51	Ju88A	Crashed Stuttgart – Ulm, two killed, two injured	100%
I/KG51	Ju88	Crashlanded Weilhaim	100%

20th June 1940

9/KG1	He111H2	Bordeaux: combat and Flak. Crew missing	100%
4(H)/22	Hs126	Missing Bourges	100%
1/KFl Gr.506	He115	Crashed Drontheim	100%

21st June 1940

III/KG53	2 x He111H2	Missing	100%
2(F)/122	Ju88A1	Crashed at Brussels	100%

22nd June 1940

2/ZG1	Bf110	Destroyed at Paderborn	100%

23rd June 1940

– nil –

24th June 1940

5(H)/13   Hs126   Combat Beaumont – Montieux, Oblt John killed   100%

****

END

Transcribed from Luftwaffe Quartermaster General Daily Returns of Aircraft Losses held at Imperial War Museum.

Bibliography

The Following is suggested reading for those wishing to pursue research further, especially the files at the Public Record Office, Kew.

Air War Over France 1939-40. R. Jackson. Ian Allan.
Bristol Aircraft Since 1910. C. H. Barnes. Putnam.
British Bombers Since 1914. Peter Lewis. Putnam.
British Fighters Since 1912. Peter Lewis. Putnam.
British Rearmament and the Treasury. G. C. Peden. Scottish Academic Press.
Current of War. B. H. Liddle-Hart. Hutchinson.
Fairey Aircraft Since 1915. H. A. Taylor. Putnam.
Fighter Pilot. Paul Ritchie. Batsford.
German Aircraft of the Second World War. J. R. Smith and A. Kay. Putnam.
German Combat Aircraft. R. Wagner and H. Nowarra. Doubleday & Co.
Hawker Aircraft Since 1920. Francis Mason. Putnam.
Hawker Hurricane. F. K. Mason. Aston Publications.
Hurricane. E. Bishop. Airlife Publishing.
Hurricane Squadron (87 Sqn.) P. Adams. Air Research Publications.
Lysander Special B. Robertson. Ian Allan.
Per Ardua. Hilary St George Saunders. Oxford University Press.
Rolls-Royce, The Merlin at War. Ian Lloyd. MacMillan.
Royal Air Force, Vol. 1. The Fight At Odds. Denis Richards. HMSO.
Stuka at War. P. C. Smith. Ian Allan.
The Birth of the Luftwaffe. Hanfried Schliephake. Ian Allan.
The Call to Honour. Charles de Gaulle. Collins.
The Fall of France. R. Jackson. Arthur Baker Ltd.
The Rise and Fall of the German Air Force (1933–1945). HMSO.
The Rise of the Luftwaffe. H. Molloy Mason. Cassell.
The Rommel Papers. E. Rommel. Collins.
The Second World War. Sir W. S. Churchill. Cassell.
1940 – The Last Act. Basil Karslake. Leo Cooper.
2 Group. Michael J. Bowyer. Faber and Faber.
Public Record Office Files. AIR2/2851, 2921, 3130, 3149, 3190, 3193, 3917, 3214, 3234, 3697 and 4203.
AIR14/74, 78, 412, and 2502.
AIR16/352. AIR20/323, 768 and 2064.
AIR41/21.
AVIA46/107, 110 and 114.

Abbreviations

A&AEE	Aeroplane & Armament Experimental Establishment.
AASF	Advanced Air Striking Force.
ACFF	Air Component of Field Forces.
AC1	Aircraftsman 1st Class.
AC2	Aircraftsman 2nd Class.
AFV	Armoured fighting vehicle.
ALG	Advanced landing ground.
AOC	Air Officer Commanding.
ASP	Aircraft Storage Park.
ASU	Aircraft Storage Unit.
AVM	Air Vice-Marshal.
BAFF	British Air Forces France.
BEF	British Expeditionary Force.
CAS	Chief of Air Staff.
C-in-C	Commander in Chief (usually AOC-in-C).
DCAS	Deputy Chief of Air Staff.
DCR	Divisions Cuirassées (French armoured attack force).
DFC	Distinguished Flying Cross (award to Officers on flying duties).
DFM	Distinguished Flying Medal (award to NCOs and below on flying duties).
DLH	Deutsch Luft Hansa (German air line).
DOR	Director of Operational Requirements.
DR	Dispatch rider.
DSO	Distinguished Service Order.
DTD	Director of Technical Development.
EA	Enemy aircraft.
Fitter A & E	Fitter airframe and engines.
GHQ	General Head-Quarters.
HQ	Headquarters.
LAC	Leading aircraftsman.
LG	Landing ground.
MT	Motor tranport.
NCO	Non-commissioned officer.
ORB	Operational Record Book.
RAAF	Royal Australian Air Force.
RAFCBEF	Royal Air Force Component British Expeditionary Force.
RLM	Reichsluftfahrtministerium (German Air Ministry).
Typex	Encoding machine for the transmission of signals.
UK	United Kingdom.
VGO	Vickers gas operated (another name for the Vickers 0.303 inch 'K' gun).

Index